Y0-BTB-698

RETAIL DISTRIBUTION MANAGEMENT

RETAIL DISTRIBUTION MANAGEMENT

A Strategic Guide to Developments and Trends

Edited by

JOHN FERNIE

First published in 1990

Kogan Page Limited
120 Pentonville Road
London N1 9JN

British Library Cataloguing in Publication Data
A CIP record for this book is available from the British Library.

ISBN 0 7494 0030 7

Typeset by BookEns Limited, Baldock, Herts.
Printed and bound in Great Britain by Biddles Ltd,
Guildford and Kings Lynn

Contents

List of Contributors

David Brady graduated in Social Sciences from the University of Leicester in 1983 . He currently holds the post of production projects manager at Grattan's distribution centre in Bradford. In October 1990, David completed his MBA in Retailing and Wholesaling by distance learning from the University of Stirling.

Lawrence Christensen is Group Distribution Director of Safeway plc. He has worked in the food industry for 15 years and was the distribution director with Cavenham Foods when the company was acquired by Argyll. Previous to this experience he worked in general management in the plastics industry, in industrial engineering in the ship-building industry and he also served as an officer in both the Merchant and Royal Navies.

John Dawson is Professor of Marketing at the University of Edinburgh and at the Edinburgh University Management School. Dr Dawson has been a visiting professor, spending time teaching and researching, at universities in Japan, USA and Australia. He is a graduate of the Universities of London and Nottingham. His research interests are in retailing and channels of distribution, and his projects have received support from agencies of the European Community, by the British and foreign governments and by large companies, including retailers and wholesalers. He is co-editor of *International Review of Retail, Distribution and Consumer Research.*

Dr John Fernie is a senior lecturer in management at Dundee Institute of Technology. His main research interest is in the field of retail distribution management, with particular reference to contract distribution. He is editor of the *International Journal of Retail and Distribution Management.* Dr Fernie is a member of the Institute of Logistics and Distribution Management and he sits on its Scottish committee. He is also a member of the Chartered Institute of Marketing.

Philip Hammersley OBE is currently commercial director for the British Shoe Corporation (BSC). His responsibilities include co-ordinating the sourcing of footwear in the UK and abroad. During the last nine years he has worked in a variety of roles for BSC, including factories director and managing director of Freeman Hardy Willis and Trueform. Prior to joining BSC he had spells with the Stride Rite Corporation in the USA, Clarks Ltd in the UK and ICI, where he was a plant and design engineer. He is chairman of the East Midlands Regional Council of the CBI.

Julie Harrison graduated in Industrial Technology from the University of Bradford in 1988. She currently holds the post of training officer in the personnel division of Grattan and the distribution operation is part of her remit.

Dr Alan McKinnon is a lecturer in the Heriot-Watt Business School, Edinburgh. He holds a Masters degree in transport from the University of British Columbia and a PhD from the University of London for research on physical distribution in the British food industry. He has lectured and researched in the fields of transport and distribution for over ten years and undertaken numerous consultancy projects for private firms and government agencies. His current research includes studies of the employment generated by distribution centres and of regional variations in inventory levels. Dr McKinnon is the author of a textbook *Physical Distribution Systems* (Routledge, 1989) and many articles on physical distribution, and is currently the European editor of the *International Journal of Physical Distribution and Logistics Management.*

Martin Pellew is divisional sales and marketing director of Exel Logistics, at their international headquarters. Prior to this appointment he was development director in the hotels business of Ladbroke plc. He has also worked with Hoechst, George Wimpey and Morgan Crucible. He joined National Freight Consortium plc as sales and marketing director in 1987 and was responsible for the 1989 rebranding of the £400m logistics division as Exel Logistics. He is a member of The Marketing Society and the Institute of Marketing and has spoken on a number of European and USA platforms on a variety of logistics and distribution subjects.

Alison Pinnock, who has been with the Institute of Grocery Distribution (IGD) for five years, currently heads the management systems research group, looking at all aspects of the development and use of information systems in the grocery trade. Having been involved in the development of the IGD unified DPP model over the past few years and the Euro DPP model, her current responsibilities include the development of the trade communications programme at the institute. This currently includes the development of product and fixture measurement standard guidelines, account profitability modelling and many concerns relating to data exchange. Prior to joining the IGD, Alison was market analyst for Loctite International, and graduated in mathematics and management from Brunel University.

David Quarmby is joint managing director of the UK's leading food retailer, J Sainsbury plc and a director of its American supermarket subsidiary, Shaw's Supermarkets Inc. His principal responsibilities are for overall company operations. He joined Sainsbury's as distribution director in 1984. He is a member of the London Education Business Partnership Council and an external examiner for Loughborough University. From 1970 to 1984 he was with London Transport; he joined as head of research and planning; in 1975 he joined the board with responsibilities for fares, marketing and planning; and in 1978 he became managing director (buses). For six years he was responsible for the planning and operation of London's 5,500 red buses. From 1966 he was an economic adviser at the Ministry of Transport. He had previously spent four years at Leeds University, where, after a diploma in management studies, he lectured for three years while working on his PhD, in modal choice for commuter travel. His first degree was in engineering and economics at King's College, Cambridge.

Susan Shaw is Professor of Marketing in the School of Management at University of Stirling. A graduate of the University of Cambridge, Susan Shaw has researched extensively on food marketing in European countries. Recent research has focused on changing forms of marketing channels and on the marketing of aquaculture products in Europe, North America and Chile. She has worked on projects for EC, FAO and national governments as well as consulting for major food companies. Recent books include *Salmon: Economics and Marketing, Marketing the Products of*

Aquaculture and *An International Study of the Marketing of Farmed Salmon*.

Alan Slater is director of logistics consultancy at Price Waterhouse in Manchester. The majority of his recent work has been with rapidly growing businesses, in areas as diverse as food and drink, fashion, electronics, consumer products, engineering and the distribution services section. He has been a management consultant since 1982 after industrial experience including managerial responsibility for distribution operations with Sony, British Oxygen, Rank and Plessey. He is a regular speaker at conferences, has published over thirty articles on specific distribution issues, and is the author of *A Handbook of Physical Distribution Software* published by Kogan Page.

Trevor Thomas is distribution and logistics consultant to Exel Logistics (European Division), part of National Freight Consortium plc. He obtained his MA in economics from St Andrews University in Scotland and from there he qualified as a chartered accountant with one of the top firms of chartered accountants in London. He has worked on specific inventory and stock management assignments with companies such as Coats Paton and Jaegar, Trust House Forte and Debenhams. He has also worked for Hill Samuel Group plc and a conglomerate which became part of the Tarmac Group, being responsible for all aspects of finance, transport and distribution. He joined Comet in 1986 to conceive, formulate and implement a new central distribution and stock management strategy.

Jonathan Weeks has spent 30 years in the distribution field with occasional time off for excursions into general management and marketing. He is currently managing director of Entertainment UK, part of the Kingfisher Group. Prior to that he was operations director of Woolworths plc. His career includes spells as managing director of SPD Distribution Limited, the Unilever transport subsidiary, and as distribution manager for Hoover, Eastern Region, during which time he worked in Europe, South Africa and Australia. Before that he was general manager for one of the Black and Decker subsidiaries, marketing manager, industrial division of Black and Decker and materials controller for the UK company. His early experience was as National Distribution Manager for Canada Dry and as a trainee and work study engineer in SPD in the early 1960s. He is a fellow of the Institute of Logistics and Physical Distribution Management, a Council Member and in 1990 was elected chairman for a two-year period of office.

Preface

British retailers experienced their worst trading conditions for many years in the late 1980s, with the prospects for the early 1990s not promising much improvement. Continued high interest rates and the introduction of the community charge have both contributed to the slowing down of consumer spending. Meanwhile, as retail sales stabilise, costs continue to rise with increasing labour, development and occupancy charges, exacerbated by the introduction of the uniform business rate (UBR). Companies which borrowed to finance expansion policies or used leveraged buy-outs to gain control of particular groups have experienced most difficulty. On the day that this introduction was written, Lowndes Queensway, the UK's largest furniture retailer, went into receivership. Other retailers are also facing crippling interest charges at a time when the market for their products has slumped, such as MFI and Magnet.

The collapse of Lowndes Queensway illustrates the rapidly changing fortunes of retailers dependent upon discretionary spending. The Harris Queensway empire was built by Sir Phil Harris and the takeover was spearheaded by Sir James Gulliver. These charismatic entrepreneurs and other retail barons of the 1980s – Conran, Davies and Monk – have all been deposed as their groups experienced tough times in the late 1980s. The retail sector has lost favour with the City and the stores sector has been in constant decline relative to the FTA all share price index since 1986. This does, however, conceal the relatively sound performance of companies in the food retailing sector and others with a broad portfolio of businesses which have enabled them to weather this short-term storm.

It is perhaps no coincidence that the best performers in recent years have either a reputation for their centrally controlled distribution – Marks and Spencer, J Sainsbury, Boots and Argos, or they have successfully implemented changes to their distribution strategy – Kingfisher, Tesco and the Argyll Group. Where profit performance has been poor, the cost of modifying the distribution system has been a contributing factor, for example in the cases of Asda, Budgen, John Lewis and Storehouse.

When trading conditions are poor, it is imperative that the old distribution cliché is applied, namely that the stock has to be in the right store at the right time in the right condition. Quick response to customer needs will be a feature of the 1990s; a market-driven system requires sound distribution to ensure availability to minimise stock-outs and lost sales.

Many UK retailers have been at the forefront of innovation in logistics and distribution management. In the 1990s, with the emphasis on cost controls and productivity improvements, distribution will play an important role in retailers' corporate strategies. It is therefore appropriate to bring together contributions by academics, a consultant, a trade association expert and industry practitioners in one volume to give an overview of logistics and retail distribution management in the UK today.

The book comprises three main parts. Chapters 1 to 5 deal with the major strategic issues in retail distribution management, chapters 6 to 8 look in more depth at the trade-offs between customer service and cost, the use of DPP in such an analysis and the role of information technology as a facilitator in the decision-making process. Chapters 9 to 12 focus on specific retail sectors – grocery, footwear, retail warehousing and mail order, with industry practitioners providing examples from their own companies, namely J Sainsbury, British Shoe, Comet and Grattan.

In chapter 1 John Dawson and Susan Shaw identify the major changes in retailer-supplier relationships in recent years. While acknowledging that a consistent and continuing trend has been the shift of power towards the retailer in relationships, the growth of more stable relationships is evident in all types of channel. What is important here for logistics management is the type of channel relationship which is *associative* in nature. In horizontal markets this has existed for some time through consumer co-operatives and buying consortia but is relatively new in vertical markets. This form of value added partnership is increasingly being eschewed by UK retailers as they implement the principles of supply chain management.

One of the reasons invariably cited for the shift in the power relationship from manufacturer to retailer in vertical markets is the increased concentration of power in the retail industry in the hands of fewer large multiple retail groups. In a mature industry, many retailers have pursued a strategy of growth through acquisitions and mergers in order to diversify into new product markets or to penetrate new geographical markets. From 1982 to 1988, 507 acquisitions were carried out in the UK retailing sector, valued at £17.5 billion. Lawrence Christensen in chapter 2 comments upon these mergers, prior to discussing the consequences of merger activity on the distribution operation of the combined group. By using his own company as a detailed case, he illustrates the problems that have to be resolved in integrating two very different distribution divisions, that of Presto and Safeway, within the overall corporate objective of continued growth.

Not suprisingly, limits to domestic growth have led UK retailers to seek market opportunities overseas. Around £2.9 billion out of the £17.5 billion of transactions on acquisitions can be attributed to UK retailers' purchases abroad. Martyn Pellew charts the trend of internationalisation of retailing during the 1980s in chapter 3. He then discusses the strategies of leading international retailers and how they have geared their distribution to these new markets. Distribution companies are also acting constructively to make the most of these international opportunities, especially in view of the coming liberalisation of the European market.

Chapters 4 and 5 discuss two of the main changes which have occurred in retail distribution in the last 10 – 15 years, namely the move to greater centralisation of stock in retail-controlled warehouses and the contracting out of the distribution function to third-party specialists. Alan McKinnon identifies the extent of retail-controlled centralisation, claiming that 50 major multiples operate or contract a total of 187 distribution centres with around three million square metres of floorspace located along the major motorway corridors of the UK. In discussing the pros and cons of centralisation he strongly favours the move to centralisation, arguing that it provides a host of operational, financial and marketing advantages. Although some retailers have encountered well-documented problems, these tend to be short term and transitional in nature. In chapter 5 the editor discusses the trend of contracting out distribution by UK retailers. Although most of the recent distribution developments have been contracted out, the editor feels that the major contracts have now been awarded and the only prospects for growth in the contract market are in DIY, convenience store retailing, mail order home delivery and the confectionery, tobacco and newsagent markets. Even then, recent large contracts awarded by grocery retailers tend to conceal the importance of own-account distribution operated by many major retailers.

In the second part of the book a more detailed analysis of supply chain principles is discussed. In chapter 6 Jonathan Weeks identifies the main trade-offs which have to be made in the retail supply chain and the costing of trade-offs in areas of packaging, handling systems, inventory and systems (from final customer in the store to warehouse to the supplier). Identifying trade-offs is only the start. Agreement has to be reached on the strategy to be pursued and a detailed specification has to be laid down on issues such as order capture, availability, delivery times, packaging, etc. DPP can then be used to describe all costs throughout the supply chain.

This theme is pursued by Alison Pinnock in chapter 7 when she outlines the historical evolution of DPP from its earliest applications in the USA in the 1960s to its revival with the IT revolution in the 1980s in both the USA and Europe. She warns that DPP cannot be the panacea in terms of decision making, rather it is a tool to make better decisions based on a sound technical understanding of the supply chain. Nevertheless, she offers numerous examples from both sides of the Atlantic – Quaker Oats, Boots, Woolworths, Procter and Gamble, Scott and Coca Cola and Schweppes – to illustrate the successful application of DPP techniques.

Alan Slater argues in chapter 8 that the basic costings required for DPP analysis are only the tip of the iceberg of potential data available within the physical distribution system to assist management in making sound decisions to achieve competitive advantage. He maintains that the applications of IT are generally targeted at achieving objectives such as lower costs or the improved speed, reliability or dependency of information transferred. However, maximum added value is gained where systems are inter-linked to transfer stock data between elements within the supply chain (EDI) and to optimise stock levels and resources throughout the chain. He concludes by suggesting a procedure for selecting software suppliers to ensure that the most appropriate system is chosen for the defined user requirement.

The final section of the book gives case study evidence of how particular companies have managed their distribution in such a dynamic retail environment. The editor reviews the major changes which have occurred in UK grocery retailing in the 1970s and 1980s and David Quarmby outlines the major trends in physical distribution over this time period in chapter 9. He concurs with the evidence presented in chapters 4 and 5 that the two major trends are the shift to retail-controlled networks and the greater use of contract distribution in the grocery sector. He concludes by using J Sainsbury as an example of how a major grocery chain has adapted its distribution operation in response to the changing needs of its branch network.

In chapter 10 Philip Hammersley re-emphasises the benefits of a supply chain management approach to identifying market opportunities. In the highly competitive footwear market he shows how it is imperative that the right stock is available in the right shops at the right time as end of season mark-downs are already high and a high percentage of lost sales occurs because the correct shoe for the customer is not available. He notes that if restocking time could be reduced, substantial improvements in gross margin would result, benefiting both the supplier and retailer. Furthermore, improvements in response time can be made in the planning process. For example, it only takes half an hour of direct labour to make a shoe but it takes the average footwear retailer 22 weeks to sell it. He advocates building stronger partnerships with suppliers to aid quick response and the development of an appropriate corporate culture to grasp the marketing opportunities available.

The retail phenomenon which has experienced most growth in the last 10 years has been the development of the retail warehouse concept. Now accounting for 50 million square feet of gross floorspace from over 2,000 warehouses, the concept has shed its downmarket image of the early years to be a major force in out-of-town retailing in the form of retail parks. In chapter 11 Trevor Thomas and the editor monitor these changes and the evolving patterns of distribution as new companies, including established high street retailers, move to retail parks. Trevor Thomas then discusses how he implemented a central distribution system at Comet from March 1987 to March 1989. Using Scotland as the pilot scheme, Comet now have three Regional Distribution Centres (RDCs) which supply all their stores. He discusses the systems used, why Comet contracted out its distribution and the fine-tuning of the strategy on implementation.

The final chapter focuses on the mail order sector where distribution is crucial to the success or failure of the business. David Brady and Julie Harrison trace the development of mail order from its northern roots with catalogues and agents, to the upmarket *Next Directory*. In this sector, quick response is crucial to competitive advantage, and Grattan, the subject of an in-depth case study, has radically overhauled its distribution system in order to respond to anticipated customer needs in the 1990s. The commissioning of a £55 million warehousing complex in Bradford has replaced a multi-site system with transport from each site. The new single site and the enhancement of systems to improve the utilisation of space and productivity will increase the speed of delivery, the standard of product, the availability of stock and will improve communications with customers – the key to competitive advantage.

John Fernie, August 1990

1

The Changing Character of Retailer-Supplier Relationships

John A Dawson and Susan A Shaw

Introduction

The channel of distribution for consumer goods over the last 25 years has changed fundamentally across several dimensions. A simple list illustrates the size of the change which has taken place. These changes are not limited to the UK but are evident, to varying degrees, throughout western Europe. They result from the restructuring of European economies which began before, but was accelerated by, the events subsequent to the oil crisis of 1973. The changes in distribution channels have been incremental and gradual, but the totality of the change is substantial. Major changes have occurred in the following ways.

- Increases in volume and value of the goods passing through the channel.
- Greater variety in the characteristics of goods passing through the channel with new goods having new characteristics. One consequence is that previously specialist distribution facilities may now be considered standard requirements and new special needs have appeared.
- Increases in the international nature of channel activity not only in terms of products, but also in respect of various types of facilitators.
- Increases in horizontal market concentration at all levels in the channel resulting in fewer, larger participants in channel processes but with a continuing large number of small firms with little market power.

- Increased acceptance by manufacturers and suppliers of services of the concepts of trade marketing.
- Increasingly complex technologies which are often substituted for labour with fewer people directly involved in channel activity.
- Greater use of support agencies and facilitators in channel activity while at the same time a tendency for there to be fewer levels of institution in the channel taking title to products for resale.
- More variety in channel relationships with increasing use both of non-traditional organisational forms, such as joint ventures, strategic alliances, administered channels and contractual channels, and also of non-traditional methods, involving techniques such as Just In Time (JIT) and Value Added Network (VAN).
- Attempts being made to manage vertical relationships (integrated supply chain management) with the objective of maximising horizontal competitive performance.
- Changes in behaviour and expectations among channel participants, usually associated with shifts in power which make retailers more powerful in the channel.

The list of changes above illustrates the range of evolution which has occurred in the channel since the mid 1960s and it must be remembered that the various changes are not independent but interact strongly with each other. Further, although almost universally characteristic of distribution channel evolution, the extent and significance of these various components of change in the distribution channel differ in degree among product groups and among countries (Burt, 1989).

The modelling of changing relationships

The way the changes have occurred may be modelled in a variety of ways. There has been substantial research literature on the changing form and character of relationships in the distribution channel. Carlisle and Parker (1989) have suggested a three-phase model of the relationship between a distributor and supplier at the micro level. Figure 1.1 illustrates the sequence of phases through which progress is made via a series of crises and their resolution. Progression to the next phase results from resolution of the crises in the usual sequence of shock, defensive retreat, acknowledgement, adaption and change (Fink *et al*, 1971). In phase one the relationship is purely a trading relationship. From the buyer's viewpoint the supplier is one of many and vice versa. Considerable time may be spent searching the market for suppliers or for buyers. Buyers play off suppliers against each other and vice versa. This phase ends when, for some reason, the buyer or supplier gains a dominant position and obtains a better negotiating stance. For example, a supplier may become dominant because it controls the leading brand; a buyer may become dominant because it controls a substantial market share. A variety of conflicts arise at this transition as the winner establishes and exploits its superior position and the loser seeks ways to minimise losses. Phase two of the relationship is a phase of negotiation with each party having a set of objectives related to their perceived relative position. Both buyer and supplier are trying to negotiate improvements in their respective power positions. This phase involves changes in power and dependency relationships as successive negotiations are undertaken. Carlisle and Parker consider this to be the 'rational/scientific' phase when information is used as a major tool in the negotiations which adjust the power relationship. Phase two breaks down as conflicts increase, for example as suppliers or buyers establish pacts among themselves to improve their negotiations and as the complexity of negotiations increases to an extent in which negotiation (transaction) costs become prohibitive. At this stage phase three occurs which is termed 'integrated'. In this stage joint activities and joint ventures are undertaken or activities become internalised within a firm (Anderson and Weitz, 1986). The move to joint activities means that mutual benefits are sought as the outcome of negotiations between buyers and suppliers who aim to manage the supply chain. Anderson and Narus (1990) suggest that in the development of co-operative relationships joint activity is an antecedent rather than a consequence of trust between distributor and manfacturer. Power ceases to be used as a tool to resolve negotiation but is used externally to enhance competitive positions to the advantage of both buyer and supplier and internally to optimise the efficiency and effectiveness of the total supply chain.

It is claimed that this general model parallels the phases of an

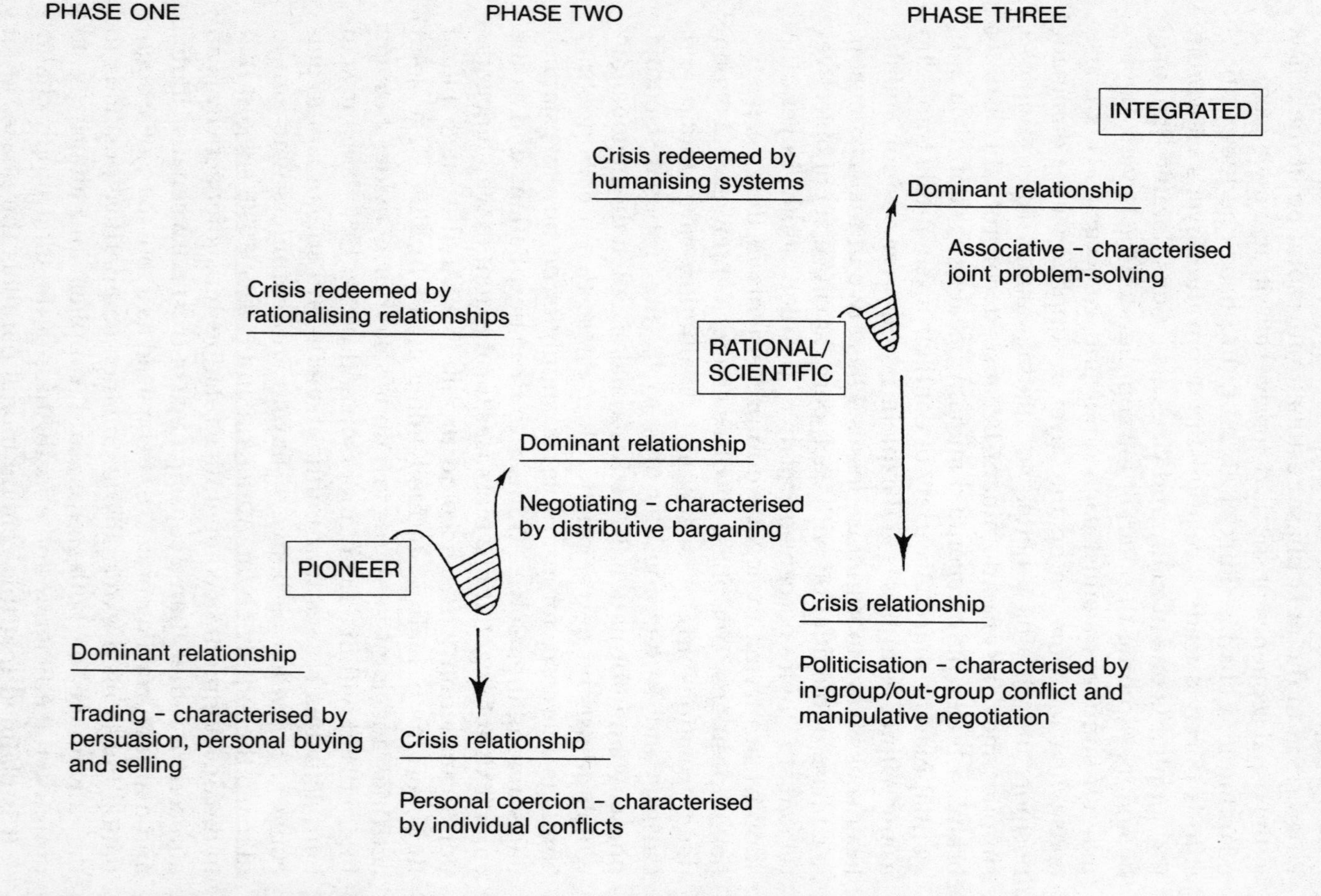

Figure 1.1: *Phases in the changing nature of retailer-manufacturer relationships*

organisation's development as it moves from personal and entrepreneurial management, through the stage of rational management where efficiency is uppermost and bureaucracy develops, to a more effective integrated management phase which is more consumer responsive and marketing directed.

Empirical evidence of the changes in relationships in the distribution channel points to a move towards either manufacturer or retailer domination, and then to a subsequent shift towards a more associative form of relationship in which relationships are more stable and mutually supportive (Mallen 1963; Frazier and Sheth 1985; Jeuland and Shugan 1983; Narus and Anderson 1987; Reve and Stern 1979). Table 1.1 provides a list of factors encouraging more stable relationships between retailers, in particular large retailers, and their suppliers both of goods for resale and also of business services. The list is long and while all factors are neither of the same importance, nor of increasing importance, none the less several strong processes are at work encouraging a more associative form to retailer-supplier relationships. Hogg (1987) suggests that in the UK clothing market co-operation between Courtaulds and retailers, enabled by investments in information technology, has enabled faster response to consumer fashion change to the mutual benefit of the retailer, through fewer mark-downs, and the supplier, through improved production planning. Such co-operation involves the joint use of information collected at several points in the distribution channel. It is interesting to note that while the move to more stable relationships between suppliers and retailers has become established, so in general there has been a move towards less stable relationships between retailer and consumer. For example, a number of factors point towards a decrease in store loyalty among consumers. It would be illuminating to explore whether the instability in consumer relationships is linked to more stability elsewhere in the channel. These more stable relationships are evident in both the supply of goods for resale and in the provision of business services.

Transactional and integrated relationships

The full spectrum of relationships in the distribution channel runs from the entirely transactional, in which each individual relationship is complete in itself with both parties undertaking a market

Table 1.1: *Factors making for stability in relationships between large retailers and their suppliers*

Factor	*Role*	*Directions of change*
(1) High and consistent quality	Stability important where regular delivery of major range items required, and with items difficult to manufacture, or where high quality, hygiene standards mandatory. Simpler administrative routines are possible when quality and consistency is high	Becoming more important as quality increasingly is used as a competitive weapon by major multiples and consistency is sought to simplify and hence reduce costs of administration
(2) Need for flexible response to respond to changes in consumer	More likely to be achieved when supplier well adapted to working with retailer, ie within context of long-term working relationship. More significant for delivery of goods in continuous demand (groceries) than for bi-annual seasonal ordering (clothing)	Becoming major factor as: (a) 'Just in time' delivery systems introduced and lower stockholding by retailers (all sectors) (b) fashion changes more frequent and flexible quicker response required by manufacturers (clothing)
(3) Joint product development work required	Most critical with retailers with pro-active approaches towards new product development work. This is a function of (a) size of retailer, (b) market niche sought. The more precisely targeted the retailer's marketing concept, the larger the retailer, the greater the degree of product differentiation, the more significant this factor becomes	Large retailers have buying teams and expect considerable interaction between themselves and their suppliers: set-up costs are high encouraging stability. However, some retailers are using this interaction to encourage more pro-active approaches by manufacturers
(4) Specific delivery systems required	Most critical with products requiring specialist distribution into stores, eg meats, fresh fish, and some chilled food	Probably becoming less important to manufacturers as third party distribution systems have grown particularly in specialist areas but this is of increasing importance for suppliers of distribution services

Factor	*Role*	*Directions of change*
(5) Frequent contact through frequent ordering	Most critical for goods ordered continuously	The development of computerised systems which link retailers and manufacturers with different technologies may make switching between supply sources easier in the long term but presently these technologies increase stability because of start-up costs and their relatively slow diffusion
(6) Wide produce ranges required for a limited number of suppliers	This increases the costs of changing suppliers because of the greater complexity of business	Becoming less important for distribution reasons in some sectors with increased availability of third party distribution. Still significant in sectors where demand related products and where manufacturer performs a product assembly role for retailers
(7) High physical degrees of product differentiation	With products which are difficult to replicate the retailer is more likely to stay with same supplier	Becoming more important particularly with products with special effects and designs (some areas of fabrics and furnishings) and retailers who seek to compete on individuality of their products
(8) Strong manufacturer brands	Retailer will wish to stock these lines	Retailer-label and brand developments have affected non-promotion-supported manufacturer brands, but have not significantly eroded the market shares of manufacturer brand leaders. In some sectors (eg toys) manufacturer brands are dominant

Factor	*Role*	*Directions of change*
(9) Number of suppliers	When there are few alternative sources of supply, degree of stability higher but this will depend on intensity of competition among these suppliers	International sourcing of higher value products such as clothing increased the number of sources of supply and reduced need for stability as long as point 2 not relevant. Overall, very variable depending on manufacturing sector involved
(10) Development of retail buying groups	As groups develop the evolution of suppliers becomes more rigorous and decisions to use a supply source are the result of a joint decision which because of its joint nature is less likely to be rescinded	Buying groups are of increasing importance with recent joint moves on European buying groups by large food retailers
(11) Buyer decision-making	The span of responsibility of buyers is increasing so that they are responsible for more products which reduces their ability to review constantly new suppliers. Shortage of buying staff in retailers also increases likelihood of remaining with an existing supplier	Likely to increase in importance as buyers come under more pressure to cover a wider range of products. Learning curve for new buyers related to product complexity
(12) Technological complexity	Important factor in suppliers of IT equipment to retailers	Becoming more important as costs of changing IT supplier can be considerable and are likely to increase with technological complexity
(13) Consistent product range	Emergent large suppliers are able to supply extensive co-ordinated product ranges	Convenient, but not essential, to obtain range co-ordination from a single supplier. Reinforces point 11
(14) Changes in organisation of export marketing by suppliers	Most critical where foreign production sources are highly variable in product quality, etc and an export agent/wholesaler is used	Long term relationships with the agent/wholesaler enables cultural differences between supply sources and retailer to be over-

Factor	*Role*	*Directions of change*
		come. This factor varies consider-ably in importance with product type
(15) Person-alities and personal obligations	Personal relationships of buyer and account manager may extend over many years. Depends very much on individuals	With fewer companies in the market this will be a more important factor but corporate obligations become less important as firms get larger
(16) Structure of deals made	Increasingly complex structure of deals and discounts allow deal structures which 'reward' stability	Suppliers likely to try to increase stability rewarding deals
(17) Strategic management issues	Stable vertical relationships are more easily planned and can generate more reliable forecasts which enable horizontal competitive policies and tactics to be calculated with more accuracy	Likely to be more important until such time as management systems can cope with forecasting the effects of rapidly changing vertical relationships

transaction, to the entirely integrated, whereby the relationship is internalised within a single organisation. Traditionally channel relationships have tended to be towards the transactional end of this spectrum, with some notable exceptions where fully internalised (vertically integrated) relationships occurred. Moves in recent years, certainly in respect of relationships involving retailers, have been away from both these extreme positions (Dawson and Shaw, 1989). Even with the relationships of single firms this pattern may be evident because a typical retail firm has a wide range of types of relationships with its suppliers of products and services. For different products in a retailer's product range a firm may choose to establish different types of channel relationship supported by different buying practices. For other products and services purchased by the retailer, for example its IT equipment or its security services, quite different channel relationships will be involved. For the supply of products for resale perhaps the previously transactional nature of relationships may become more administered with moves into retailer label and brands or because of some of the other reasons listed in Table 1.1. At the same time previously internalised relationships for the supply of services, such as transport/distribution, security, cleaning, for example and even the supply of capital equipment have moved towards being more transactional with third party transport, specialist service providers and the leasing of capital equipment. Even functions such as employee recruitment have become provided on a more, but not totally, transactional basis by specialist employee agencies.

The situation in respect of physical distribution provides an interesting illustration of the trend. Relationships can vary from a position in which both the warehousing and transport functions in physical distribution are vertically integrated within the manufacturer who delivers to the shop, through various combinations of integration and administration of both warehousing and transport by both retailer and manufacturer and within administered cases possibly including other specialist service providers, to an opposite extreme situation in which parcels are sent by postal service, courier, parcel carrier, etc on a totally transactional basis (McKinnon, 1989). The potential, and actual, variety is considerable even within one product area and even involving one retailer using a range of suppliers. The reasons for a particular form to the relationship or even a particular portfolio of relationships are complicated and imperfectly understood.

Transaction costs theory (Williamson, 1975; 1989) can make a contribution to an understanding of the factors which lead a channel to externalise activities. This has been developed in the marketing literature (Ruekert *et al*, 1985) where the efficiency of internal versus external organisation is seen to be dependent on the uncertainty and complexity of macro-environmental conditions, the number of bargains, the frequency, specificity, duration of the task and ease with which the performance of the task can be assessed. As a generalisation, external transactions are likely to replace internal organisation when no idiosyncratic assets are required, many competitive suppliers are available, when tasks are repetitive, the task environment is stable and not complex and, finally, when performance outcomes can be easily and accurately assessed. In a current portfolio of relationships in a company there is probably also a strong inertial component. Some of the issues for grocery retailing and whether to use a retailer-owned distribution depot or whether to use direct store delivery by manufacturer have been listed by Harris (1987), but information on cost relationships of the various alternatives is difficult to obtain.

Types of channel relationships

It is generally assumed that channel relationships may be divided into four main types: conventional; administered; contractual; and corporate (McCammon, 1970). The conventional channel is characterised by transactional relationships and although termed 'conventional' it is probably no longer the most common type. The corporate channel is characterised by internalised, corporately integrated relationships. Between the two extremes are:

- administered systems in which one party in the channel undertakes the co-ordination of activity and of relationships on the basis of leadership or power;
- contractual systems in which members are bound together by formal agreement, such as a franchise relationship.

Both these intermediate positions involve the manager and the managed in a relationship. Power differentials exist and are exploited either informally or formally. Within both administered and contractual systems there is great variety depending on:

(**1**) span of control exercised by the dominant agent;
(**2**) the power differential between the parties involved;
(**3**) the extent of policing, reward and punishment involved in the relationship;
(**4**) the tightness with which responsibilities in the relationship are specified;
(**5**) the extent and boundaries to which entrepreneurialism is tolerated or encouraged;
(**6**) the extent to which information and communication are integrated among members of the relationship.

Despite the potential dimensions of variation in all administered or contractual relationships there is an element of inequality and dependency implicit in all relationships of this type (Mattsson, 1985).

The rise of the retailers

One of the consistent and continuing trends in administered channels has been the shift of power towards retailers in relationships. Most evident in administered channels, it is also present in contractual channels. Although this is a widely held view there have been surprisingly few attempts to evaluate or measure the change. Several studies provide qualitative evidence for the shift (Mintel, 1987; Davies *et al*, 1986; Howe, 1990). Grant (1987) defines power as the ability of large retailers to extract preferential discounts from suppliers. The evidence from the Monopolies and Mergers Commission (1981) *Report on Discounts to Retailers* suggests that the larger retailers can obtain larger discounts than small retailers, but the subsequent updating of this study carried out by the Office of Fair Trading (1985) pointed to a reduction in the differential in discounts between large and small retailers which might be taken as a decrease in the power of large retailers. Difficulties exist with these studies in their equation of power and buying discount. The basis of retailer power is more broadly based than the negotiation of discounts. The basis of the channel power of retailers is the ability to influence other channel members to make decisions which otherwise would not have been made. There are many ways that this power is exercised and made manifest. The degree of power may be related to magnitude of change which can be made to the decisions of others. The measurement of the power may be in financial terms or in many other ways including, for example, the ability to call meetings according to the timetable determined by the more powerful group, the capacity to define when particular activities will take place, the influencing of advertising of the brand of the less powerful partner, the capability of the more powerful group to alter the strategic direction of others. The definition, use and measurement of power in distribution channels has been widely researched and it is intended here neither to review nor to add to these studies (Lusch and Ross, 1985; Mallen, 1978). It is, however, useful to consider some of the reasons why retailers apparently have become more powerful.

There are many reasons for the relative and often absolute increase in influence of retailers within supply chain or channel relationships. Some of these reasons are listed below.

- Large retail companies have resulted in greater actual and potential buying power for products for resale, capital equipment, marketing services (eg advertising) and other goods and services, even finance. Suppliers of goods and services have become aware of the potential extent of this power.
- Proximity to consumers and point of sale information collec-

tion allow retailers to become aware rapidly of consumer reactions to products and of changes in consumer demand.

- Retail label development has increased retailer involvement in traditional manufacturer areas of new product development, product testing and 'brand' (retail label and store) advertising.
- Product related variables, over which the manufacturer has control, are of lesser importance in the retail marketing mix than formerly was the case.
- The shortening of product life cycles results in retail strategy being built on factors other than the product and on factors over which the retailer, rather than the manufacturer, has control.
- Resale price maintenance now exists on very few products.
- Improved market searching and market information by retailers (particularly on non-UK suppliers) increases retailer opportunities to use multiple sources for products.
- Retailers' awareness of the real costs of in-store space has encouraged tighter management of space by retailers and the exclusion of manufacturer involvement in activities in-store merchandising.
- Retailers' decisions to seek more control over physical distribution has removed one of the activities traditionally managed by manufacturers and in the process retailers have expected and obtained financial and other benefits formerly held by manufacturers.
- More professional management practices have become widespread in retailing.
- Increased international sourcing by retailers has increased the number of manufacturers in competition with each other for retail sales.
- Aggressive short-term negotiation tactics by retailers are used to reinforce dependency relationships.

Few, if any of these factors, are likely to diminish in significance in coming years and several will increase in importance. The reasons are of different significance in different broad retail sub-sectors such as specialist, fashion or convenience and also may have different significance in respect of product groups, such as toys, confectionery or ambient grocery. The shift in influence is a broadly based feature of distribution channels in the UK, elsewhere in Europe and in the USA. The results of the Annual Report of the Grocery Industry published in *Progressive Grocer* illustrate the trend. Tables 1.2 and 1.3 summarise results over several years of this survey of retailer-manufacturer relations. Table 1.2 shows perceived changes in the balance, year on year, by respondents to the survey by *Progressive Grocer*. Respondents are drawn from manufacturers, retailers and wholesalers. The proportion perceiving a change on the previous year is usually a little over half, but over 60 per cent of those perceiving a change see it as a move which enhances the power of the retailers. Cumulatively, over the 1980s, this represents a significant shift.

Table 1.3 shows two components of manufacturer-retailer relationships as perceived by chain store respondents to the survey. Despite a change in the response sample structure in 1986, the pattern of perception of change is very clear with a notable increase in the proportion of retailers seeing an increasing number of deals and discounts being offered and a shift towards more dis-

Table 1.2: *Perceptions of grocery industry executives in USA on changes in retailer-manufacturer relationships*

	% saying		of those saying change % saying	
	no change	change	towards retailer	towards manufacturer
1981	40	60	67	33
1982	not available	not available		
1983	54	46	70	30
1984	48	52	62	38
1985	42	58	63	37
1986	50	50	63	37
1987[1]	46	54	72	28
1988[1]	33	67	83	17
1989[1]	35	65	83	17

[1] Responses of the chain store respondents; respondents from other groups see an even greater degree of change.

Source: *Progressive Grocer*, Annual Report of the Grocery Industry

Table 1.3: *Perceptions of chain store executives and managers in USA on changes in character of retailer-manufacturer relationship*

	Number of deals and allowances offered		Amount of merchandising and display material	
	% saying		% saying	
	less now	more now	less now	more now
1978	47	31	67	13
1979	41	37	66	18
1980	34	43	64	20
1981	33	43	58	27
1982	22	51	50	28
1983	23	52	52	27
1984	23	51	49	27
1985	24	50	48	31
1986[1]	11	65	33	30
1987[1]	14	58	29	33
1988[1]	11	59	32	17
1989[1]	9	56	38	18

[1] Figures refer to respondents who are chain store executives only.

Source: *Progressive Grocer*, Annual Report of the Grocery Industry

play materials being offered. The implications drawn in the commentary to the survey is that retailers are expecting and obtaining more benefits coming to them in the deals which are struck. The commentary on the 1990 survey says, 'One fact everyone can agree on is that in the 1980s the balance of power shifted decisively to the retailer and is still shifting that way. . .until the industry finds a new equilibrium, until retailers understand the breadth of their power and manufacturers accept this change, relationships promise to stay stressed' (*Progressive Grocer*, 1990 p34).

The situation in the USA is explicitly shown in this survey of perceptions of channel relationships in the grocery sector. A variety of implicit studies (Bain and Co, 1990) and reported interviews in the European trade press suggests that the position in Europe is perhaps less acute, but a strained relationship does exist. This is a point explored by Moir (1990) in his review of retail competition. Many of the participants in these channel relationships profess dissatisfaction with the levels of conflict which have developed in recent years.

There are several factors likely to encourage questioning of the channel domination by retailers. Inter-manufacturer co-operation is likely to increase particularly as a response to increasing retailer concentration. The larger groupings will be more likely to question retailer domination. A second factor is the realisation in some sectors that overdomination of a channel by one partner can stifle creativity. Helleberg and Engh (1990) argue, 'closer buyer/seller co-operation should also result in faster and more effective product development' (p43). The pace and character of reaction to a situation of overdomination will vary considerably by sector and will be heavily influenced by the attitudes of key individual senior executives.

Associative relationships

A fifth type of channel relationship may be observed which again is intermediate between the transactional and corporate integrated extremes, but which is *associative*. In this type of relationship participants jointly undertake the necessary activities in a value adding partnership (Johnston and Lawrence, 1988). Difficulties arise over definitions of competition and collusion in this type of relationship. The form of the relationship has been present in horizontal markets for some time, whether at the consumer level through consumer co-operatives or at retail level with buying consortia and joint ventures. Although present for some time the pace of development appears to have quickened in recent years with several major cases.

Significant examples are the joint agreement of Boots and WH Smith in the UK to establish a joint venture with their respective DIY retail operations, the international agreement between J Sainsbury and GB to establish DIY outlets in the UK, and an agreement between Eroski and Consum in Spain to develop jointly hypermarket-based shopping centres, the several European based buying and marketing consortia involving major retailers in the food sector. What is relatively newly recognised is the potential for such activity in vertical markets. The basis of the associative relationship is that interdependence is seen as mutual. The relationship is not seen as competitive with decisions made in a zero-sum game framework of profit apportionment, but is seen as complementary with decisions made in a prisoner's dilemma game framework of increasing total added value to the benefit of all parties.

A radically different management culture is required for these associative relationships than is commonplace in the highly aggressively competitive transactional relationships or power exploitative administered and contractual systems. Furthermore, this approach to marketing relationships has implications for a variety of other functions in the firm (Lyons *et al*, 1990; Cespedes, 1988; Miles, 1989). Axelrod (1984) has suggested that each member of co-operative groups with shared objectives should not be first to play 'competitive' games, nor should they seek to gain an upper hand on other members of the association. Such almost altruistic behaviour can be culturally painful for managers who have been encouraged, throughout their career and development, to compete. It requires a different approach to insiders of the associative relationship than to outside competitors.

Associative systems are enabled by networks which allow simultaneous sharing of information among network members but exclude non-members (Miles and Snow, 1987). This allows co-ordinated responses to the environment outside the channel and to the activities of non-members of the network. These networks of shared information also work positively to increase interdependency and efficiencies of members of the network such that new cost economies of network membership arise which become exclusive to the particular vertical relationship. Baligh (1986) argues that while vertical decisions may be shared horizontal decisions are unshared with the higher implementation costs implicit in vertical co-operation offset by increased horizontal competitiveness. These associative relationships may exist for particular functions rather than across the whole channel. Senker (1986) has shown how such relationships may exist in technological co-operation for new product development.

The vast majority of retailer-supplier relationships is of one of the four more widely recognised types. There appears to be an increase in the proportion of administered systems of channel relationships at the expense of the two extreme positions. Such a move to channel relationships which have an explicit power and dependency component is quite distinct from the creation of associative relationships. Such relationships have several phases within them. Dwyer *et al* (1987) suggest a five-phase sequence of awareness, exploration, expansion, commitment and dissolution. The move to more stable relationships in the case of administrative systems represents a consolidation and logical use of power to reduce transaction costs while in associative relationships stability is linked to the supportive relationships and joint decisions which occur in associative channels. These types of move would suggest a greater emphasis is being placed by members on the expansion and commitment phases in the Dwyer *et al* model. At the same time, associative channels are starting to appear and this type of relationship seems likely to become more widespread and important in the future. The growth in importance of this type of channel has paralleled changes in concepts of business management associated with the establishment of networks (Mintzberg, 1989) and it is interesting to surmise on potential parallels with the post-modernity arguments prevalent in social science philosophy (Harvey, 1989).

Summary

This chapter has suggested that relationships between retailers and their suppliers have undergone fundamental changes in recent years as a result of many factors, including emerging techniques for managing the supply chain. These techniques have been applied as firms have become larger and as distribution channels have taken more variety of form, structure and process. These approaches to supply chain management have been enabled by new information technologies associated with the collection, transmission and analysis of information through networks of firms (Pilotti, 1988).

The changes in the structure and operation of the distribution channel are substantial. Although more stable relationships are evident, the relationship between retailers and suppliers is not static. The number of options for different forms of relationships have increased. Neither does stability mean a reduction in competitive pressures. Alongside the increasing stability there has also been a shift to retailers having more influence in both the form and operation of the supplier-retailer relationship. The question to be asked about the supplier-retailer relationship in the future is, will retailers, from a position of increased market power and under conditions favouring more stable relationships, use their growing influence to create truly associative relationships or will they use their power to reinforce relationships of long-term domination ?

References

Anderson, JC and Narus, JA (1990) 'A model of distributor firm and marketing firm working partnerships' *Journal of Marketing 54* : 45–58.

Anderson, E and Weitz, BA (1986) 'Make or buy decision: vertical integration and marketing productivity' *Sloan Management Review 27* (3): 3–19.

Axelrod, R (1990) *The Evolution of Co-operation* Penguin Books, London.

Bain and Co (1990) *The Battle for the Value Added Chain* Bain and Co, Munich.

Baligh, HH (1986) 'Co-operating and competing in shared and unshared marketing decision variables' *Research in Marketing 8*: 131–80.

Burt, S (1989) 'Trends and management issues in European retailing' *International Journal of Retailing 4* (4): 1–97.

Carlisle, JA and Parker RC (1989) *Beyond Negotiation* Wiley, Chichester.

Cespedes, FV (1988) 'Channel management is general management' *Californian Management Review 31*(1): 98–120.

Davies, K, Gilligan, C and Sutton, C (1986) 'The development of own label product strategies in grocery and DIY retailing in the UK' *International Journal of Retailing 1*(1): 6–19.

Dawson, JA and Shaw, SA (1989) 'The move to administered vertical marketing systems by British retailers' *European Journal of Marketing 23*(7): 42–52.

Dwyer, FR, Schurr, PH and Oh, S (1987) 'Developing buyer-seller relationships' *Journal of Marketing 51*: 11–27.

Fink, SL, Baek, J and Taddeo, K (1971) 'Organisational crisis and change' *Applied Behavioural Sciences 7*: 15–37.

Frazior, GL and Sheth, JN (1985) 'An attitude behaviour framework for distribution channel management' *Journal of Marketing 49*: 38–48.

Grant, RM (1987) 'Manufacturer-retailer relations: the shifting balance of power' in Johnson, G (ed) *Business Strategy and Retailing* Wiley, Chichester: 43–58.

Harris, DG (1987) 'Central versus direct delivery for large retail food outlets' University of Stirling *Institute for Retail Studies, Working Paper 8703*.

Harvey, D (1989) *The Condition of Post-modernity* Blackwell, Oxford.

Hellberg, RB and Engh, MMO (1990) 'Buyer-seller relations: improving the effectiveness of materials supply' *International Journal of Logistics Management 1*(1): 36–43.

Hogg, C (1987) 'How manufacturers are responding to retailers' needs' paper to *Retail Consortium Conference on the Retail Environment* London: May 1987.

Howe, WS (1990) 'UK retailer vertical power, market concentration and consumer welfare' *International Journal of Retail and Distribution Management 18*(2): 16–25.

Jeuland, AP and Shugan, SM (1983) 'Coordination in marketing channels' in Gautschi, DA (ed) *Productivity and efficiency in distribution systems* North Holland, New York: 17–34.

Johnston, R and Lawrence PR (1988) 'Beyond vertical integration: the rise of the value-adding partnership' *Harvard Business Review* July/August: 94–101.

Lusch, RF and Ross, RH (1985) 'The nature of power in a marketing channel' *Journal of Academy of Marketing Science 13*(23): 39–56.

Lyons, TF *et al* (1990) 'Mixed motive marriages: What's next for buyer-supplier relations' *Sloan Management Review 31*(3): 29–36.

McCammon, BC (1970) 'Perspective for distribution programming' in Bucklin, LP (ed) *Vertical Marketing Systems* Scott, Foresman & Co., Glenview, I11.

McKinnon, AC (1989) *Physical Distribution Systems* Routledge, London.

Mallen, B (1963) 'A theory of retailer-supplier conflict, control and cooperation' *Journal of Retailing 39*: 24–32, 51–2.

—— (1978) 'Channel power: a form of economic exploitation' *European Journal of Marketing 12*(2): 194–202.

Mattsson, LF (1985) 'An application of a network approach to marketing: defending and changing market positions' *Research in Marketing (Supplement) 2*: 263–88.

Miles, RE (1989) 'Adapting to technology and competition' *Californian Management Review 31*(2): 9–28.

Miles, R and Snow, C (1987) 'Network organisations: new concepts for new forms' *California Management Review* Spring: 62–78.

Mintel (1987) 'Food retailing: retail buying practices' *Retail Intelligence*(1): 74–85.

Mintzberg, D (1989) *Mintzbergon Management* Free Press, New York.

Moir, C (1990) 'Competition in the UK grocery trades' in Moir, C and Dawson JA (eds) *Competition and Markets* Macmillan, London: 91–118.

Monopolies and Mergers Commission (1981) *Discounts to Retailers* HMSO, London.

Narus, JA and Anderson, JC (1987) 'Distribution contributions to partnerships with manufacturers' *Business Horizons 30*: 34–42.

Office of Fair Trading (1985) *Competition and Retailing* OFT, London.

Pilotti, L (1988) 'Technological and informative efficiency for flexible retail services' *CESCOM*, Research Note: 15.

Progressive Grocer (1990) 'Annual Report of Grocery Industry 1990' *Progressive Grocer 69* (5): 4–67.

Reve, T and Stern, LW (1979) 'Interorganizational relations in marketing channels' *Academy of Management Review 4*(3): 405–16.

Ruekert, RW, Walker, OC and Roering, KJ (1985) 'The organisation of marketing activities: a contingency theory of structure and performance' *Journal of Marketing 49*: 13–25.

Senker, JM (1986) 'Technological co-operation between manufacturers and retailers to meet market demand' *Food Marketing 2*(3): 88–100.

Williamson, O (1975) *Markets and Hierarchies* Free Press, New York.

—— (1989) 'Transaction cost economics' in Schmalensee, R and Willig, RD (eds) *Handbook of Industrial Organization vol 1* Elsevier, Amsterdam: 135–82.

2

The Impact of Mergers and Acquisitions upon Retail Distribution: The Safeway Case

Lawrence R Christensen

Introduction

The 1980s witnessed a major transformation of ownership patterns in UK industry. The retail sector was prominent in the acquisition fever of the period, thereby transforming the face of the British high street. This chapter will outline the scale of these acquisitions, the major players involved and the consequences of these growth strategies for logistics management, using Safeway as a case study.

Retail acquisitions and mergers in the 1980s

According to research undertaken by the Corporate Intelligence Group (1989) a total of 507 major acquisitions and mergers were carried out within the UK retailing sector from 1982–8; these transactions were valued at £17.5 billion (Tables 2.1a and 2.1b). Growth in the annual value of transactions was continuous until the stock market crash of October 1987. Even then, 105 transactions valued at £3.2 billion were carried out in 1988. The reasons for this level of activity are varied but in general terms UK retailing is a mature industry offering limited opportunities for organic growth. Companies have therefore used an acquisition strategy to increase market share in their own specialised area of business or they have diversified away from their core business into other potential growth areas of retailing. The former strategy has been adopted by several food retailers, most notably the now defunct Dee Corporation, the Argyll Group and Tesco. The mixed retailers have been active in diversifying away from their variety or department store image. Woolworth, now Kingfisher plc, has been the most energetic

Table 2.1a: *Summary of UK retailing acquisitions and mergers: number by sector, 1982–8*

Selling sector	Numbers						
	1982	1983	1984	1985	1986	1987	1988
Food retailers	4	10	8	6	14	19	8
CTNs	–	3	3	5	4	10	5
Off-licences	–	4	8	13	3	3	5
Clothing retailers	2	3	3	5	9	16	12
Footwear retailers	1	4	1	3	2	8	4
Furniture, carpets and household textiles retailers	4	2	4	7	4	8	10
Electrical and music goods retailers	1	–	4	7	7	14	5
DIY and hardware retailers	4	1	4	2	4	5	8
TV rental and other hire operators	–	1	1	3	–	4	1
Chemists	1	1	–	2	3	13	9
Booksellers and stationers	–	–	–	5	2	4	2
Jewellers	–	2	4	1	4	3	6
Mixed retail businesses (incl department stores)	1	–	3	6	1	1	7
General mail order houses	–	1	–	2	2	3	4
Others (incl opticians)	1	6	2	4	8	12	10
Total UK purchases	**19**	**38**	**45**	**71**	**67**	**123**	**96**
UK retailers' purchases abroad	2	–	5	8	10	14	9
Total all acquisitions and mergers	**21**	**38**	**50**	**79**	**77**	**137**	**105**

Source: Corporate Intelligence Group research

of these companies with its acquisition of B and Q, Comet and Superdrug although the most recent acquisition of Ward White has taken Boots into DIY, through Payless, and auto accessories (Halfords). It is in both the food and mixed retail business sectors that the greatest concentration of activity occurs in a small number of large firms.

Not surprisingly, limits to domestic growth have led UK retailers to seek market opportunities overseas. As can be seen from Table 2.1b, the value of acquisitions abroad increased markedly from 1984 to 1987, slowing down in 1988 after the stock market crash. Much attention has been focused by UK retailers on the USA. From 1984 to 1989, UK companies made a total of 37 acquisitions in US retailing valued at around $3.9 billion (Table 2.2). Hamill and Crosbie (1990) show that 1987 and 1988 were peak years with a total

Table 2.1b: *Summary of UK retailing acquisitions and mergers: value by sector, 1982–8*[1] *(£ mn)*

Selling sector	1982	1983	1984	1985	1986	1987	1988
Food retailers	107.5	322.7	275.4	73.9	832.2	1,104.6	260.9
CTNs	–	6.8	51.8	39.2	72.7	340.8	75.3
Off-licences	–	10.8	45.9	10.3	24.1	50.0	18.0
Clothing retailers	5.1	46.9	6.7	145.1	36.5	105.4	115.9
Footwear retailers	6.0	47.0	15.3	30.1	6.0	72.2	28.5
Furniture, carpets and household textiles retailers	14.9	4.8	17.7	662.6	163.6	750.7	545.7
Electrical and music goods retailers	30.0	–	428.3	26.6	79.3	32.0	53.3
DIY and hardware retailers	14.0	–	9.4	–	302.0	187.6	477.7
TV rental and other hire operators	–	–	120.0	65.5	–	256.5	0.5
Chemists	0.5	0.3	–	–	21.1	325.6	136.7
Booksellers and stationers	–	–	–	14.4	0.8	26.3	6.6
Jewellers	–	2.2	11.1	0.3	232.8	27.6	200.3
Mixed retail businesses (incl department stores)	310.0	–	23.7	2,760.4	7.0	9.8	162.8
General mail order houses	–	1.7	–	0.8	310.0	4.5	480.0
Others (incl opticians)	–	269.5	57.9	30.5	70.5	422.0	21.2
Total UK purchases	**488.0**	**712.7**	**1,063.2**	**3,859.7**	**2,158.6**	**3,715.6**	**2,583.2**
UK retailers' purchases abroad	33.6	–	28.7	395.6	548.5	1,251.3	641.8
Total all acquisitions and mergers	**521.6**	**712.7**	**1,091.9**	**4,255.3**	**2,707.1**	**4,966.9**	**3,225.0**

[1] Value of transactions where known

Source: Corporate Intelligence Group research

of 22 acquisitions worth $2.3 billion. The main deals were made by Marks and Spencer, Dixons, Sainsbury and Ratners Group (see Table 2.3). This preference for the US rather than the European market can be attributed to the size of the US market, the liberal political environment with regard to foreign direct investment and

Table 2.2: *British acquisitions in the USA: 1984–9*

	Total		Retailing	
Year	Number of Acquisitions	Acquisition Value ($m)	Number of Acquisitions	Acquisition Value ($m)
1984	119	3,604	1	12
1985	147	5,200	5	862
1986	208	13,592	6	536
1987	262	31,725	13	1,061
1988	385	31,708	9	1,197
1989	262	11,743	3	204
Total	1,383	97,572	37	3,872

Source: Hamill and Crosbie, 1990

Table 2.3: *The ten largest British acquisitions in US retailing: 1984/89*

Acquiring Company	Acquired Company	Principal Activity	Value ($m)	Year
Marks and Spencer	Brooks Brothers	Menswear retailing	750.0	1988
Dee Corp	Builderama Inc	Retailing	414.0	1986
Dee Corp	Herman's Sporting Goods	Sporting goods retailer	406.0	1985
Dixons Group	Cyclops (Silo)	Electrical retailing	400.0	1987
Grand Met	Pearle Health Services	Eye care products	386.0	1985
J Sainsbury	Shaw's Supermarket	Supermarkets	261.0	1987
Ratners Group	Sterling	Jewellery retailing	203.0	1987
Panfida Group	Majik Market (90%) Tenneco	Convenience Stores	152.0	1988
Grand Met	Eyelab	Optical superstores	142.0	1989
Marks and Spencer	Kings Supermarkets	Food retailing	108.0	1988

Source: As Table 2.2

planning constraints and the short-term considerations of a strong pound and relatively depressed stock market prices. It is likely that companies will reorientate their strategies post 1992 and beyond, especially with the unification of Germany and the development of other markets in eastern Europe. To date, however, UK retailers have not been so active in European markets as in the USA, limiting developments to small acquisitions or joint ventures with cross shareholdings among groups. The latter approach is one adopted by Argyll in collaboration with Casino and Ahold.

The distribution consequences of merger activity

While much attention is invariably focused on how the predator or senior partner in an acquisition or merger will run the combined group, the consequences for distribution should not be ignored in discussions on store formats, merchandising, marketing and the future utilisation of property assets. It is unlikely that the harmonisation of distribution systems between the two merged parties will be an easy task. Depot networks will be analysed with regard to the number and sites of existing warehouses. Current operational procedures at these sites and the agreed work practices with labour unions in both warehouse and transport operations will be reviewed. The best way to illustrate how to manage such change is to give a detailed example, namely that of Safeway plc, the company created through the merger of the Argyll food retailing business of Presto and the UK division of Safeway in 1987.

The case of Safeway plc

The key statistics of the two companies at the time of the acquisition were:

	Presto	Safeway
Stores	540	135
RDCs	10	4
Personnel	40,000	20,000
Turnover	£m 1,824bn	£m 1,040bn

In the year prior to the acquisition, profits were:

PROFIT	£m 71.8	£m43.8
PROFIT	3.9%	4.2%

In addition, there were the north-west companies of Lo-Cost and Cordon Bleu which operated limited range and freezer stores in England and Wales, as well as Mojo Cash & Carry, North West Vintners and Snow King.

The chairman and chief executive, Alistair Grant, set as the companies' objective – that from the separate mainstream retailing businesses of Presto and Safeway would emerge a single, much more powerful and efficient force, broadly based upon the retailing and product skills of Safeway and the trading, information technology and distribution skills of Presto, while all stores not suitable for this format would convert to Lo-Cost limited range discount stores.

This approach resulted in the Safeway 1990 programme which involved tremendous change in all areas of the business, while still retaining the quality of service, product, stores, people and most of all the profit. The key to success is to maintain quality through such a period of rapid change.

First, what is meant by quality and change?

The quality aspect of the job can be defined as follows.

- delivering the product ordered by the store:
- on time;
- in good condition;
- within code;
- at the correct temperature and intact;
- by a vehicle which is clean both inside and out;
- by a driver whose appearance confirms the company image;
- and with documentation which is the minimum required for accuracy and efficiency of operations;
- and all of course at minimum cost.

Change would be defined as any movement in company policy or strategy which could effect the efficiency or the quality of the operation during the transitional period. The objective must be to accomplish the change while holding the quality in place. This skill, for skill it is, has become known in Safeway as 'the management of change'. Put in more simple terms, neither the store managers nor the customers must be able to see the join.

How is change and quality managed within Safeway?

In February 1987 the distribution divisions were as follows. The Presto network was completed just before the acquisition of Safeway and consisted of centres at:

Abbotsinch	–	Glasgow
Bathgate	–	T/P Glass Glover
Felling	–	Newcastle
Stockton	–	Teesside
Birtley	–	T/P UCD
Wakefield	–	Yorkshire
Welwyn Garden City		
Chadwell Heath	–	T/P UCD
Hayes	–	T/P Glass Glover
Bristol		
Exeter	–	T/P UCD

The Safeway network consisted of distribution centres at:

Aylesford	–	Kent
Hedge End	–	Southampton
Warrington	–	Cheshire
Cambuslang	–	Glasgow

In addition there was a speciality chilled operation out of Atherstone. The total output of both divisions was some 208 million cases per annum, or 4 million cases per week, which remarkably split almost evenly into 50 per cent to Presto and 50 per cent to Safeway with 70 per cent of the products going via central distribution in Presto and 85 per cent in Safeway.

The chief executive's strategy for one major trading fascia by 1991 (excluding Lo-Cost) with a target of 380 Safeway stores (originally there were 135) placed the following demands on the distribution division.

(**1**) To design and implement a distribution strategy to cope with projected outputs of 350 million cases per annum by 1991 – an increase of 168 per cent on current volumes of the combined operation, resulting in a weekly output of some 6.7 million cases per week.

(**2**) To install Argyll's computer systems into the Safeway environment.

(**3**) To resolve industrial relations issues with two very different union agreements and two different unions.

(**4**) To merge and rationalise stock ranges into one single increased range.

(**5**) To cope with immediate store fascia changes and new openings.

(**6**) To resolve method differences between Safeway distribution and Presto distribution.

(**7**) To bring together two management teams with very different philosophies.

It is very easy to take each of these issues in hindsight and look at them in isolation, but in fact they all happen at much the same time in a very dynamic situation.

Therefore it is essential that there is a very detailed planning system forming the basis for regular review meetings of all the key executives involved from all the various departments within the company.

Meetings were held every two weeks to review progress against the objectives. Use was also made of the special computer systems which allow for the production of critical path analysis charts and for the production of statistical information of individual stores' outputs, by commodity group and the capacity of warehouses based on actual and forecasted data.

Using the company's five-year sales plan including the location of known new store sites, a computer model was used to locate and size the ideal network. This was then overlaid on top of the existing locations. Each location was then evaluated as to its potential and fit in the new environment. This initial study was made against the background of using the original Safeway stock range as the range to be carried. This amounted to some 9,000 lines.

The trading and marketing teams then completed their work which changed the terms of reference to the requirement to handle in the order of some 16,000 lines. This requirement no longer worked within the proposed strategy, as the only workable alternative was twin distribution centres with two locations delivering to all the stores in wide geographic areas, for example Scotland, with the consequential impact on transport costs.

A new strategy was needed to cope efficiently with the same output – but over a much wider range of product, which confirmed that any system developed for this kind of evaluation must be flexible in both its approach and application to be successful.

This took several months of detailed work and took us from the current network of 16 locations to the new proposed network – 12 locations – which includes, at the tactical level, the use of narrow aisle and crane systems, and at the strategic level, an investment of £64 million in new locations, such as:

- Bellshill (near Glasgow), which is one of the largest distribution developments currently in the UK which when complete will be able to handle 1.4 million cases per week across the total range of 16,000 lines;
- investment in the Bristol distribution centre with a 190,000 square foot extension, mainly temperature controlled to service stores with fresh produce and perishables in the south-west;
- a major reorganisation and capital investment in the Aylesford site to improve vehicle movement and productivity;
- as well as converting our Wakefield RDC to a common item warehouse, warehouse handles all the slow moving products in the ambient range for distribution to all stores in England and Wales, through a trunk operation to other centres or direct to store in its own delivery area.

This network will, with the exception of Wakefield and Atherstone, work on a four region basis (See Table 2.4).

The 79 stores in Scotland would be serviced by Bellshill and Bathgate, with Bathgate delivering a fast moving ambient range to stores on the eastern side of the country. Bellshill would deliver the total range across all commodity groups. Thus a store on the east coast would receive its deliveries from both Bellshill and Bathgate while a store in Glasgow would receive all its deliveries from Bellshill.

The 37 planned stores in the north-east would be serviced by both Felling and Stockton – who in turn would be supported by Bellshill for frozen and perishable foods and Wakefield and Atherstone for slow moving. The 145 stores in the Midlands and south-west would be serviced by Warrington, Bristol and a new, as yet to be developed, third party distribution centre in the Wolverhampton area. This region would be supported by Wakefield and Atherstone as already described for the north-east. The 118

Table 2.4: *Safeway 1990's programme distribution division – proposed network*

Region Serviced	*Location*	*Sq ft K*	*Operation*	*Operator*	*Stores*
Scotland	Bellshill	500	Composite	Christian Salvesen	79
	Bathgate	220	Ambient	Glass Glover	
North-east	Felling	207	Composite	Own Account	37
	Stockton	203	Ambient	NFC	
Midlands and South-West	Warrington	340	Composite	Own Account	145
	Wolverhampton	200	Ambient	Third Party	
	Bristol	351	Composite	Own Account	
South-East	Aylesford	554	Composite	Own Account	118
	West London	50	Frozen	Third Party	
	Welwyn G City	186	Ambient	Own Account	
England and Wales	Wakefield	206	Ambient Common Item Warehouse	Own Account	301
National	Atherstone	20	Speciality Chill Products	UCD	380
Total		3,037			

Previous total	2,607 k sq ft	
an increase of	430 k sq ft	Index 116
	Cases output	
Compared to an	4.0 million	
output increase of	6.7 million	Index 168
	2.7 million	
Moving the cases per sq ft to	2.2 from 1.5	

stores in the south-east would be serviced by Aylesford and Welwyn Garden City working broadly to the same method of operation as Bellshill and Bathgate supported by a new frozen third party operation with Wakefield and Atherstone supporting as before.

Had this new strategy been in place on day one, it would have made life relatively easy – however once this network was approved in principle the task was to commence implementing it while at the same time coping with all the changes brought about by the commencement of the retail conversion programme to Safeway.

The chairman stressed the need to commence the conversion programme before facilities were in place in order to generate our profit as soon as possible so as to demonstrate to both our existing and potential shareholders the profitability of our acquisition of Safeway.

To enable the conversion programme to start (which commenced in the south), it was essential to install the Argyll integrated distribution computer systems into existing Safeway locations in order to capture information such as store orders, depot replenishment, stock files and print picking lists and cover such issues as branch accounting, etc. This involved some 14 installations, while still handling case volumes in the order of 2 million per week on a short lead time, 24 hours per day, in a seven day per week operation. It was an enormous and risky task. It was achieved over a six-month period by first selecting key people who were trained as the implementation/training team.

Most of the problems encountered at this stage were not systems related, but people related – with such comments and feelings expressed as 'we've done it for years our way, we are successful – why should we change'. This was overcome in four ways:

- the commitment, confidence and skill of the implementation team;
- formal briefing meetings in small groups of all employees;
- informal involvement of senior distribution management at all levels;
- wide publicity within the company of the success of the initial implementations.

It was a very tough six-month period but at the end of it the objectives had been achieved and all 14 locations were operating on our systems very successfully.

It is not possible to manage an intense fast moving short lead time operation on a day-to-day basis and manage change as well. A strategy has been developed which is to have two teams reporting to a senior executive responsible for the site. The first team leader (who is normally the ongoing site manager) is responsible for day-to-day operations. The second team leader is responsible for the project – for example, the management of the change. It is the responsibility of the senior executive to ensure that the efforts of the two teams are well co-ordinated, thus ensuring there is no clash and no duplication of effort.

At the same time as installing systems, the different methods used by the two divisions were being examined. The major issues were as follows.

Presto had moved to case labels from picking lists because of the benefits to the store and for checking. Although a cost penalty to distribution, the company benefits outweighed the cost. Safeway on the other hand used a gross picking list.

To protect the business a healthy mix of third party operators was normal Presto policy, while Safeway in the main used large distribution centres totally in-house.

Presto had adopted a quad picking system in which superfast picking was separated and the picker picked orders from a quad which consisted of ten base points – five each side of the aisle – the products within the quad positioned on the basis of their volume movement. Safeway picked product up one side of an aisle turning at the top to pick the other side.

Presto – in line with the rest of the industry – used 90 per cent roll cage pallets with 10 per cent on pallets to the larger stores. Safeway delivered totally on wooden pallets with product retained using shrink wrap.

Presto – whose store staff completed shelf filling during the day – required loads delivered by a specific time to meet store staffing requirements, deliveries were guaranteed within a fixed two-hour window. Safeway who operated a night fill could handle the goods at any time during the day.

Presto – in order to take advantage of a longer picking period and to allow for the latest possible supplier delivery window – picked perishable goods by line into roll cages as the product was received. This also meant that similar volumes for branch pick could be handled in a much smaller area. Safeway laid all perishable products out into picking points and when all products were in the picking began. This resulted in a very condensed picking period to meet delivery requirements and required stock to be held.

Presto had developed a keen sense of hygiene through investment in equipment and the high standards of the management team. Safeway were not quite so good in comparison.

A small joint study team was set up to identify the best method for the new division which could have been something entirely new and not necessarily one of the two available alternatives. Some of the findings were surprising. For example, as a result of this study we moved to the wooden pallet operation instead of roll cages – probably the only major food retailer to do so.

In this scenario all options must be considered and decisions must be based on what is best for the new business. There was much opposition in some of these issues and barriers had to be broken down. But the one issue that could not be compromised was the retention of the highest possible hygiene standards.

The one possible error in the findings was perhaps the move from case labels to picking lists. Subsequent experience has led to a reversal of this decision. Where this has already been done, an immediate improvement in picking accuracy has been achieved.

In order to enable optimum use of facilities throughout the conversion programme with minimum product waste, it was necessary initially to set up temporary facilities. The Midlands and south-west region, for example, were serviced by Bristol for Presto and Warrington for Safeway. If no other changes were to be made, as stores converted to Safeway, they could only go to Warrington to be serviced by the Safeway range. The end result of this would be Warrington no longer able to cope with demand, and Bristol standing empty and unused.

To avoid this situation, a temporary third party warehouse was set up adjacent to Bristol using Rockwood Distribution Services at Avonmouth. Bristol and Avonmouth together could then carry:

- the common lines to both fascias;

- Presto specific lines;
- Safeway specific lines.

This meant that because we had implemented our systems and they were now common, a Presto store serviced by Bristol/ Avonmouth could receive its range until it became a Safeway, when it drew the Safeway range from the same source.

At the same time the longer-term project of producing a common stock range was ongoing, such that by the time the conversion programme has reached Scotland there will be a common range to both fascias, and by the time the new facilities come on stream, the much increased range of 16,000 lines will be available. The greatest problem encountered in this area was the correct tagging of every line in our computer system to ensure that it appeared in the store catalogues correctly.

As has been explained, the conversion and new store opening programme commenced while the new distribution facilities were still in the planning stage. So, how have we managed in the interim, with the increased volume and ranges with which we have had to cope? Three examples can serve as illustrations. First, to look at volume – our Aylesford site has the following space:

Cold store	1	64K	sq ft
Cold store	2	87K	sq ft
Cold store	3	69K	sq ft
Grocery		334K	sq ft
Plus			
Salvage		32K	sq ft
Vehicle Maintenance		8K	sq ft

Under previous management, this operation peaked at 1.4 million cases per week in the week before Christmas 1987. In 1988, in the week before Christmas, we successfully handled 2 million cases off this site and now on average handle 1.3 million cases per week on an ongoing basis. This has been achieved by:

- improved productivity;
- improved site organisation; and
- a management structure designed to cope more effectively with a 'multi-shed', multi-discipline site.

The second example is Scotland where, ahead of Bellshill coming on stream, we have 'tripled' our existing locations of Cambuslang, Abbotsinch and Bathgate – in other words part of the stock range for all stores is held in each location.

The final example fits into both our long- and short-term strategies – that was the setting up of Wakefield as our common item warehouse for England and Wales, and Atherstone as our national speciality chill operation. The commissioning of both these operations enabled immediate significant range improvement by releasing picking points in other locations, reduced inventory by having all slow movers in one place and improved stock service levels for the same reason.

As a result of the trunking operation we took full opportunity to back haul store deliveries to stores located on the return route to Wakefield.

These actions have taken us from 4 million to 5 million cases per week output, albeit at some interim cost penalty. However, the benefit at the store end and the ability to press ahead with conversion and new store opening programmes ahead of new distribution facilities has paid dividends well in excess of the interim distribution cost penalty.

At the time of the acquisition the Presto distribution division had negotiated agreements with the Transport and General Workers' Union (TGWU) and had within its network a liberal sprinkling of dedicated third parties as a deliberate policy. Safeway on the other hand was totally own account and dealt with the General Municipal, Boilermakers and Allied Trades Union (GMBATU). So, there were two totally different union agreements with higher rates of pay within the Safeway agreement.

Achieving harmony was a problem. The trick was how to achieve this without significantly increasing distribution costs, while maintaining good industrial relations. A strategy was developed which took the TGWU regional distribution centres to the Safeway rates of pay but in return for the following:

- Six-day cover (six-day cover means Saturday is part of the normal working week with Sunday as a day off together with one other day dependent on store demand). Productivity standards have been significantly improved with increased picking rates and improved vehicle fill.
- Total flexibility within a 40-hour week, whereby staff work to meet the demand. This could well mean five hours on a

Tuesday, ten hours on a Thursday, etc – all without premium payments.

- We were able to negotiate a totally clean slate and eliminate all local agreements that had crept in.
- A new sick pay scheme was implemented to eliminate casual sickness and absenteeism.

All this took some 12 months to achieve – but it is now in place.

In general terms, industrial relations must always be uppermost in mind. Communications must be good and it is important to care for, train and develop staff but, even if the policy is perfect it must still be possible to supply the store in times of difficulty, such as a major fire or systems breakdown at a single location. Contingency plans must therefore be in place as part of the strategy and will probably include the use of dedicated third parties as part of the network.

Nothing is possible without people. Of the key issues described in this chapter without doubt the most important is people. Without the right kind of leadership and the right people around you, none of the other objectives are even remotely achievable.

The initial difficulties of bringing together two divisions with strong traditions and 'dripping' with professional pride was not easy. The author is very well supported by an extremely professional team at head office in such areas as operations, systems, personnel, finance/administration, industrial engineering, engineering, and security.

Each distribution centre has its own team covering the same areas as head office. We have worked very hard over the past four to five years to develop structures which create the right kind of opportunities and career progression when taken in parallel with our assessment, training and management development programmes and, of course, the needs of the business.

In conclusion, the logistics team of Safeway has contributed significantly to the company's success by 'managing quality' throughout our operations and through the tremendous challenges and changes which had to be faced in integrating Presto and Safeway.

References

Corporate Intelligence Group (1989) *The Retail Rankings* CIG.

Hamill, J and Crosbie, J (1990) 'British Retail Acquisitions in the US' *International Journal of Retail and Distribution Management* vol 18 no 5, forthcoming.

3
The Internationalisation of Retailing - The Impact on Physical Distribution

Martyn T Pellew

Introduction

The trend towards the internationalisation of retailing has been strong over the past ten years. Today it is strengthening in Europe as leading European retailers seek to relieve the pressure of their own domestic markets, protect their profits and spread their risk. For some years, many retailers in the non-food sector have successfully expanded their concepts into other markets, for example Habitat, C&A, Mothercare and IKEA to name but four (see Table 3.1).

Now the major players in the food sector are following suit and moving into foreign markets, albeit more tentatively and in different ways, which will be gone into in more detail later. The rush to become international is certainly being boosted by the hype about '1992' and the feeling that it will be essential for companies to have an international presence in order to compete against foreign invaders. It is anticipated that the big players will get bigger, in manufacturing as well as in retailing, and many companies, large as well as small, will be swallowed up or will fail to survive in the increasingly competitive environment that is likely to result. But the internationalisation of retailing is happening on a wider scale than merely a European one.

European companies have moved into North and South America, and certain important figures in the industry have expressed a strong preference for transatlantic rather than cross-channel expansion. In many cases, there is a considerable trade-off between the two areas. Some European companies will consider that they have the flexibility and linguistic ability to develop a Europe-wide business. Others, particularly UK companies, will prefer to stick to markets that have close links to their own markets, be they economic, linguistic or cultural.

Table 3.1: *Leading international retailers by % of turnover*

		Country of Origin	*Foreign t/o as % of total t/o*
(1)	IKEA	Sweden	80%
(2)	Bally (Oerlikhon)	Switzerland	72%
(3)	Benetton	Italy	70%
(4)	Laura Ashley	UK	59%
(5)	Mr Minit	Belgium	56%
(6)	Mothercare (Storehouse)	UK	53%
(7)	Hermes	France	53%
(8)	C&A	Germany	46%
(9)	H&M Hennes	Switzerland	42%
(10)	Continent	France	41%
	Habitat (Storehouse)	UK	41%

Source: OC & C Strategy Consultants (*Retail Week* 10.11.89)

In this chapter we will consider how the internationalisation of retailing will affect the area of physical distribution. Initially an assessment of the current retailing climate will be made, looking at the trends identifiable in the market, and in the different sectors and countries, briefly commenting on the different distribution conditions in various markets today. This picture will be completed by a look at the progress of retailers who have already made moves to internationalise their business, and their approach to physical distribution in their new markets.

What of the future? What current and new trends are likely to have the greatest effect on physical distribution? How should logistics companies respond to the new demands of the international retailing environment? What will the retailers' new requirements be? An attempt will be made to address some of the many interesting questions that arise, as the physical distribution industry considers the advancing internationalisation of retailing.

Current developments

At the time of writing, it is the end of an extended period of buoyant retail sales in many of the major industrial markets of Europe. At the very beginning of the 1990s, the threat of an end to the retailing boom period of the mid and late 1980s is very real, at least in the UK. High interest rates, the government's method of controlling inflation, are finally having a serious effect on people's perceptions of their buying power, and both manufacturing and retailing companies are beginning to feel the squeeze. Economists are still undecided about whether the US economy is in for a 'hard' or 'soft' landing, which would have the usual knock-on effect on European economies.

New factors have emerged to give the economic outlook a completely different face in central Europe. With the unification of the Germanies and the liberalisation of eastern European economies, these areas will be key targets for manufacturers and retailers of consumer goods.

The dominant trend in retailing throughout Europe and the USA over the past few years has been the concentration of buying power and market share into the hands of fewer and fewer players. This has been true particularly in the UK, where the top five grocery retailers now claim about 60% per cent of the market, according to the Institute of Grocery Distribution. This in itself has had serious implications for the logistics industry. Previously, the distribution chain followed product from the manufacturer to wholesaler or distribution company, and then to the largely independent and relatively small retail outlets.

In many cases, the manufacturer served the retailers directly, which often meant a large number of vehicles delivering to the same shop each day. The emergence of the third-party shared-user distribution company, which developed in many cases from the in-house operations of major manufacturers such as Unilever, Imperial Group and Tate and Lyle, provided manufacturers with a more efficient method of serving the retailers, while reducing their own investment in transport and warehousing and maintaining a certain level of control. This manufacturer-driven system was gradually undermined by the rapid growth of the multiple retail chains during the 1970s and 1980s, when the retailers took control of distribution by building their own dedicated warehouses into which the manufacturers were obliged to deliver their product in given quantities and at specified times. The most forward-looking of the third-party distribution specialists moved with this trend and provided the new powerful retailers with a professional and dedicated distribution management service, bringing in additional added value services and new technology to suit the particular requirements of the retailer.

At the end of the 1980s the leading multiples have moved a step further and now have a network of composite or multi-temperature warehouses which supply almost the entire range of products to their stores. These depots, too, are often run by the third-party logistics specialists with the retailers maintaining some of the work in-house for the control and measurement of service levels, as well as to maintain the expertise that they too have gained over the years. UK retailers have developed highly-advanced computer systems to control their logistics operations. This technology has helped them become highly efficient, profitable and potentially well placed for expansion into Europe and elsewhere.

It is not only food retailers that have benefited from the relative freedom of planning controls that exists in the UK. We have seen a boom in DIY retailing with superstores opening in great numbers, in spite of the shortage of sites, particularly in the south-east, and the extremely high cost of land. In fact, the relatively easier conditions and the considerably higher margins that UK retailers can make in comparison to their European counterparts, may make some of them targets for aggressive international competitors.

Trends in continental Europe and USA

In France the restrictions on the construction of new retail stores are significant. During the 1960s, the wave of new hypermarkets and out-of-town superstores swept France, but by the 1970s, the French government had passed laws restricting the size and number of such stores. This was a key factor in the decision of some French food retailers to be in the vanguard of international expansion. It was also a sign for them to diversify, and very successfully, into the non-food and catering sectors, while investing heavily in modern technology. Concentration in terms of buying groups has also been a major trend in France and hypermarket stores have achieved as much as 80 per cent of the grocery market. However, many of these remain independent, or semi-independent, such as members of the Leclerc or Euromarche chains.

The level of logistics sophistication remains behind that of their UK competitors. While centralised distribution depots have been developed for the faster-moving lines, the slower-moving products tend to remain to a large extent within the domain of the third-party consolidator, or still come direct from the manufacturer to the store. The concept of composites has not been taken on board yet by either the retailers or the French distribution specialists. It may be significant that it was a UK distribution company, Harris Distribution (in conjunction with its French transport sister-company), that in 1989 won the contract to run a new central depot for the French food retail chain Auchan.

Germany also has strict out-of-town development laws, although this has not prevented certain sectors of retailing from showing good growth in recent years, including the DIY and mail order sectors. Germany is unusual in that it is characterised by a large number of regional retail chains and discount stores. The regional nature of the industry obviously has important logistics implications, which beg a different approach from other markets.

This is a particular difference which highlights the need for distribution companies with international pretensions to have a presence in foreign countries in order to learn about the different requirements as soon and as quickly as they can. The discount chain concept pioneered by Aldi is also a major departure from the trading format in the UK. The logistics requirements of a retailer whose aim is to 'pile them high and sell them cheap' are bound to be different to those of the increasingly quality-orientated UK retailers.

In Germany, one cannot overlook the fact that most retailers are private companies – only 2.1 per cent of the stock market capitalisation in 1989 was accounted for by retailing. With private owners unwilling to water down their level of control in order to take over attractive-looking UK or French publicly-quoted competitors, the most likely route of expansion for the Germans will be through start ups, or the formation of international buying groups. (Asko has set up the buying group Interbuy International with other German, French and Far East companies.) Several friendly mergers (Horten with Batig, Kaufhof with Metro) have already taken place. Disputed takeovers are virtually unheard of in Germany where company law and tradition make a hostile bid unlikely to succeed.

In spite of the regional nature of some sectors, there are some very big players in the German retail market. The big four (Karstadt, Kaufhof, Hertie and Horten) claim 75 per cent of the department store market, while Aldi and Tengelmann figure among the top three retailers in Europe by turnover. Specialist retailers and discount stores such as Aldi have taken much business away from the department store sector in recent years. Now the department stores are fighting back by buying into hypermarkets and specialists and taking them on, on their own patch. As in France, German retailers have also kept much of the physical distribution function in-house, and it will be interesting to see if Aldi, for example, continues this policy should it achieve a significant market presence in the UK, as it is aiming to do.

Other markets in Europe have been equally restrictive and in Belgium both the leading supermarket chains GB – Inno and Delhaize have been forced to look abroad and to diversify due to serious planning restrictions. Meanwhile, in the USA, the level of interest in internationalisation among the major retailers has been relatively low. Only four out of the ten largest retailers in the USA had retail interests outside the USA in 1988. Indeed, several major players, including FW Woolworth and Sears Roebuck have been divesting of foreign interests after poor performances. The sheer size of the US market means that many of the largest retailers are still only dominant on a regional basis. The relatively restricted nature of the European markets suggests that the opportunities are more attractive in the less regulated and still growing American market. Certainly, UK retailers consider the USA to be a key target, as we shall see later.

Internationalisation – ways and means

Development has varied by sector as well as by country. Well differentiated niche retailers such as Body Shop, Laura Ashley and Tie Rack, find success on the international scene accessible because they present a highly-specialised and instantly recognisable product range. Food and mixed product retailers find it much more difficult to differentiate themselves by the products they sell, since their range is likely to be virtually identical to those of the local competitors. They may be able to gain an advantage through technology or know-how but this can soon be copied and negated by the competition.

Due to the considerable differences in taste and also in retailing methods between countries and even regions, pan-European food retailing is likely to take a relatively long time to develop. Logistics companies will have to be able to compete on regional, as well as national and international terms. One sector which defies this characterisation of the food market in Europe is the fast-food sector. Various restaurant chains have succeeded in exporting different concepts, usually from the USA, and implanting them completely into markets all over the world. In this sector, distribution specialists have managed to provide a good logistics service, and are now looking to extend their contracts from the national to the international scale.

Alan Treadgold (1988) has classified the international strategies of retailers by the extent of their geographical commitment and by the level of cost and control that is involved in entry and operating strategy. There are four levels of geographical presence, and three grades of entry and operating strategy, according to Treadgold. Geographical presence is categorised as follows.

(***1***) Concentrated – this is the most cautious path, which sees a retailer moving into a neighbouring country or a country with similar culture or language. This is the preferred route for most UK retailers (eg Sainsbury, Ratners and Marks and Spencer in the USA).

(***2***) Dispersed – here a retailer will have extended his interests, perhaps via former colonial ties, into various unconnected and culturally diverse markets. This is a transitional stage of development towards a multinational presence (eg Carrefour, Storehouse).

(***3***) Multinational – this is where a retailer has developed an interest in a large number of markets (eg Laura Ashley, Body Shop).

(***4***) Global – some retailers have succeeded in achieving a truly comprehensive global presence (eg Benetton, McDonalds).

Not only is it important to consider these four different approaches to internationalisation, but it is also appropriate to analyse the different entry and operating strategies that retailers have used. Then by looking at individual cases an attempt can be made to understand how their geographical and strategic moves have affected or been affected by their logistics operations, and how logistics requirements could change in the future.

Strategies

The three strategic approaches are based on the level of cost and control. A high-cost strategy, for example an acquisition or a major-

Table 3.2: *The international retailers October 1989*

	Country of origin	*Accounting year*	*Total Foreign T/O (system sales excl home country $m)*	*Foreign T/O as % of total T/O*	*Number of foreign countries*	*Average foreign T/O per foreign country $m*
(1) McDonalds	US	1988	3656	20%	53	69
(2) Carrefour	Fr	1988	2901	25%	4	725
(3) C&A Brenninkmeyer	WG	1987	2386	46%	7	341
(4) Ikea	Sw	1987	1841	80%	19	97
(5) Aldi (Albrecht)	WG	1987	1780	20%	5	356
(6) Auchan	Fr	1988	1762	20%	3	587
(7) Kentucky Fried Chicken	US	1988	1639	36%	55	30
(8) Continent (Promodes)	Fr	1988	1448	41%	3	483
(9) Benetton	I	1988	836	70%	14	60
(10) Dixons	UK	1987	749	34%	2	374
(11) Circle K	US	1987	717	25%	4	179
(12) Burger King/Wimpy (Grand Met)	US	1988	622	10%	32	19
(13) Asko	WG	1987	608	10%	5	122
(14) 7–11 (Southland)	US	1988	575	32%	13	44
(15) Bally (Oerlikhon)	CH	1988	450	72%	4	112
(16) Pizza Hut (Pepsico)	US	1988	376	13%	14	27
(17) Toys R Us	US	1987	373	11%	6	62
(18) Baskin Robbins (Allied Lyons)	US	1987	344	26%	41	8
(19) Printemps	Fr	1987	335	12%	6	56
(20) H&M Hennes (Hennes & Mauritz)	Sw	1987	325	42%	5	65
(21) Mr Minit	B	1987	322	56%	24	13
(22) WH Smith	UK	1987	318	12%	2	159

(23) Midas (IC Industrial)	US	1988	265	24%	17	16
(24) Laura Ashley	UK	1988	252	59%	12	21
(25) Mothercare (Storehouse)	UK	1988	222	53%	5	44
(26) Wickes	UK	1988	121	19%	2	60
(27) Habitat (Storehouse)	UK	1988	79	41%	2	40
(28) Stefanel	I	1988	76	29%	4	19
(29) Kwik Fit	UK	1988	61	23%	2	30
(30) Hermes	Fr	1988	55	53%	4	14

Source: OC&C Strategy Consultants *Retail Week* 10.11.89

T/O = turnover

ity shareholding, implies a high level of control, while a low-cost strategy, such as a McDonald's franchise arrangement, implies less control.

We will now look at several of the international companies in more detail.

The international retailers and their distribution

The leading international retailer in terms of turnover is the fast-food chain McDonald's (Table 3.2). They have pursued a global franchising and therefore low-cost strategy. However, McDonald's have maintained a considerable amount of control of the production and logistics chain in the UK, one of their major overseas markets, by acquiring their own ingredients producer and distribution company. This company manufactures a large part of the range of ingredients and carries out the distribution for the total requirements of the outlets. This contrasts with the approach of the Pepsico pizza chain Pizza Hut. Pizza Hut have elected to contract out their distribution requirements to Exel Logistics, the UK's leading third-party distributor.

Exel supplies warehousing and distribution of the entire product range to the chain's restaurants, including cutlery and furniture. These distribution set-ups remain contained within national boundaries, but as fast-food restaurant chains continue to expand throughout Europe, one must ask how long it will be before distribution will be required on a pan-European scale.

The leading international food retailer has been the French Carrefour chain. Carrefour set up its chain of hypermarkets and supermarkets in France during the 1960s. The discount prices, one-stop shopping and good parking were new concepts and were a great success. The restrictive laws passed by the French government forced Carrefour to look abroad, but not in Britain, Germany or Belgium, where the already well-established chains left little room for new competition. (As we will see, the German discounter Aldi has a much more positive attitude about the UK at the present time). However, Carrefour chalked up major successes in Spain, Brazil and Argentina, where no major chains were established. Obviously, the opportunities for European logistics companies to take advantage of the South American development are difficult to assess, but Carrefour's move towards third-party distributors in

France certainly opened doors for, among other specialists, the UK-based Christian Salvesen, who proceeded to carry out consolidation operations for Carrefour in both France and Spain. However, as yet the Spanish grocery distribution market remains relatively underdeveloped with the major retailers only just beginning to look at the benefits of centralised distribution.

The influence of the more advanced French retailers such as Carrefour and Promodes will continue to be a major factor in the development of retailing in Spain. The proximity of Spain to France may even lead to a certain level of common sourcing of products in the long term, although food retailing is likely to lag behind in this, due to the strength of local tastes as far as food is concerned. Although the two countries are neighbours, Paris is separated from Madrid by almost 800 miles.

Carrefour's attempts to enter several unconnected markets by acquisition reflects a policy of 'dispersed internationalisation' and a high cost strategy. This contrasts with the policy of their hypermarket competitor Euromarche, who took the low cost and more limited route. Euromarche took a 20 per cent stake in an American chain, Hyper Shoppes, that succeeded where Carrefour failed by imitating the French version.

Aldi, fifth in the international retailers stakes by foreign turnover, began its cross-border expansion in 1967, understandably enough in Austria. This was followed by Holland in 1972 and later on Belgium and Denmark. Since then, the more daring move into the USA has been made by looking for sites on which to build stores. Now, however, Aldi is planning to make a concerted bid to enter the UK market and has bought sites and distribution premises. This is preferred to outright acquisition of an existing chain since it is a family-owned company unwilling to go through the stock exchange. This policy continues the Aldi trend of building an international presence by acquiring sites rather than the un-German act of a contested bid.

Aldi's entry into the UK could have serious repercussions in the grocery retail market, should it succeed. In the past, the discount sector has been relatively free and left largely to two major players, Argyll (Lo-Cost) and Kwik Save, as other retailers have moved upmarket. If Aldi decides to fill this potential hole, it is reputed to have the potential to decisively undercut the supermarket competition (see, for instance, *Supermarketing*, October 1989). Furthermore, it may be prepared to lose money for the first few years in order to get into a market where margins are much higher than in Europe.

The buying power of Aldi, Europe's largest retailer, is phenomenal, with own-brand products making up 75 per cent of the range. Although expansion may be relatively slow due to Aldi's methods and the problem of local tastes, in the long term a European-wide Aldi organisation would have huge potential for buying, marketing and logistical economies of scale. Until now, the elusive Aldi ownership has steadfastly kept to an in-house distribution operation, but it will be interesting to see whether this policy is maintained in the unknown and logistically sophisticated UK market.

Grocery retailers in the UK have shown little inclination until recently to internationalise their business. However, Marks and Spencer has pursued an expansion policy rare for British retailers, by encompassing both the USA and Europe. In the USA, this has been by acquisition of the Brooks Brothers and Kings Supermarkets chains, while in Europe, Marks and Spencer has opened a number of stores in France and Belgium, as well as operating stores-within-stores in other countries.

The move into France gives another example of the opportunities that cross-border retailing presents for the logistics specialists. In the UK, Marks and Spencer has been one of the leading exponents of contracting out physical distribution services and has been largely served by four main companies, Exel Logistics – Fashionflow, BOC Transhield, Christian Salvesen and Tibbett & Britten. When the decision was made to centralise distribution to all Marks and Spencer outlets in France at a composite depot, the decision also was taken to go for Exel Logistics – Fashionflow, a UK specialist with long experience of the Marks and Spencer philosophy and practices, rather than a French company with greater knowledge of the local area and its peculiarities. Added to the success of Harris (TGD) in winning a contract with Auchan in France and of Christian Salvesen in supplying various retailers in France, Germany, Belgium and Spain, this suggests that UK logistics specialists are well placed to take advantage of retailers' moves into new markets in Europe.

The Atlantic has not presented an impossible barrier to UK logistics companies. In the USA, Sainsbury has made the acquisition of Shaw's. Sainsbury's have followed the route, popular among UK retailers, of entering a new market with strong cultural links to Britain, in preference to the more 'foreign' markets of Europe with specialist companies running many of their central distribution depots. Sainsbury's too has made extensive use of third-party contract distribution in the UK. In this case, the links between retailer and distributor have been sufficiently strong to warrant the extension of the relationship to the other side of the Atlantic. The Exel Logistics subsidiary Dauphin Distribution has been awarded the distribution contract for Shaw's and will therefore be able to bring the experience of working for many years with the Sainsbury's organisation as well as the local knowledge and expertise of the US operator.

The strategy of three more of Europe's leading food retailers may have the greatest implications for the future of physical distribution in Europe. In 1988, Argyll from the UK, Ahold from Holland and the French group Casino carried out a cross-shareholding deal to cement their European Retailing Alliance (ERA). Argyll invested £70m in a relationship that will look at several areas for potential co-operation, such as physical distribution, information systems, new store formats, product development and marketing. The group is going as far as to examine the possibilities of a European own-label brand. This would commence with the importing and exporting of each partners' own-brands and could well be developed into a European network with common product sourcing. The implications of this for the physical distribution process are clearly significant, and ERA is already looking at the potential for packaging, labelling and distribution across Europe. The competitive advantage that such a set-up could give the members of ERA is unlikely to be allowed to materialise without similar agreements being formed by other major retailers. Although the rate of change is likely to be fairly cautious and slow over the next few years, the pace of internationalisation is bound to quicken as more retailers gain their first experiences of the benefits of the cross-border exchanges of ideas, technologies and tastes.

The effects of the single European market

A further boost to this process will come from the eventual liberalisation of the European market during the 1990s, if not by the end of 1992. If one looks at the progress that is being made towards the Single European Market in the area of road transport, it is clear that for the time being, full liberalisation remains a distant ideal.

For example, the 'cabotage' or the carrying of product between two points within a foreign country is forbidden for transport companies. Furthermore, licensing remains a formidable hurdle, particularly in Germany. Largely as a result of the restrictions on third-party transport, it is estimated that up to 25 per cent of international haulage vehicles currently run empty. Nevertheless, this emphasises the significant savings that could eventually be made by retailers, particularly when using third-party contractors, when the latter are subject to a period of more effective use of capacity, the entry of new competitors to the market and a downward pressure on rates. The eventual realisation of the Single European Market will enable retailers and distribution specialists to set up more efficient and more extensive logistics operations. So, how will the distribution industry react to these changes in the international structure of retailing?

The response of the logistics specialists

Distribution companies will respond differently to this question depending on their own expertise, size and ambitions. The major logistics service suppliers are already coming to terms with the need to offer a potentially Europe-wide service. They will need to extend and develop their quality and range of added value services such as packaging, labelling, merchandising, systems design and traffic planning. Particularly important will be their response to the new advanced technological requirements of international retailers. Distributors will need to show a capability to develop new services such as the tracking of individual items from the factory, through the retailer to the consumer, in-cab communications and new vehicle technology. They will be expected to be able to implement new international distribution operations that will depend on advanced systems technology developed by the retailers.

Many distribution companies are already acting constructively to make the most of the opportunities. We have already seen the examples of Exel Logistics, Christian Salvesen and TDG moving into Europe with an extension of their UK activities, but many of the larger companies are also actively looking for acquisitions and joint ventures. Smaller and medium-sized companies are looking for reciprocal agreements with partners of similar size in order to improve their competitiveness. Smaller companies are not necessarily at a disadvantage in the emerging internationalised market. A recent survey on transport operators by the Frankfurt Transport and Logistics Association (GVB) in Germany showed that 60 per cent of decision-makers in 13 sectors of business would prefer to use smaller distribution companies to larger ones. This reflects the regional nature of the German market, and the high degree of private ownership.

As yet, few retailers have embraced a truly international strategy. Now, however, the pace of internationalisation is accelerating. The impact on physical distribution may well be as significant as the centralisation of retail distribution has been in the UK over the past ten years. Once again, technological advances will be to the fore and logistics companies will need to invest heavily to keep pace with the leaders and to offer retailers the new services that they may require.

References

Corporate Intelligence Group (1989) *Retailing and 1992 – The Impact and Opportunities.*

Euromonitor (1989) *Retail Trade International.*

Survey on transport operators by the Frankfurt Transport and Logistics Association (GVB) (1989) *Verkehrszeitung* 18 November.

Treadgold, A (1988) 'Retailing without frontiers' *Retail and Distribution Management*, Nov/Dec.

4
The Advantages and Disadvantages of Centralised Distribution

Alan McKinnon

Introduction

The centralisation of retail inventory in warehouses and consolidation of branch store deliveries have been important features of multiple retailing since its inception in the UK over a hundred years ago. Multiple retailers recognised at an early stage that by setting up their own depots they could receive supplies in bulk loads directly from producers and thereby reduce their dependence on wholesalers.[1] From this initial, very modest involvement of retailers in physical distribution, motivated primarily by a desire to bypass the middleman, have evolved the sophisticated logistical systems upon which much of the success of modern retailing is based.

Over the past century, the degree of control that retailers exercise over the supply chain has grown as a result of two processes: the expansion of multiple retailing; and the increasing propensity of multiples to assume responsibility for distribution upstream of the shop. These processes have been mutually supportive. By developing systems, the multiples have strengthened their competitive position and gained market share. As they have grown they have acquired greater capital resources to invest in distribution facilities.

AT Kearney estimated that in 1983 around 35 per cent of all shop supplies in the UK were channelled through warehouses (or 'distribution centres') controlled by retailers (ie either operated by the retailers themselves or by outside contractors on their behalf).[2] If one excludes sales through independent retailers and small multiples, which do not generally have separate depot facilities, it appears that around 55–60 per cent of the goods sold by the larger multiples (with ten or more branch stores) in 1983 were distributed via warehouses they controlled. Over the past seven years this proportion has increased significantly and is probably now in the region of 65 per cent.

Retailer-controlled distribution centres have, therefore, become the main intermediate nodes in the retail supply chain. In terms of the volume and value of product flow, they are today much more important than either manufacturers' distribution depots or wholesalers' warehouses. A recent survey of 50 major multiples involved in physical distribution found that collectively they either operated or contracted a total of 187 distribution centres, comprising around 3 million square metres of floorspace. Five retail organisations accounted for roughly half of these premises, while 23 firms in the sample had only one. Most of the distribution centres are located along motorway corridors, particularly those of the M1, M6 and M8, with pronounced clustering in and around the conurbations of Greater London, West Yorkshire and Greater Manchester (see Figure 4.1).

The establishment of a typical distribution centre of 15–20,000 square metres requires an investment of around £20 million. Tesco and Asda have each spent over £150 million in the past few years on the development of new distribution systems comprising, respectively, seven and six regional distribution centres. To justify investments on this scale retailers must derive substantial benefits from their involvement in physical distribution. This chapter weighs up the advantages and disadvantages to a retailer of centralising its distribution.

Advantages of centralised distribution

Retailers derive a host of advantages from channelling supplies through a distribution centre. The most tangible benefit is the bulk discount that can be obtained by receiving supplies in full lorry loads. Many manufacturers offer a discount of around 1 per cent for the delivery of full loads directly from the factory. In the 1960s and 1970s, some manufacturers tried to preserve their direct links with retail outlets and discourage the diversion of supplies to distribution centres by granting little or no discount for bulk deliveries. As the move towards centralised delivery has gathered momentum, however, most of these firms have begun to accept the inevitable, awarding more generous bulk discounts and scaling

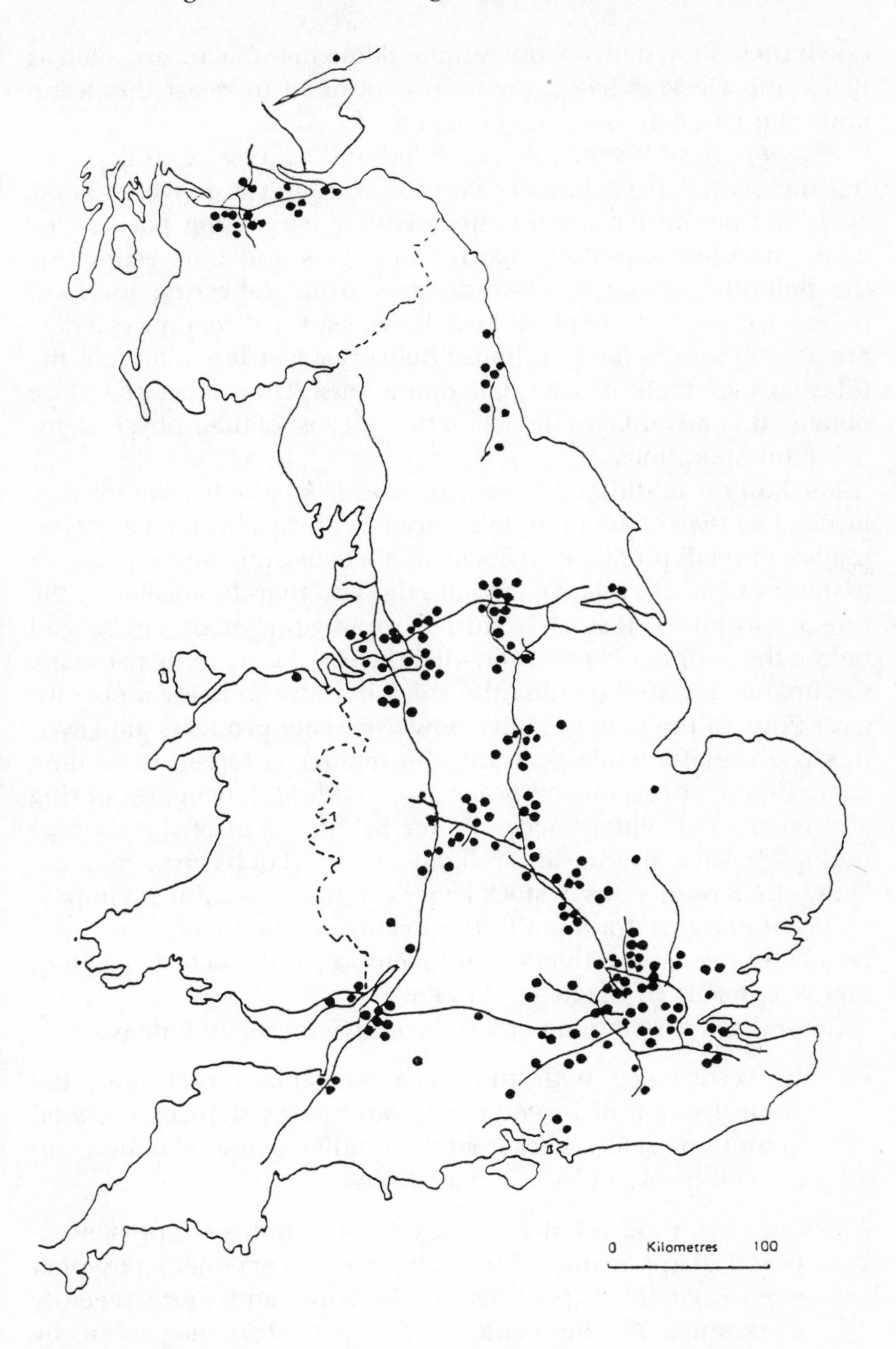

Figure 4.1: *Distribution of 50 multiple retailers' central warehouses relative to the motorway network*

down their shop delivery operations. Some manufacturers, such as Black and Decker[3] have, however, continued to resist this trend and retain an extensive shop delivery network.

Retailers have become more skilled and aggressive in negotiating the switch from branch store to warehouse delivery. Some, such as Comet,[4] have strengthened their bargaining position by analysing their suppliers' distribution costs and thus estimating the potential saving they would gain from delivering to warehouses rather than shops. At best, however, the discounts retailers are able to secure for warehouse delivery cover less than half the total cost of their distribution operations. They must therefore obtain other advantages to recoup the full cost of their physical distribution operations.

Much of the additional benefit accrues from a reduction in stock levels. The management of inventory has always been a key determinant of retail profitability. Retailers are constantly under pressure to minimise stocks relative to total sales and thereby accelerate the rate of 'stockturn'. If stock is 'turned' rapidly the goods can be sold before the supplier is paid, allowing the retailer not only to escape the financial cost of owning the stock but also to enjoy a positive cash flow. In the case of many slower-moving products, however, this is an unattainable goal and the retailer is forced to assume some financial responsibility for stockholding. Financing, storing and insuring inventory accounts for 6–7 per cent of the average multiple's sales revenue and roughly one-third of its gross margin.[5] Quite small reductions in stock levels can have a significant impact on profit margins: for a multiple working on a net margin of 4 per cent, a 10 per cent reduction in inventory could, *ceteris paribus*, increase profits by about 15 per cent.

Centralised distribution can reduce inventories in four ways.

- In accordance with the so-called 'square root law', the centralisation of inventory in warehouses reduces the total amount of 'safety stock' that the retailer requires to maintain a given level of product availability.[6]

- Concentrating retail inventory in warehouses represents a practical application of the principle of postponement which was originally expounded by Bucklin[7] and more recently elaborated in the context of logistical management by Bowersox.[8] This suggests that the longer a retailer can postpone committing stock to individual branch stores, the lower the probability of supplies being misallocated at the retail level relative to short term variations in local demand. It is very difficult to forecast these variations accurately by product and outlet over the typical time interval between suppliers' deliveries. It is also costly to redistribute stock among branch stores where misallocation occurs.[9]

- As branch stores receive much more frequent deliveries from the retailer's central warehouse than from individual suppliers, order lead times are much shorter and safety stock requirements correspondingly lower. It is becoming increasingly common for retailers to operate 'quick response' systems with reaction times of less than 24 hours from receipt of order to shop delivery. The reliability of retailer-controlled deliveries is also generally superior to that offered by suppliers, further reducing the need for stock cover.[10]
- Inventory can be more closely monitored and tightly managed when concentrated in a distribution centre. When responsibility for stock control is devolved to shop level, managers are often prone to order excess stock either as a contingency measure or in response to promotional offers. The loss of stock through damage, deterioration and pilferage is also greater when it is dispersed throughout the retail chain.

In addition to reducing the total volume of stock, centralised distribution effectively concentrates it in locations where it can be stored more cheaply. Storage space can be provided much more economically at a warehouse in a suburban or out-of-town location than at the back of a shop, especially when the latter occupies a prime retail site. The displacement of stock from branch store to distribution centre releases former storeroom space for more productive use as sales display area. Mothercare, for example, attached considerable importance to the improved utilisation of retail floorspace in its decision to move to a system of centralised distribution.

The general efficiency of the retail operation can be enhanced in other ways. Goods arriving in large consolidated drops from central warehouse can be offloaded much more quickly and efficiently than those delivered in small quantities by a multitude of separate suppliers. Deliveries from central warehouse can be much more tightly scheduled and, unlike most suppliers' vehicles, can arrive outside normal trading hours. The retailer's own handling system can be more closely related to the characteristics of its branch stores and goods even arranged on pallets in accordance with shop layout. All these measures improve the productivity of retail staff whose wages can account for 50 per cent or more of total shop operating costs.

The centralisation of distribution and purchasing relieves shop managers of the need to meet large numbers of sales representatives and to prepare orders in accordance with a range of different replenishment procedures specified by suppliers. This allows them to focus their attention on the internal management of the store and customer care. By concentrating responsibility for buying at head office, retail chains can strengthen their negotiating position *vis-à-vis* suppliers and economise on associated administrative and clerical work.

Centralised distribution can help retailers to generate additional sales per unit of sales area. The more frequent and rapid delivery of supplies from central warehouse can raise the level of product availability in shops, reducing sales losses from stock-outs. Furthermore, retailers can enforce higher standards of quality control when supplies are channelled through a central warehouse. By acquiring a reputation for being well stocked and selling high quality merchandise a retailer can build up longer-term customer loyalty.

Multiples with central warehouses can also attract more customers by expanding their product range. Throughout the retail trade, firms have been stocking a greater diversity of products and buying from a larger number of suppliers. In many retail chains, the ordering systems and reception facilities of individual shops could not have coped with the proliferation of products and suppliers. Many small, specialist producers lack the necessary resources to provide branch store delivery but can transport supplies economically in bulk loads to retail distribution centres. Even larger producers, which could support a more extensive shop delivery network, often set minimum drop sizes at a level beyond the reach of individual branch stores.

The development of centralised systems of distribution has been closely associated with the practice of 'own-branding'. In the grocery trade, for instance, 'own-label' products increased their share of retail sales during the 1980s from around 23 to 33 per cent.[11] The own-label product has become an important instrument of retail marketing, strengthening customer loyalty to the shop while, in most cases, earning a larger net margin. As multiples are expected to take responsibility for the intermediate storage, distribution and merchandising of own-label products, a centralised system of distribution is a prerequisite for the development of an own-label range. This was an important factor in Asda's decision in the mid 1980s to establish a network of regional distribution centres.[12] The relationship between own-label development and centralised distribution does not operate in both directions, however. Kwik Save, for instance, which Sparks[13] describes as a 'very centralised-distribution driven company' has eschewed the general trend towards own-branding.

Disadvantages of centralised distribution

Channelling supplies through a central warehouse is not always entirely beneficial, as several major retailers have discovered to their cost over the past 20 years. The concentration of stockholding and delivery operations in a few locations, or even at a single point, can increase the vulnerability of a firm's supply chain to industrial action, fire or extreme weather conditions. In the 1970s, for instance, the distribution systems of British Home Stores and J Sainsbury were temporarily paralysed by industrial disputes and shops starved of supplies. More recently, wind damage at Mothercare's national distribution centre at Wellingborough has disrupted the flow of merchandise.

The development of an in-house distribution system requires heavy capital investment in warehousing, handling systems, computing and vehicles, absorbing resources that could otherwise be used to expand and improve the retail chain. It increases overheads and can reduce flexibility. Heavy dependence on centralised distribution can constrain the geographical expansion of a chain, and complicate the integration of retail organisations following a merger.[14] Firms investing in more expensive, capital-intensive forms of distribution, involving, for instance, refrigeration or highly automated sorting, increase their financial exposure to the risk of a drop in demand.

It is important, however, to put the level of capital expenditure on distribution facilities into perspective. The costs of acquiring prime sites for retail development, constructing the shops and furnishing them to modern specifications have risen significantly faster than the cost of developing the typical distribution centre. Consequently, in many parts of the UK, the amount of retail capacity that can be purchased for the capital cost of a regional distribution centre has fallen. For example, it can now cost more to set up a couple of superstores than to construct and equip a 20,000 square metre distribution centre.[15]

Retailers establishing a new distribution system or radically modifying an existing system can experience serious transitional problems. Teething troubles with new distribution operations have been blamed for a deterioration in the trading performance of chains such as Asda, Budgen, Gateway and Mothercare. Asda, for example, has estimated that the problems it encountered in incorporating fresh foods into its new system of centralised distribution reduced its profits by £16 million in the 1989–90 financial year.[16] Budgen has attributed much of the 30 per cent drop in its profits over the same period to difficulties in relocating its distribution operation from north London to Northampton.[17] Tesco and Safeway, on the other hand, have demonstrated that it is possible for large retailers to undertake a fundamental reorganisation of their distribution systems without jeopardising sales growth or profitability.

Many retailers have had difficulty recruiting managers of sufficient calibre to run large-scale distribution operations, which increasingly involve the use of sophisticated computing and materials handling equipment. Bamber and Lansbury[18] have observed a tendency to 'redeploy unsuccessful store managers into distribution', despite the fact that in distribution centres they frequently encounter much more serious management problems and make decisions with more far-reaching consequences. By means of a comparison of two similar distribution centres serving an Australian supermarket chain, Bamber and Lansbury demonstrate the critical importance of 'management competence and style' to the successful operation of these facilities.

None of the difficulties outlined above are insurmountable, though they have clearly deterred some retailers from becoming heavily reliant on centralised distribution. As outlined below, many retailers have found that they can avoid most of these difficulties by contracting out at least part of their distribution operation.

Factors promoting the development of centralised distribution

Over the past 20 years, circumstances have been generally conducive to the development of centralised distribution, both strengthening its advantages and alleviating some of its problems.

The increase in the number, size and quality of contractors providing an integrated distribution service has made it easier for retailers to extend their control over intermediate storage and shop delivery without becoming directly involved in the development and/or management of physical distribution systems.[19] Many contractors have acquired the necessary capital resources and managerial skill to handle large-scale distribution operations on retailers' behalf and have vigorously marketed their services. They have relieved retailers of the need to invest heavily in distribution facilities. Some retailers, nevertheless, prefer to assume ownership of warehouses and fleets of vehicles but find it advantageous to contract out their management. A common strategy has been for retailers to increase their reliance on centralised deliveries by supplementing in-house distribution operations with the use of outside contractors. Some contractors provide a parallel distribution service, reducing the risk of the flow of supplies being disrupted and accommodating overspill at peak periods. They have also supported the geographical expansion of retail chains and the broadening of product ranges into categories of merchandise for which in-house systems are ill-equipped.

Major advances in information technology have greatly enhanced the relative advantages of centralised distribution. Multiple retailers' distribution operations generate exceptionally large quantities of information because of their extensive product range, high turnover, broad supply base and numerous outlets. Information handling is further complicated by the need to monitor and control stock at two levels in the distribution channel and regulate the flow of supplies between them.[20] Large sophisticated computer systems essentially drive the retailer's distribution operations and are the medium through which it controls the activities of dedicated contractors.[21] This allows retailers to 'concentrate their efforts on moving data, not lorries'.[22] The installation of electronic points of sale (EPOS) and development of direct links between the computer systems of retailers, their suppliers and distribution contractors through electronic data interchange (EDI) networks helps firms to derive even greater benefit from centralised buying and distribution.[23]

Improvements to the transport system have proved especially beneficial to the distribution operations of multiple retailers. These operations are characterised by a high degree of stock centralisation, long delivery distances and the use of maximum-sized lorries in a shop delivery role.[24] Vehicles carrying large consolidated loads from regional or national distribution centres use the trunk-road network more intensively than lorries making more localised deliveries from depots operated by manufacturers or wholesalers. The construction of the motorway network and general upgrading of other trunk roads has, therefore, favoured the more centralised distribution operations of retailers.[25] It is not surprising, therefore, that retailers' distribution centres have gravitated to points of high accessibility on the motorway network (Figure 4.1). Increases in the maximum weight and dimensions of lorries and the development of new multi-temperature, compartmentalised vehicles have also permitted a higher degree of load consolidation, substantially improving the relative efficiency of retailer-controlled deliveries.

During the 1980s, sharp rises in real interest rates greatly increased the financial cost of stockholding and induced widespread destocking throughout the retail sector. The ratio of year-end stocks to total sales fell by around 7 per cent between 1979 and 1987.[26] Some of this reduction is likely to have been the result of tighter inventory control within centralised distribution systems. Woolworth, for example, claim that by reorganising their supply chain they have managed to reduce stock cover in their distribution centres from 16 to 6 weeks and eliminate around £250 million worth of stock.[27]

Retailers have also come under increasing pressure to use retail floorspace more intensively, partly as a result of rising site costs, but also to accommodate expanding sales volumes within existing outlets. One obvious way of doing this is by holding less stock in retail premises and converting storage space into sales display area. Changes in the relative costs of developing shops and distribution centres, mentioned in the previous section, have reinforced this trend. The pressures created by escalating property charges have been particularly strong in town centres and have given high street retailers a major incentive to centralise their distribution. They have also, however, been partly responsible for the decision of firms, such as Asda, Comet and B&Q, operating superstores or retail warehouses on cheaper sites outside town centres to reverse their earlier policy of reliance on direct delivery and dispersed stockholding at shop level. By shifting the burden of local taxation from warehouses (and factories) to retail premises the introduction of the uniform business rate from 1990 onwards and associated revaluation of commercial premises is likely to promote a further transfer of stock from shop to distribution centre. Advances in materials handling and storage systems are also making it possible to use warehouse floorspace much more intensively, reducing site costs per unit of throughput. Foster Brothers' new national distribution centre, for example, has 267 per cent more storage space than its predecessor, but only 75 per cent more floorspace.[28]

Variations in retailers' dependence on centralised distribution

Given the numerous benefits of centralised distribution listed earlier, one might expect multiple retailers to channel most, if not all, their supplies through distribution centres. In practice, however, there are significant differences in the level of retailers' dependence on centralised distribution. This level of dependence is conventionally measured in terms of the proportion of supplies passing through a warehouse controlled by the retailer. Several surveys have shown that this index varies both between and within retail sectors.[29] The fact that intra-sectoral variations are often greater than variations in sectoral averages indicates that dependence on centralised distribution is not simply a function of product type. Some products are, nevertheless, more suited to distribution via retailer-controlled warehouses than others. Items, for instance, that are highly perishable, bulky or difficult to handle and store are often delivered directly to the shop.

Several attempts have been made to explain why retailers, particularly within a given sector, differ in their relative use of central warehouses.[30] These differences have been attributed to the sizes and locations of branch stores, the composition of the product range, the nature of the retailing operation, the pattern of growth and the underlying business philosophy.

Differences in distribution strategy appear to have narrowed considerably during the 1980s. Retailers, such as Asda, Mothercare,

Comet and B&Q, have begun using distribution centres for the first time, while others, such as Tesco and Woolworth, have sharply increased their reliance on centralised delivery. This gradual convergence on a high level of centralised distribution can be largely ascribed to two processes.

First, many more firms have come to recognise the merits of centralised distribution. During the 1960s and 1970s distribution management was still in its infancy in many retail organisations and it generally lacked clout. There was much less appreciation, particularly at board level, of the possible contribution of improved physical distribution to net margins. The success of firms that have traditionally placed heavy emphasis on centralised distribution, most notably J Sainsbury and Marks and Spencer, has encouraged imitation. J Sainsbury, for example, have estimated that efficient distribution contributes around 1 per cent of their net margin of 6.2 per cent and that further improvements to their logistical operations could raise this margin by another 0.5 per cent.[31]

Even in the late 1970s, however, there was still considerable uncertainty about the optimal level of retailers' involvement in physical distribution. A survey of 23 supermarket chains in 1978 revealed marked differences in what they regarded as the optimal level for their own particular operations (Table 4.1). Today, the major grocery multiples in the UK believe it is desirable to channel at least 75 per cent of supplies through central warehouses.

Table 4.1: *Optimal Levels of Centralised Distribution: Opinions of 23 Supermarket Chains in 1978–9*

	% of supplies through central warehouse						
	0	1–20	21–40	41–60	61–80	>80	Total
No. of Retailers	2	0	4	8	6	3	23
	9%	0%	17%	35%	26%	13%	100%

Second, many of the retail chains that have grown primarily by acquisition have begun to rationalise their distribution operations. These firms were traditionally less dependent on central warehouses than chains whose growth was essentially 'organic'.[32] It has been easier for retailers in the latter category to co-ordinate the development of the distribution system with the expansion of the retail chain. The integration of distribution systems after a merger can be a complex, laborious and costly exercise, particularly where there are wide differences in firms' relative use of central warehouses, product ranges, handling systems, trade union agreements and management styles. The simultaneous restructuring of the combined retail operation further complicates the operation. During periods of frenzied merger activity in the retail sector in the late 1960s, late 1970s and 1981–7, many of the more acquisitive multiples had neither the time nor the inclination to develop a new comprehensive distribution strategy. This applied particularly to retail conglomerates formed by the acquisition of firms in different retail sectors.

Over the last few years, the level of merger activity has dropped and several of the larger retail organisations have begun to consolidate their operations. This has created the more stable conditions required for a fundamental redesign of retailers' distribution systems. Chains such as Safeway, Gateway and Storehouse have substantially restructured their distribution operations in recent years, in each case raising their dependence on centralised distribution. Not all 'merged' chains have attempted to integrate their distribution operations, however. Retail conglomerates such as Kingfisher and Ward White (prior to its recent takeover by Boots) have granted their various subsidiaries considerable autonomy in the formulation and implementation of distribution strategy.

Conclusion

A consensus has developed among large British retailers that it is desirable to control the intermediate storage and delivery of the majority of branch store supplies. In addition to conferring a host of operational, financial and marketing advantages, involvement in physical distribution can transform the 'culture' of a retail business, redefining its role within the supply chain and broadening managerial horizons. It is often hard to quantify the benefits of centralised distribution, particularly at the planning stage, but the experience of numerous retailers suggests that, if the system is properly designed and managed, it can improve trading performance by a significant margin. The problems that some retailers have recently encountered with centralised systems have been essentially short-term, transitional problems often related to their individual circumstances. They have done little to undermine the general case for centralised distribution. For most large retailers the question is no longer whether or not it is right to channel supplies through a centralised system, but how their particular system can be improved to gain additional competitive advantage.

Notes

(1) Jefferys, JB (1954) *Retail Trading in Great Britain, 1850–1950* Cambridge University Press, Cambridge.

(2) National Economic Development Office (1985) 'Factors affecting the cost of physical distribution to the retail trade' Unpublished Report, EDC for the Distributive Trades, London.

(3) Monopolies and Mergers Commission (1989) *Black and Decker*, HMSO, London.

(4) Thomas, T (1988) 'Comet stores – strategic case study' *Focus on Physical Distribution and Logistics Management, 7* (7): 29–31.

(5) Institute of Logistics and Distribution Management (1989) *Survey of Distribution Costs: Results of a Study into Current Distribution Costs and Trends in UK Industry, 1988–89* Corby.

(6) The theoretical basis and practical relevance of the 'square root law' is discussed in McKinnon, AC (1989) *Physical Distribution Systems*, Routledge, London, 101–4.

(7) Bucklin, L (1965) 'Postponement, speculation and the structure of distribution channels' *Journal of Marketing Research 2*: 26–31.

(8) Bowersox, DJ (1983) 'Emerging from the recession: the role of logistical management' *Journal of Business Logistics, 4* (1): 21–34.

(9) Westwood, JB (1978 'Retail inventory movement – a case study in rationalisation' *International Journal of Physical Distribution and Materials Management 8* (4): 180–8.

(10) Murrell, G (1988) 'Management of the retail supply chain' *Logistics Today, 7* (2): 5–8.

(11) Anon (1982) 'Own label sales set to break more records' *The Grocer*, 17 April, 5. Keynote (1988) *Supermarkets and Superstores: An Industry Sector Overview* London.

(12) Van de Vliet, A (1988) 'Can Asda deliver the goods' *Management Today* April, 58–63.

(13) Sparks, L (1990) 'Spatial-structural relationships in retail corporate growth: a case-study of Kwik-Save Group plc' *Service Industries Journal 10* (1): 25–84.

(14) Christensen, L (1989) 'Managing change and quality' *Focus on Physical Distribution and Logistics Management 8* (7): 2–12.

(15) Tesco recently purchased three sites for superstore development from Asda for £54.75 million (*Financial Times*, 4 May 1990). Once allowance is made for construction and equipment costs, each superstore will cost around £24 million, roughly equivalent to the average cost of the 24,000 square metre 'composite' distribution centres the firm set up in the late 1980s (Allcock, RE (1988) 'The planning approach of a major food chain', Paper presented to the Town and Country Planning Association Conference on 'Freight – Planning for the 1990s London).

(16) *The Grocer*, 21 July 1990.

(17) *Financial Times*, 26 July 1990.

(18) Bamber, GJ and Lansbury, RD (1988) 'Management strategy and new technology in retail distribution: a comparative case study' *Journal of Management Studies 25* (3): 197–216.

(19) Fernie, J (1989) 'Contract distribution in multiple retailing' *International Journal of Physical Distribution and Materials Management 19* (7): 1–35.

(20) Hill, RM (1989) 'Allocating warehouse stock in a retail chain' *Journal of the Operational Research Society 40* (11): 983–91.

(21) Quarmby, DA (1985) 'Distribution in the next ten years – the market place' *Focus on Physical Distribution Management, 4* (6): 3–6.

(22) Rudd, T (1987) 'Trends in physical distribution' in MacFadyen, E (ed) *'The Changing Face of British Retailing'* Newman, London, 84–93.

(23) McKinnon, AC (1990) 'Electronic data interchange in the retail supply chain: the distribution contractor's role' *International Journal of Retail and Distribution Management 18* (2): 39–42.

(24) McKinnon, AC (1986) 'Multiple retailers' distribution strategies – effects on patterns of land use and traffic flow' *The Planner, 72* (7): 16–20.

(25) Quarmby, D (1989) 'Developments in the retail market and their effect on freight distribution' *Journal of Transport Economics and Policy, 23* (1): 75–87. Sparks, L, *op cit*.

(26) Central Statistical Office *United Kingdom National Accounts* HMSO, London (annual series). Central Statistical Office *Economic Trends* HMSO, London (monthly series).

(27) Wiggett, C and Grange, B (1988) 'Woolworths: achieving supply chain control' *Logistics Today, 7* (2): 31–5. Bowring, JA (1989) 'Centralised distribution in the non-food sector' *Retail and Distribution Management 17* (6): 42–4.

(28) Barrow, B (1989) 'Distribution centre makes better use of cubic space' *Logistics Today 8* (3): 37–8.

(29) National Economic Development Office, 1985, *op cit*. Simpkin, LP, Maier, J and Lee, WM (1987) 'PDM and Inventory Management' *Retail and Distribution Management 15* (1): 57–9.

(30) Thorpe, D, Kirby, DA and Thompson, P (1973) *Channels and Costs of Grocery Distribution*. Retail Outlets Research Unit, Manchester Business School, Manchester. McKinnon, AC (1985) 'The distribution systems of supermarket chains' *Service Industries Journal 5* (2): 226–38.

(31) Christopher, M (1989) 'The logistical approach' *The Director 43* (1): 66–9.

(32) McKinnon (1985) *op cit*.

5
Third Party or Own Account – Trends in Retail Distribution

John Fernie

Introduction

It has already been shown in earlier chapters that much of the responsibilities for intermediate storage and onward delivery of goods to retail outlets has shifted from manufacturers and wholesalers to multiple retailers. The concentration of inventory into one or a small number of central warehouses and the ensuing benefits of such a strategy have been discussed at length by Alan McKinnon in chapter 4. Commensurate with this aspect of change in retail distribution practice has been the trend to contract out distribution to specialists. This chapter will identify some of the trends in this growth market, discuss the pros and cons of contracting out and review results of survey work undertaken by the author on the role of contracting out in retailers' distribution strategies.

Market trends

Any reviewer of the trade press would quickly come to the conclusion that UK retailers have awarded substantial contracts to third party specialists in recent years. The trend has been to contract out, but attempts to qualify the size of this market are fraught with difficulties. Most surveys on distribution have been carried out by either the Institute of Logistics and Distribution Management (ILDM) or consultants, for example, Kitcat and Aitken (1987), Syfa (1990), Corporate Development Consultants (1988) and KAE (Gouldborn, 1988). These surveys have tended to overstate the case of contracting out, no doubt because leading distribution companies commissioned the research! Thus sweeping statements such as 'in the grocery sector up to 71 per cent of distribution expenditure was spent on outside contractors' (Bedeman, 1989, 6) have to be treated with caution. Such assertions are often based on general market surveys of which the retailing sector is only a part. Indeed, most of the works cited above are based on relatively small sample surveys. Furthermore, estimates of market size have been largely equated with the road freight transport market. Buck (1987) and Kitcat and Aitken (1987) assume a £2.4 billion market, while Harvey (1989) estimates £3.5 billion. The most comprehensive survey of the contract distribution market was undertaken by Corporate Development Consultants (CDC) (1988). CDC covered around 500 organisations in the retail, consumer goods manufacturing, local government and other assorted industrial sectors. The retail sector comprised roughly 10 per cent of the sample. The expenditure on distribution by all these organisations was estimated at £6,808 million, £2,221 million of which was spent on contract distribution, £4,587 million for own facilities. In the retail sector it was claimed that £1.9 billion was spent on distribution; £0.6 billion on own account, £1.3 billion on contracting out. It is not clear from the report on what basis distribution expenditure was calculated but it is likely that expenditure is synonymous with warehousing and transport costs. The most recent ILDM survey of distribution costs (ILDM, 1989) is much more comprehensive than previous years with 385 respondents taking part. Of this number, 44 companies with a turnover of £21.1 billion were retailers. Distribution costs in this survey include inventory, administration, packaging in addition to warehousing and transport. This sample size, not dissimilar to that of CDC, has total expenditure of £2.03 billion. A rule of thumb estimate based on distribution costs as a percentage of retail sales would calculate the UK market at around £9 billion.

In terms of market trends, CDC (1988) anticipate growth in the overall contract distribution market of 5–10 per cent per annum for five years with most potential coming from medium-sized organisations that currently do not use contractors. Nevertheless, this research revealed that 84 per cent of the companies did not use contract distribution. Retailers and consumer goods manufacturers were the sectors with most experience of dedicated distribution, whereby the management of the fleet and depot is dedicated to a single client. Indeed, it was these sectors which were the main users of contract distribution services and were still envisaged to account for much of the potential growth in the future.

The pros and cons of contracting out

Although much has been written about market trends in the distribution market, little research has been undertaken on the reasons why firms decide to contract out all or part of their distribution business or, alternatively why they decide to keep distribution 'in-house'. Later in the chapter the results of the author's research to date on this topic will be presented; here, an overview of the factors generally cited as being important by companies deciding to contract out or not will be given.

Table 5.1: *The benefits of contract distribution*

(1) *Strategic reasons*
- (a) Flexibility
- (b) Spread risks

(2) *Financial reasons*
- (a) Opportunity cost of capital investment
- (b) Economies of scale
- (c) Off balance sheet financing
- (d) Better planned budgets

(3) *Operational reasons*
- (a) Accommodate seasonal peaks
- (b) Enter new markets
- (c) Reduce backdoor congestion at warehouse/store
- (d) Provision of 'specialist' services
- (e) Improve service levels
- (f) Minimise industrial relations problems
- (g) Management expertise

Fernie (1989) has listed all of the factors considered to be influential in the decision to contract out. These are shown in Table 5.1. It should be noted that the reasons cited by retailers for using third-party contracting are numerous and invariably involve a combination of several of these factors. Fernie (1989) classifies the reasons into three categories: strategic, financial and operational. In a strategic sense retailers can use contractors to give them flexibility when implementing a new distribution strategy, for example, because of a move to centralisation (Thomas, 1988) or the integration of two merged chains (Christensen, 1990). As a result the retailer can minimise the risk of disruption to the total distribution system in a period of rapid change within the company. Interestingly, two general surveys which sought to discover the key reasons for contracting out concentrated upon financial and operational factors (CDC, 1988; Cooper and Johnstone, 1990). The aforementioned CDC report established that contract distribution was used primarily because of its cost-effectiveness. Similar conclusions were drawn by Cooper and Johnstone (1990). Secondary factors in contracting out were 'provides access to specialists', 'allows effort to be concentrated on core business' and 'provides a more flexible system' in the CDC report. Cooper and Johnstone concur with the argument concerning the concentration of management and financial resources in the core business, adding higher level of customer service as another highly ranked factor.

It is not surprising that the argument that a retailer should stick to its mainstream business and contract out its peripheral functions such as distribution to specialists is often presented. In the last five years, many of the major retailers in the UK, especially in the food business, have embarked upon ambitious store development programmes with systems back-up costing hundreds of millions of pounds per annum. The pay-back period for a new superstore is considerably less than that from a distribution depot and a fleet of vehicles, thereby encouraging the use of contractors who invest in the new capacity on behalf of the retailer. An added bonus here is that changes in accountancy practice in the 1980s, especially the phasing out of the 100 per cent capital allowance, have encouraged companies to contract out (an expense) rather than own the asset (a fixed asset). This off balance sheet financing improves a company's return on capital employed by contracting out.

Of the operational reasons cited in Table 5.1, research by CDC and Cooper and Johnstone (1990) would appear to suggest that the availability of management expertise was of most importance, with the minimisation of industrial relations problems and the entering of new markets being of secondary significance.

Undoubtedly, the depth of expertise now available to retailers has developed considerably in the 1980s. No longer can one equate distribution with traditional road haulage. The leading professional distribution companies have grabbed the marketing opportunity offered to them as contracting out became a growth segment of the freight transport market. The leading players – NFC, TDG, Tibbet & Britten, Hays, TNT, Christian Salvesen and Glass Glover – have recruited and trained management in all areas of logistics management. They are the experts and, as predicted by Harvey in 1989, rationalisation of the industry is occurring as these UK companies restructure in an attempt to tackle international markets.

Although not mentioned by the above researchers, contracting out is invaluable to retailers in harmonising seasonal variations in volume levels and spatial variations in volumes distributed. As retailers experience surges in demand at Christmas and Easter, not to mention excessive demand for particular product groups in 'atypical' circumstances such as the 1989 and 1990 heatwaves, contractors are used to meet peak demands to supplement the own account operations. Similarly, the geographical margins of a company's operation may be contracted out, at least in the market entry stage, because of the low volumes of goods involved.

Although the range of reasons outlined above would seem to indicate an overwhelming case for contracting out, most companies in the UK (84 per cent) use own account distribution. In the CDC report, 78 per cent of the retail companies surveyed were own account operators. Table 5.2 lists the main advantages of own account distribution (Fernie, 1989).

Many of the arguments cited as advantageous for own account distribution are similar to those presented by contractors extolling the virtues of their services. One major difference is that concerning loss of control over the distribution operation. In essence, companies claim that they can shape their own destiny. Retail outlets will be served by their own depots ensuring flexibility to respond to changing circumstances as they arise. Flexibility was ranked highly in the CDC report as a reason to remain 'in-house'. Overall, using own account distribution should lead to better customer service levels, greater loyalty to the retail group and security

Table 5.2: *The advantages of own account distribution*

(1) *Cost*
  (a) Cost plus argument
  (b) Monitoring costs
(2) *Control*
  (a) Total responsibility through the supply chain
  (b) Better customer service
  (c) Loyalty to one, not several companies
  (d) Security in relation to new product development
(3) *Technological innovation*
(4) *Economies of scale*

of new product development. The question about loyalty and new product development is normally associated with the manufacturing sector. However, the proliferation of own-label brands has given greater credence to the view that company image and loyalty are relevant in keeping distribution 'in-house'. Indeed, in the CDC report 'better control of the distribution' was cited first (54 per cent of responses) in the retailing sector compared with 42 per cent overall. In consumer goods manufacturing, control (43 per cent) was ranked second after 'cost-efficiency' (51 per cent). It can therefore be argued that retailers perceive control as more important than any other sector in the sample. Some of the larger food retailers would question this, for example, David Quarmby, joint managing director of J Sainsbury plc, has argued in the past that retailers can control distribution by information, rather than by doing, thereby information systems give retailers control and it is irrelevant who actually runs the operation, contractor or own account operator (Quarmby, 1989).

Cost-effectiveness is clearly important in the decision to contract out or not. It was ranked as the most significant factor for firms contracting out in the research cited above, but paradoxically is almost as important a factor for companies who run their own facilities. It is often argued by own account operators that contractors are in business to make a profit and will therefore be much more expensive than the 'in-house' operation. Furthermore, if a switch to contracting occurs, extra costs will be incurred such as redundancy costs, asset disposals or write-offs. Whatever option is taken, some management expertise will still have to be retained to monitor the performance of the contractor. This will also have to be considered in the cost analysis.

Some of the larger own account operators can claim that they have much more expertise than contractors in certain lines of business because they have been at the leading edge of technological development over the last 20 years. Indeed, several own account operators are, or have been, third party operators. They would therefore claim that they can benefit from scale economies and derive buying power advantages over their suppliers in the same way as contractors. Also, as experienced operators they have been able to adapt and innovate in areas of product handling, storage and transport because they are specialists in their line of business.

The role of contracting out in retailers' distribution strategy

In 1987/8, the author conducted exploratory research on the role of contracting out in the distribution strategy of the major multiple retailers. This research was published in 1989. Subsequently, further interviews were conducted with directors/managers of regional companies and more specialist retail chains. Currently, a postal questionnaire is being distributed to senior distribution personnel of smaller retail businesses in order to ascertain the importance of company size, the extent of branch networks and the historical evolution of the company's distribution in the decision to contract out or have 'in-house' distribution. The remainder of this chapter comprises a review of the current research to date.

The food retailers

The major multiple retailers currently channel between 80 and 90 per cent of their products through retail-controlled distribution to the extent that around half of all grocery products purchased in UK stores are delivered from 75 distribution centres. Much of the 'hype' concerning the importance of contracting out can be attributed to the sizeable contracts awarded by Tesco, Asda and Safeway to third party specialists in recent years when these major food retailers embarked on major distribution investment programmes. It is true that much of the new depot development by food retailers has been contracted out but this has often been misconstrued to imply that food retailers contract out most of their distribution. This is not the case. The major food retailers, with the exception of the Marks and Spencer's food business, including the largest regional multiples, retain a sizeable own account operation.

The own account/contracting out mix has evolved in response to the changing store portfolios of food retailers. Tesco has trimmed its 800 plus store network of the early 1970s in half, progressively replacing small shop units with the opening of new superstores. As the average size of store rose and superstores began to feature more prominently in the store portfolio, a move away from smaller, product category warehouses to larger, composite depots became a viable option. Conversely the superstore pioneer, Asda, has been able to plan its distribution network around a small number of large composites. However, as the depots were being commissioned the company bought 61 superstores from Gateway in 1989 for £700 million, necessitating a further modification to the distribution plan. Composite depots are less important to operators with smaller-sized stores in their network. Not only did Gateway and Argyll have hundreds of small stores but these networks evolved as a result of aggressive acquisition strategies in the 1980s. It was shown in an earlier chapter that Safeway is now the flagship of the Argyll group and the depot network has had to be developed in an adaptable way to respond to the major strategic changes carried out by the group in the 1980s.

The changes outlined above have hastened the move to centralised distribution and given contractors the opportunity to seek this new business. *But* prior to such changes, distribution to stores was either carried out directly by manufacturers or by the in-house operation of the retailer. Contracting out was mainly confined to particular product categories, most notably chilled, frozen and wines and spirits lines. An exception to this was Marks and Spencer which collaborated with the BOC group in the late 1960s to build a series of depots to supply Marks and Spencer stores with chilled products.

In essence, the role of contracting out in a food retailer's distribution strategy is dependent upon a range of factors, most importantly the management expertise 'in-house', the geographical spread and variation in size of stores, the competing claims for capital investment in the company's business and the stability of the existing network. The latter factor relates to the scale of change being implemented in a new distribution strategy.

The main reason cited by the larger retailing chains for contracting out much of their recent distribution developments is the inherent flexibility that can be achieved through a mix of own account and contract distribution. With the aid of sophisticated information technology the network can be controlled by information from the company headquarters. This allows companies to respond quickly to market changes with dynamic sourcing of products from alternative depot locations and a degree of immunity from industrial relations problems. The key factor, however, is the ability to be able to control and monitor costs. The constant comparison of performance levels between contractors and the own account operation instills competition among operators. This should raise industry standards and control costs. For example, each year at Safeway the distribution manager of the depot which achieves the best performance levels receives a special shield. The distribution director looks forward to the day when a third party operator will be good enough to win it (Christensen, 1990)!

The larger companies also cite the opportunity cost of capital in their mainstream business rather than distribution activities as a contributory factor for contracting out. The level of capital investment by major food retailers has risen markedly in the late 1980s. Debenham, Tewson Research (1990) claim that the level of investment has risen from £700 million in 1986 to £1.7 billion in 1989. The race for good supermarket sites as saturation is reached is pushing prices up for land, for example, in May 1990 Tesco paid Asda £55 million for three sites (undeveloped) with planning permission in the south of England. Site acquisition, store opening programmes and investment into systems development have all absorbed capital often at the expense of the distribution function. It is no coincidence, therefore, that the companies with the largest capital investment programmes – J Sainsbury, Marks and Spencer, Tesco and Safeway – have contracted out most of their distribution in recent years. Asda, on the other hand, invested in all of its regional distribution centres (RDCs)* and vehicles but this was in the wake of its disposal of MFI and prior to its purchase of the Gateway superstores. With a debt of £900 million, it is unlikely that this decision would have been taken in 1990. Nevertheless, Asda contracted out the operation of all of these RDCs, except two at Falkirk and Wakefield, close to the sites of previously run 'in-house' produce depot operations. Unlike its competitors, Asda centralised its distribution late, depending on suppliers' deliveries to its superstores. The in-house operation was limited to produce and meat lines, with a previously owned subsidiary, Associated Fresh Foods, delivering direct dairy and chilled lines. The value of management expertise in running large RDCs was therefore an important consideration for Asda in its decision to contract out six of its eight distribution centres.

Although the larger food retailers have tended to contract out, the main regional multiples retain much of their own distribution. The successful 'regionals' Wm Low, Morrisons and Waitrose could claim to have more efficient distribution systems than their larger national competitors. Indeed, by centralising early, store develop-

*Its largest site at Lutterworth was originally purchased by MFI.

ment has been impaired by the geographical constraints imposed by the furthest distance to which a depot could deliver. It can be argued that as regional chains grow and achieve national penetration, more of the arguments presented above for contracting out come into play. The consistently most successful national operator was primarily a south-east of England chain until the 1970s. J Sainsbury in moving north has contracted out all of its depots as it developed its product range and spread into new geographical markets.

Own account distribution is also important in specialist retail markets. The largest specialist, Iceland, has developed in-house expertise in distributing frozen food to its stores. This was enhanced with its takeover of Bejam in 1989, a company that did not use third party contractors (Measures, 1989). The frozen food sector requires special handling and transport facilities and many of the larger general food retailers with a large number of small stores have tended to contract out this part of their business, for example, CRS and Gateway.

At the other end of the food retailing spectrum, major changes in distribution are also taking place in the cash and carry and convenience store sectors. Central distribution is changing the face of cash and carry (C and C) operations with the larger groups – Booker, Nurdin and Peacock (N&P) and Makro – building up the percentage of volume that is going through the centralised network. In terms of contracting out, the most recent entrant to the cash and carry market, Makro, the Asda of C and C in that it has a small number of large C and Cs, contracts out its centralised distribution, whereas the companies with a history of delivering wholesale to the catering and grocery trade have undertaken their own distribution.

With the resurgence of the small shop in the form of convenience store retailing, operators have been improving performance through the implementation of new systems linked to either wholesalers or their own depots. Circle K has recently opened a central depot through which most of its products will be channelled to its 240 stores and in July 1990 awarded a £4 million, five-year contract to BRS Western to supply vehicles, drivers and manage the transport operation from this new distribution centre. Clearly this is a sector which may provide a marketing opportunity for third party specialists and is worthy of further research investigation.

Non-food retailers

Although similar general trends can be identified in the non-food sector to that of food retailing – greater centralisation and a move to contracting out parts of the distribution operation – the nature of non-food retail distribution poses more complex logistical problems to the distribution manager than in the food retailing sector. The larger mixed retail business operators, including the mail order houses, carry two to three times the number of product line items than their grocery counterparts and most of these lines are relatively slow moving compared with the fast moving stock of grocery businesses. To further complicate matters, distribution managers have had to contend with major changes in corporate strategy such as the integration of merged chains (Burton Group), rationalisation of product range (Woolworths) and the movement into new lines of business (Marks and Spencer, Boots).

In view of the complexity of the larger non-food retail operations, these companies have taken a supply chain approach to tackle these logistical problems (see chapter 10). The integration of buying, purchase order management and distribution can streamline an unwieldy organisational structure and improve customer service to stores. The Woolworths operation provides a good example of the implementation of supply chain management in the 1980s when the company introduced its focus strategy, thereby rationalising the number of its departments and product lines. Woolworths introduced a formal centralisation policy establishing clear guidelines to suppliers on specifications such as packaging, palletisation, lead times, etc. Ultimately, Woolworths reduced its number of suppliers from 8,000 to 1,000, average stock holding fell to 4.7 weeks from 12 weeks, the number of invoices issued fell from 7 to 2 million pieces of paper and the depot network was rationalised from 14 to 5 sites.

Interestingly, as these mixed retail businesses have widened their business portfolios diversifying away from their 'variety chain' image, similar distribution policies have been applied through the group, for example the supply chain philosophy, initially initiated in Woolworths, was implemented first in Comet and now in B&Q.

In terms of contracting out their distribution, the current own account/contracting split is strongly influenced by the historical role which distribution has played in the company. Of the larger companies, the Burton Group, Next, Great Universal Stores (GUS), British Shoe and, to a lesser extent, Woolworths have mainly own account operations. Boots, on the other hand, contracts out most of its distribution, a policy which has also been pursued by Marks and Spencer in the 1980s. In both these cases, however, a strong 'in-house' element within the network acts as a quality control factor to monitor performance at various sites. Indeed, both Boots and Marks and Spencer contract out to a range of contractors to instil competition among these companies. In the case of Boots all transport is contracted out, but different contractors run their RDCs from those trunking into these sites from their primary warehouses.

The reasons for contracting out vary from company to company but the choice of contractor and the evolution of a partnership between the retailer and contractor goes back around 20 years in the case of Marks and Spencer and Boots when they initially developed an RDC network. Until relatively recently, Marks and Spencer awarded their RDC contracts according to the track record of existing established contractors rather than put an RDC out to invited tender. In both cases, Marks and Spencer and Boots initially contracted out to benefit from the management expertise of contractors. Boots, in a similar manner to the Asda approach discussed earlier, actually own their RDCs but contract out most of the operation on an annual open-book accounting basis – that is contractors are paid for the cost of carrying out the job, plus a fee negotiated on performance levels. Marks and Spencer have opted for the model adopted by some of the major food retailers and cite similar reasons for contracting out in the 1980s and 1990s, namely that they can concentrate financial resources on the mainstream business. Recent contracts for large RDCs are therefore for around five years on an open-book basis.

The companies which have tended to contract out most, if not all of their distribution, in recent years in the non-food sector have been firms which have reviewed their distribution strategy and decided on a policy of centralisation. In addition to the Comet case study discussed by Trevor Thomas in chapter 11, other examples can be found from the DIY sector (Homebase, B&Q) and drinks retailing (Victoria Wine). In these cases, the value of management expertise is invariably the key factor in contracting out. In the case of Homebase, the choice of Exel Logistics to carry out the distribution of 6,000 'core' lines to stores was mainly due to the size and experience of the NFC group. Centralised distribution in DIY is at the pioneering stage because of the disparate range of products stocked. Clearly, certain products will always be delivered direct. The choice of an experienced contractor was therefore important to Homebase because of the 'teething' problems which were anticipated in centralising certain product lines.

Although the use of contractors has been a feature of most retail companies' distribution strategy, several retail groups retain a sizeable own account operation. In some cases the distribution divisions of these retail groups precede many of the contractors in the market place. Indeed, High Street Transport was a major third party carrier until the 1980s when the Burton Group began its period of acquisition. Then High Street Transport came out of the third party market to concentrate upon distributing to a larger store network. When Burton acquired Debenhams, an existing contract with Federal Express was not renewed.

Other companies with a 'tradition' of own account distribution are GUS, British Shoe, Next (formerly Hepworth) and Argos. In these cases, as within the Burton Group, these firms have developed 'in-house' expertise in specialist markets – parcels, shoes, hanging garments, catalogue shopping – that can better the package offered by contractors. The main reasons cited for not contracting out are cost, customer service and control. Clearly, constant monitoring of costs is carried out to allow comparisons with those quoted on the open market but a key factor tends to be the level of control that can be achieved across the whole network of different stores and product lines.

That is not to say that these companies have not considered contracting out. In fact contractors are used for work that comes into the marginal category for own account operators, namely, seasonal business, new or geographical marginal markets and difficult product groups. For example, when Argos first test marketed its superstore concept, NCCS (now Exel Logistics) was used to supply these stores. The contractor is also used for seasonal peaks. GUS contracts out its transport in Ireland.

It must be stressed that most retailers contemplating contracting out tend to consider the transport operation rather than warehousing. This trend confirms the annual evidence produced by ILDM in their cost surveys which show that UK companies have generally adopted this approach. British Shoe reviewed its distribution strategy in the mid 1980s and seriously considered contracting out its transport operation. Instead, it upgraded its existing operation using draw bars trunking from its one million square foot warehouse to six outbases for onward delivery to stores. Next contracted out its transport in the mid 1980s but reverted back to own account at the expiry of the contract. Woolworths contracts out all of its transport treating vehicles and drivers as a commodity while retaining management of the routeing and scheduling.

Future prospects

Contract distribution has played a significant role in the distribution strategy of many retail companies in recent years. The pros and cons of contracting out and own account distribution have been discussed and the reasons for adopting any given strategy are dependent upon each individual company's overall corporate strategy. Major influencing factors are:

- the scale and complexity of the distribution operation;
- the financial status of the company and current capital investment programmes;
- the level of management expertise in distribution;
- the nature of labour relations.

Although analysts tend to be optimistic about the growth of the contract distribution market in the 1990s, the retail distribution market offers fewer opportunities for the third party contractor. Most of the large grocery contracts have been finalised now that Tesco, Asda and Safeway have implemented their distribution strategies. These RDCs which cost £15–20 million to commission, £10 million per annum to operate and employ 300–400 staff are at a mature stage of development in grocery retailing. Indeed, as most of these large contracts are for five years, there is the possibility that the retailer could opt to buy back sites and revert to own account operation if the circumstances were appropriate.

Areas which are currently attracting the interest of contractors are in the fields of DIY, confectionery, tobacco and newsagents (CTNs), mail order home delivery and convenience store retailing. In DIY, CTN and convenience store retailing, the traditional method of delivering to stores – through wholesalers or direct delivery – is changing as companies centralise their distribution, thereby offering market opportunities for contractors. However, in Britain the best prospects appear to be in non-retail areas. It is not surprising that contractors have turned their attention to foreign markets, notably the USA and western Europe, where the contract market is poorly developed in the retail sector (see Pellew in chapter 3; Bedeman, 1990).

References

Buck, D (1987) 'Third party operations are cost saving' *The Grocer* 14 February.

Bedeman, M (1987) 'Contract distribution – a market overview' in *Managing the Supply Chain*, The NFC Contract Distribution Report.

Christensen, L (1990) 'Third party versus own distribution', Paper presented at a conference 'Logistics – the European Impact', May.

Cooper, J and Johnstone, M (1990) 'Dedicated contract distribution: an assessment of the UK market place' *International Journal of Physical Distribution and Logistics Management 20* (1): 25–31.

Corporate Development Consultants (1988) *The United Kingdom Market for Contract Distribution* CDC.

Debenham, Tewson Research (1990) *Food Superstores – The Challenges of the 90s* Debenham, Tewson & Chinnocks.

Fernie, J (1989) 'Contract distribution in multiple retailing' *International Journal of Physical Distribution & Materials Management 19* (7): 1–35.

Gouldborn, B (1988) Personal communication.

Harvey, J (1989) 'Physical distribution in the retail environment' *Retail and Distribution Management 17* (1): 46–9.

Institute of Logistics and Distribution Management (1989) *Survey of Distribution Costs: results of a study into current distribution costs and trends in UK industry* ILDM.

Kitkat and Aitken (1987) *Distribution: A Revolution in Motion* Kitkat and Aitken.

Measures, C (1989) 'Why spoil the party' *Distribution* January/February: 28–9.

Quarmby, DA (1989) 'Developments in the retail market and their effect on freight distribution' *Journal of Transport Economics and Policy* January: 75–87.

Syfa (1990) *The Road Transport Industry Survey* Syfa.

Thomas, T (1988) 'Comet stores – strategic case study' *Focus on Physical Distribution and Logistics Management 7* (7): 29–31.

6
Trade-offs, Service and Cost

Jonathan Weeks

Introduction

Any retailer who is following supply chain management principles logically, will have come to the conclusion that it is a series of supply chain trade-offs which determine distribution service specification and the service specification which determines distribution cost.

This sounds too obvious to repeat in a book on the subject, but many companies still have distribution departments who are working to their own internal service specification. These departments are often run by otherwise clever management who not only understand, but are also trying to reduce their unit costs, believing this to be their main goal.

The first symptoms of this aberration can be quickly diagnosed by asking one or two questions of the distribution division and listening to their responses.

'Do you have an agreed strategy/mission/service specification?'
'Who has it been agreed with?'
'When was it last updated?'
'How are you measured against it?'

Over the years I have had such responses as 'No', 'What?' or, I have been given a beautiful PR brochure with romantic pictures of freshly painted wagons blazing through snow drifts at night – containing warm and woolly statements of love and affection for 'our customers – the stores'. All too rarely, I have been handed a clear and clinical description of the division's role within the total organisation, together with the service specification, its measurement tools and permitted failure rates.

I have also been asked these questions by clear thinking chief executives, together with less intelligent questions such as:

'What is the policy of the distribution department?'
'Your costs are too high/above budget, what are you doing to reduce them?'
'What will your budget be for next year?' (This last question was asked before we had seen a retail sales target, much less a service/ volume/order characteristic/seasonality/stock analysis of any kind.)

The responses to these questions are important.

(***1***) The distribution division can have no *independent* policy.

(***2***) Costs cannot be assessed without an agreed specification.

(***3***) The budget is driven by the *demands* of the organisation.

All these questions must be asked within an agreed company context, based, primarily, on a detailed understanding of the supply chain trade-offs. So, the burden of this chapter is, very simply, to describe how to set about identifying the overall supply chain trade-offs, agreeing the services required and costing them. Only from this can we move into the slightly narrower field of defining the role of, service to be provided by, and cost of, the distribution function itself. Any other method or approach must be flawed.

The trade-offs

In a pure marketing sense everything can be included in a trade-off calculation, from the company advertising spend (driving volume) to the training programme for store staff (improving their ordering efficiency). In order to start somewhere it is important to divide the activity of the company into two groups:

- direct supply chain trade-offs;
- external trade-offs. (External in this sense meaning outside the company supply chain.)

These external factors should not be continually ignored, but too many variables in the pot from the outset make the mixture too difficult to handle. They can often be brought in as additional variables once the basics of the trade-off model are established. Perhaps the easiest way to split the direct from the external is to take the company operating budget as the input. On this basis the directs ought to be specified (or be capable of being derived) – stores, footage, volumes, seasonality, supply chain performance.

Whereas the external would be the broader assumptions behind the operating budget – market share, promotional activity – things that could change but are not capable of being expressed in the budget document.

Most trade-offs occur at points of interface and imply a breaking down of the usual barriers and a mutuality of interests typically – *I* do this so that *your* task is easier. Some trade-offs occur late in the process and can be missed. For example, bar coding is applied by manufacturers, is not usually of any direct use to a retail distribution department and only comes into its own in stores at the final point of sale and then only if EPOS systems are employed.

The main trade-offs in a retail supply chain are shown in Figure 6.1. Before trying to analyse and balance the supply chain trade-offs we have to start by assuming you have the detailed costing data with which to achieve this. We can develop this using work study, synthetics or activity sampling. But, you have to know in advance what you are going to use the data for, otherwise the chances are they will not be in the right format to be used. If in doubt go for a direct product profitability DPP approach (see below), since this will force you to be product specific. It is product that makes you profit, it is product that manufacturers make, you handle, and your customers buy.

The awful realisation that you do not have this costing data may now dawn. You must put down this book, acquire the information, and return to it in six month's or a year's time.

* * * *

Welcome back! We can now return to the task of finding the most logical and effective way to start to analyse these trade-offs. This is to start at the end of the chain and move backwards. With EPOS in so many retail organisations today the end is at the point where the consumer is picking up the purchases ready to leave the store, with payment and wrapping completed.

The questions you are asking in this analysis are the classical method study ones:

Why am I doing this job – at all?
– this way?
– here?
– with these people?
– now?

Player	Element
Supplier	Identification Pack size Packaging Drop size Delivery – frequency – reliability Lead times/inventory Administration (order/invoice/ claims)
Retail distribution department (assumes centralisation)	Product lines Stock cover Physical handling – product characteristics – order characteristics – special requirements Distribution cost – combined order size – service frequency – store location Administration/stock control
Stores	Handling cost – unloading – to and from stockroom – counter loading – pricing Stock cover – stockroom – counter Packaging disposal

Figure 6.1: *Retail supply chain trade-offs*

Again, space pressure, rising wage costs, poor staff availability and high labour turnover will make it more attractive to push unnecessary tasks out of stores and either eliminate, reduce or move them back up the chain to places where they can be performed in production line environments.

There are several practical reasons why you should start at the end and not the beginning. The first is that if it is not the customer then it will at least be the retail store that is calling the service shots. The second is that the bulk of the labour cost is in stores and not (usually) in the supplier or distribution parts of the chain. Bear in mind that we are looking at supply chain costs not product costs (which indeed could have a high but irrelevant labour content). If you do come across a product with a higher than suspected supplier/centralised cost then the probability is that it is selling at a loss, but more on DPP below.

Your labour analysis will already have pointed you towards certain jobs which appear to be people intensive, for example:

- Manning tills – 25 per cent
- Shelf filling – 11 per cent
- Ordering product – 10 per cent

By concentrating the questioning techniques on the high labour content tasks you will find yourself straightaway in a rich seam of potential trade-offs, for example:

Q How could we reduce the labour content of shelf filling?
A By presenting *only* the product needed for that occasion:

- in shelf fill sequence;
- already unpacked;
- pre-priced;
- easily identifiable.

Q Can/should some of these tasks be carried out more cheaply elsewhere:

- in the stockroom?
- in the distribution centre?
- back at the suppliers?

A Go and find out!

This is a very exciting area of investigation, and to encourage you to try it there follow a few examples of successful trade-off areas which have saved huge, and often unsuspected, amounts of money.

Protective packaging

Have you ever looked at the output, not from the front, but from the back, of a retail store? Supermarkets and off licences can, in the main, usefully pass on their cardboard to the consumer and thence to the domestic bin, but the majority of stores are not so lucky. Separate industries have sprung up emptying, flattening, compacting and transporting the cardboard in and from our shops. And yet, with just-in-time manufacturing, much of this expensive rubbish is often only hours old.

Note that the phrase 'protective packaging' is used to differentiate product packaging – that which the consumer carries away – from any other form of protective material which is used to create a single unit of multiple items – a case, a tray, shrinkwrapping or banding – which is not usually sold with the goods.

There are two approaches to packaging trade-offs. The first is to use our questioning technique, applying it from the back end of the chain, progressively through to the point where the packaging is specified and ordered. The main questions to ask are:

(***1***) is this the most cost-effective packaging material for this product?

(***2***) is it designed so that it minimises the task of using it

- when it is being filled?
- in transit/handling?
- when it is being unpacked?
- when it comes to disposing of it?

(***3***) should it be returnable?

The second trade-off concerns disposal itself. Assume that only really useful bits of packaging have survived the first technique and then simply check the trade-off between local disposal–labour–capital cost and revenue (if any) and central disposal or even specialist and again returnable options.

In FMCG environments these problems are better thought through than in other sectors. Across the retail industry there are fortunes waiting to be made and saved!

Handling systems

A cursory examination of almost any supply chain will reveal the most extraordinary lack of congruity between handling systems in the three main divisions, supplier, retail distribution centre and store. It is almost as if the three protagonists have deliberately set out to make life difficult for each other; certainly they will never have met, and probably they dislike or mistrust one another.

There have been some successful attempts to standardise systems at point of interface, the pallet, the roll cage, the tote box, but not very many bridge all three links in the supply chain (try turning up at the back door of most stores with a pallet nowadays!). One of the few examples of three-step bridging is the set in the hanging garment industry. It moves happily from garment producer, through the retailers' distribution centres, back stockrooms and even finds its way on to the shop floor in some less salubrious emporia.

While searching for another solution as neat as the set is rather like looking for the Holy Grail, there is, nevertheless, a great deal which can be done even within the limitations of currently available systems. For example, in one major retailer only a few years ago they were using their own unique pallet, on to which every unit of intake, palletised or not, was solemnly restowed. Of course there was a reason, that their racking was too flimsy to take modern loadings, but it was only when that secondary problem was addressed that they could take advantage of something that the rest of the world had spent millions in making available, free of charge.

So how do we use our trade-off questioning technique this time? It is almost the same as on packaging, and while we are doing it, keeping an eye on the output from our packaging project, since the two can impact on each other in several obvious ways. Again we start looking for trade-offs at the back end of the process because that is where the savings are most likely to be. (You only have to compare the relative labour statistics between a retail central distribution system and the stores to see that this is likely to be true – 35:1?, 50:1?)

The overriding questions are:

'What is the ideal handling system for the final user?' (In our case the store.)
'Can the distribution centre provide the systems, (working methods and IT) to support this requirement?'

'Is there any impact even further up the chain?' (At suppliers or beyond.)
'How do the costs and benefits stack up at each point in the chain?'
'What's to stop me getting on with it then?'

If you have read this far you will not need a detailed description of all the secondary questions implied by this technique. What might be useful, and even encouraging, would be to relate the simplest and yet most exciting handling trade-off that has been identified in many businesses (most of whom appear to have kept it to themselves).

This is the story of the humble roll cage, which dramatically illustrates not only fairly obvious trade-offs, but produces some hidden benefits to boot. The location and time of the story are: any retailer, anywhere, fairly recently.

Prior to roll cage introduction, but post centralisation, produce still flowed from suppliers to distribution centres on differing pallets – loose stowed – in giant cartons (imported product) and by parcel post, parcel carrier, nominated carrier, hire transport and dedicated supplier vehicles.

Product within a distribution centre was moved and stored on original pallets, repalletised, unboxed and palletised, kept in original cartons and placed on shelves, reboxed into special cartons or containers on racks or shelves. Product was picked and then packed into new cartons, if picked singly, or selected in original outers if product was big enough, or a whole case was ordered. Smaller items were picked into jiffy bags and amalgamated into new cartons, again depending on quantity ordered. Product was delivered to stores with tailboard level docks on pallets; to large and small stores without docks, loose, or loaded on pallets which never left the vehicle.

At the stores it would take an average of three hours to unload all this, and three days to complete the process of carrying it to the stockroom, opening every carton, sorting it by department, checking the contents, date-coding it and putting it away in bins by department code. All this before store staff were even allowed to touch a packet. To get product on to the shelves the staff indented for it from their own stockroom, carrying it down the stairs or in the lift, in armfuls or using shopping trolleys. They then dumped it on the floor prior to unpacking it, pricing it, putting it on the shelves, tearing up the cardboard and other packaging among the customers, before carrying it all upstairs to bale it. Later they heaved the bales down to the back door for the council to take away (on a good day!).

The roll cage revolutionised all this. Designed in conjunction with, and entirely on behalf of, the retail stores, right down to the quality of its non-marking wheels for differing store floor finishes, it brought the following benefits.

Mobility

At the store the product now arrived fully mobile, not on a piece of equipment that suited the distribution people, but on one which was capable of being used anywhere inside the store without further handling:

- off the vehicle on a tail lift with bridging plate;
- into the lift if necessary;
- into the stockroom where it could be used as bulk storage for a while.

But most importantly – product can go straight on to the retail floor, in or out of trading hours.

Speed of handling

The comparative speed of handling saved staff from being tied up with back door duties, sent the vehicle away within, typically, 15–20 minutes and eliminated the need to take the product to the stockroom. This in turn produced further staff savings.

Stock reduction

Since there was now a positive disincentive to take stock to the stockroom their use began to wither and today backroom stocks are often either totally eliminated or at least represent less than 20 per cent of total store stocks. Prior to this mini-revolution they were often as high as 60 per cent.

As a hidden by-product, the roll cage also eliminated two to three days' stock in the system because that was the average time it took a store to check in the previous old-fashioned delivery and put it all away in the stockrooms. It was only when all this had been completed to the satisfaction of the stockroom manager that he would allow the retail staff access to the new product.

Improved sales/customer service
The roll cage made it possible to take product straight off the vehicle and place it on the counter. The whole question of availability was quickly addressed in much clearer terms. 'If there is no/little stock in the stockroom, then if it is not on the counter there is none in the store, I'd better order some'. 'If it doesn't come tomorrow I can see that it clearly wasn't sent, so I can complain directly to the distribution people or the buyer about lost sales. I have no doubts about whether I've lost the line internally.' I can give clear answers to my customers, "I'm sorry Madam, it is not on display, that means I have not got any. I will order it today. It should be here tomorrow." Not "Wait there please Madam while I go and scour the stockroom".'

Finally, among the more obvious benefits, roll cages began to be used for stacking discarded packaging, both on the sales floor at the time of unpacking and pricing, and behind the scenes, where it is now good economics to take back the cardboard to the central distribution point, compact it in a decent-sized industrial machine and sell it reasonably profitably to a waste contractor for whom full load collections have become much more attractive.

You may still doubt that this is really a trade-off. The reassurance would quickly come from any distribution manager. Roll cages mean poor load utilisation, and there is a quicker way of unloading a vehicle. The most effective way, from a purely distribution standpoint, is to load everything on to pallets, 8 ft high, and to load them on to a curtain-sided 40ft vehicle with rear access. On arrival at the store you operate the hydraulic tipping mechanism and, having secured the tailgate, you can drive away.

Inventory

At any time when the cost of money is high our financial colleagues constantly remind us of the cost to the company of owning inventory. They should also be capable of pointing out the other costs which exist even if money is cheap. The physical storage cost, the additional cost of physically working with larger inventory than you need (your labour has to travel through and past it), and the cost of shrinkage, whether damage, deterioration or pilferage. The more surplus stock you have the more people tend to feel that it is unloved, not needed and therefore easy game.

Reducing inventory to its optimum level is thus not just good housekeeping or a response to high interest rates, but an essential and continual process for ensuring the health of the business. 'Optimum' is, as you would expect, the key word here and implies yet another trade-off.

The other thing you will have spotted by now is that almost all trade-offs impact on almost all parts of the business and analysing the way inventory behaves is a classic example of this.

Availability

The biggest determinant of inventory is the company availability objective. I do not propose to expand this chapter any further to encompass this in detail, but it is clearly important to establish this criterion firmly and unequivocally from the outset. It needs to be proposed, explained, written down, understood and then generally bought into by all areas of the business and, most particularly, by customers themselves.

Once you have worked out what you want to achieve, not only will it drive your inventory, it will also drive a number of other costs. In setting your availability objectives make sure that you recognise that they can be different at various points in the chain and can be allowed to vary by product, product group, supplier and seasonally. To illustrate: in a retailing environment the crucial available index would be the one which measures what happens when a customer reaches out his or her hand to select a product off the shelf. You might be aiming to hit 99 per cent or slightly better.

Although this would be your target for branded goods or the top-selling item in the branded goods range, it is unnecessary and costly to apply that criterion to all those products and we could have lower targets for items where brand awareness is lower and substitution is acceptable. It is the difference between, say, Nescafe 200gm, a specific brand and size, and flour or sugar, where rightly or wrongly most people are happy if there is product available.

Assuming that you have agreed and set availability targets at the counter, you should then move backwards through the system agreeing reasonable standards for stockroom, warehouse and suppliers, bearing in mind the trade-offs between lead time, the physical cost of additional service and storage space, retail and warehousing. Bear in mind that at the counter the availability trade-off is between:

- the number of units of that product on the counter;

- the length of time it will take to replenish it
  - from the stockroom
  - from the warehouse;
- the cost of either of these routes;
- the cost of increasing their frequency;
- the cost of the inventory for that line.

The availability target from the warehouse ought to be the same as for the counter if there is no stockroom, but it will be lower if a significant proportion of any product range is kept in stock at the store (forced there by pack size constraints or counter space competition).

When we get to suppliers the same targets should be set but they will be less onerous in reality because the lead time will be longer. This is illustrated in Figure 6.2 which shows that because at every step we have added to the lead time we are entitled to expect that at each stage the service level will be the same.

Stock Position	*Typical Lead Time*	*Used For*
Counter	Nil (!)	Customer satisfaction
Stockroom	1 hour	Top up shelf
Warehouse	1/5 days	Centralise suppliers' orders
Manufacturer	1/2 weeks	Complete all order lines
Raw material supplier	1/2 months	Grow/extract product from worldwide sources

Figure 6.2: *Standardising availability targets through lead times*

The manufacturer would not be expected to provide the same level of availability with the lead time used between counter and stockroom, but he should be expected to provide all products demanded within the lead time he himself has offered/agreed.

The point of all this is that, in setting availability targets, you are effectively setting the physical and lead time constraints on all parts of the system and thus largely determining the inventory.

To achieve 99.5 per cent availability you have caused (numbers here used entirely for illustration):

- six packets of the product to be designed permanently into the counter of every store;
- another six to be permanently in the stockroom of every store
  - for backup
  - or because the pack size/or minimum order is 12;
- an average of 62 cases to be on roll cages on a lorry somewhere at all times (in transit stock);
- half a pallet to be in the pick slot in each of your six central warehouses;
- two pallets to be in each of the bulk storage areas of those warehouses;
- four pallets to be in their collective intake bays at any one time;
- four pallets to be on a supplier's vehicle at any time;
- another large quantity back at the supplier's factory for safety stock to cover his lead time pending your next order.

The lower the availability target the lower this stock will be, and the higher the greater! The quantity of stock is determined entirely by these steps and the decision surrounding them. It is no good shouting for inventory reduction unless you are prepared to change one of these parameters.

As an aside, whenever the author has analysed these steps it is usually found that for most products far too much is designed into the counter stock by use of planograms. Often it is impossible to cut these quantities further since it then represents a less than credible display. What you should then do, and most people don't, is to slash the availability targets at all other points – have no stockroom stock – 80 per cent or less at warehouse and similar criteria for suppliers. Actually, these slow-moving lines often defy the rules by remaining stubbornly available throughout the supply chain.

Service frequency

The second most sensitive determinant of inventory size is probably service frequency. (Probably is used because all industries differ, as do product ranges.) Seasonal products like Christmas decorations lead an inventory life of their own. The service frequency trade-off component has several facets, one obvious and two or three hidden.

The obvious facet is the effect of increasing or decreasing frequency of supply on the inventory level. It is probable that not many companies have tested the effect of upwardly increasing delivery frequency to the limits. Commonly, most retailers have moved from fortnightly to weekly, and twice or thrice weekly to daily. Some are still discovering the benefits of these moves and a few are moving on to multiple deliveries in a day.

There is a simple prejudice, which is probably reasonably safe, that to deliberately increase distribution cost, optimally a whole lorry load to a single destination, is to go too far. However, it is a measurable trade-off like anything else and should be tested vigorously. The obvious benefit is that you can eliminate stockroom stocks and even reduce counter stocks (to credible display limits) by increasing frequency of delivery, and it is very simple to measure these benefits against the cost of achieving it. The non-obvious benefits are similar to those discussed in the roll cage example above, plus better attention to stock ordering and prevention of shrinkage or deterioration on chilled or other short-life products.

Pack size

Having drained the inventory lake by setting realistic available targets and working out the optimum delivery frequency, the next rock to appear above the surface will be that of pack size. Again it is a simple matter to model the cost of decreasing pack sizes and naturally you will have to take into account the additional labour cost for handling and disposal. If you are smart you will also take the opportunity to redesign the packaging and you'll think about eliminating the pack altogether by redesigning the unit that comes into your warehouse (thus enabling you to pick in singles at no additional expense).

Systems

Finally, in this section on inventory, you must consider your inventory control and management systems. Since the purpose of this chapter is only to persuade you to take all these factors into account when establishing the trade-offs, this subject cannot receive as much space here as it deserves elsewhere.

The important points are the following.

(**1**) If your inventory *control* systems are poor you will suffer from two problems:

- out of stocks – caused by not having accurate records;

- over stocks due to the same reason.

Your out of stocks will cause lost sales and much administrative chaos (the computer thinks it is there – how do you convince it that it is not?). Your over stocks will cost you money but, since you do not know you've got these, it will be impossible to correct the situation.

(**2**) If your inventory management systems are poor you will have the same symptoms as for poor control, but for different reasons and with, usually, much worse consequences. Typically you will be ordering product you do not need through following an inaccurate forecasting system. Simultaneously you will be failing to order product your customers are desperate for, for the same reason, poor forecasting.

In addition you will probably have a high proportion of long stock which no one appears to be accountable for and which is eating you out of house and home (taking up space and capital). It is of no help but clearly the task is to ascribe accountability and wade in to improve control and put in some decent systems. The point is raised here simply to point out the potential dangers and opportunities while you are engaged in the task of setting your overall service specification.

Systems

To round off this section on trade-offs a few general points on systems will now be outlined. Too many companies treat their paperwork and computer-driven systems as if they were the sole prerogative of the IT department. Over the years I have discovered as many benefits from trade-offs associated with (or prevented by) systems, as from any of the more physically oriented activities described above. In one company there was concern at the number of times that orders got split before they were available to the picking lines. Half of these splits were imposed by the system. The effect was to increase the number of packages we produced and to increase the number of transactions and thus invoices, pods, queries and claims. All this was totally artificial and drove the operators and our clients to distraction while the carriers chuckled away on their frequent journeys to the bank. It is essential that the physical methods and the administrative methods be evaluated hand-in-hand throughout this entire process of trade-off and cost benefit analysis, leading to clear and comprehensive service specifications and optimum operating cost.

The last point to be made in this section on trade-offs is to remember that their purpose is primarily to determine the optimum supply chain methods and the place in the chain where the task is best performed. The service specification, which we will now move on to, is concerned with cost and the quality (and reliability) of the way in which those methods are applied.

The service specification

Since it has already been agreed that we cannot possibly produce a service specification until after we have had a full and detailed discussion with our customers, it will not surprise you to learn that this is going to be the most productive and exciting part of the entire process. Over the years I have had more satisfaction, and indeed sheer fun, out of exploring service needs with my clients (the stores) than almost any other facet of logistics management.

To start with, there is a very good chance that when you call for your service specification no one will be able to find it. It is not because it has been temporarily mislaid, it is because it has never been written down in the first place. And why? Well that is usually for one of two reasons, either someone didn't think it was worth writing down or, much worse, neither side had ever even thought about it!

Let us assume that you work for a very enlightened company indeed and someone has, after all, discovered your service specification document, dusted it off and brought it proudly to you. Unfortunately, you are still doomed to suffer some small twinges of disappointment:

- it may be out of date;
- it may be quite different to the expectation your customers have;
- it may be so superficial and banal as to be quite useless; and, most horribly of all,
- it will almost certainly not represent what is actually happening.

Certainly I have suffered similar problems over the years, even where a formal written document did exist. Most problems spring from (self-evidently) not having one at all or treating the exercise as a once-in-a-lifetime act at a very superficial level.

Perhaps we should begin by defining the purpose of this essential document and what it should and should not contain. First of all, it should apply to any client relationship in the supply chain, whether the customer is external or internal. Secondly, it should exist not just downwards between you and your stores, but upwards between you and your suppliers of goods or services. Of course you get the supplier to write it if he will, but if he will not you must produce a supplier service specification of your own.

The most important point, especially if you are keen to examine potential trade-offs, is that unless and until you have had those discussions with your clients you cannot possibly just publish a service specification because that would be an unthinking and arrogant act. It follows that since you cannot announce your service, you must discuss and agree it. This process is iterative and may take a great deal of time. It is iterative because you or the customer may generate some valuable trade-off options in discussion, which will have to be subjected to joint cost benefit evaluation, modified in the light of this evaluation, modified again after pilot running and only agreed and built into your specification after months of work. This gives a clue to the nature of the specification itself.

The purpose of a professional logistics based service specification is to describe in detail all the agreed points of interface between the parties:

- working methods;
- information technology; and
- the quality measurements;

in short, the services and service to be provided. (Since we are confining ourselves to retail management we do not have to include terms and conditions of trade, but if it seems likely that this new document will be more useful if it is included why not do so?)

Most service specifications, if written down at all, confine themselves to a few weasel-worded statements about speed and reliability of service, from order capture (sometimes cunningly omitted), to delivery. The service specification outlined below is bigger, braver and altogether a more useful and challenging version than most in use today. It can be an incisive weapon to give you a competitive edge, or a sword to turn back upon your overambitious or inefficient department or company. Use it if you dare!

The service blueprint

The précis

The service specification should start with a simple description of the service to be provided seen through the eyes of the people receiving the service, in our case the stores. It assumes that a great deal of effort has already gone into identifying potential trade-offs, evaluating them and agreeing them within the framework of the overall retail strategy. It is no longer a document for discussion, but a factual description in prècis form of an agreed set of operating methods. It should describe, in simple language:

- the service mission;
- the order capture systems and cycle;
- the delivered response
  - when goods will arrive
  - what availability targets are agreed
  - identification methods
  - packaging methods
  - disposal of equipment/packaging;
- other services such as
  - help desk facilities
  - management information provided.

The detail

This section tries to indicate the level of detail that you need to work to, in creating your specification. Since we are dealing in theory there is little purpose in attempting to give a real example of a detailed specification, it would have a limited application. My purpose here is to indicate most of the things that the specification must cover.

(a) Order capture:

- include a simple description of how the system works, stressing the importance of the store itself keeping to deadlines;
- specify your target response times for incoming telephone calls – explain how you monitor that and show how you propose to publish the qualitative data;

- explain overload and exception routines.

(b) Availability:

- describe the availability criteria;
- point out firmly that these are company agreed goals;
- describe how they are measured so that everyone understands and is using the same target – this is a famous area for misunderstanding
  – 'I ordered two lines – one came, the other didn't, that's 50 per cent availability.'
  – 'No, you ordered 99 boxes of Mars bars and one packet of lime green zips which we have temporarily discontinued on the buyer's instructions – thats 100 per cent availability the way we see it, or at least 99 per cent the way the consumer sees it!'
  – 'But this consumer only came in for a lime green zip so that's 100 per cent failure!'
  – 'So give him a Mars bar and phone when the zips are in – that'll be 110 per cent success!'
- explain how deletions and substitutions work and how they might affect apparent availability.

(c) The delivery response:

- explain your internal order cycle
  – what time of day the store order gets polled
  – when it is processed
  – when it gets to the distribution department
  – how their processing cycle works;
- describe your warehousing methods briefly
  – intake through to despatch;
- explain exactly how the vehicle is routed and when it should arrive
  – what leeway should be given
  – what will happen if you know it is late
  – what the procedures are for – sealing, unsealing, unloading, returning empty equipment, resealing.

(d) The product preparation:

- describe how each module (roll cage, pallet, box, tote box, parcel) will be

- identified
- sealed
- unpacked
- disposed of/returned;

- describe how each product/range will be
  - identified
  - packed
  - unpacked
  - priced
  - processed – in stockroom, on shop floor (here we are using an amalgam of distribution department and in-store procedures);
- explain the use of the paperwork/or labels
  - to aid identification
  - to aid counter filling
  - for checking/shrinkage control
  - for pricing/stock records.

(e) Information service:

- add a separate statement of your quality objectives:
  - timeliness/reliability
  - availability
  - accuracy;
- show with sample documents the format with which you expect to report on this and to whom;
- describe in detail how to
  - raise queries
  - make complaints
  - claim
  - compliment!

  and, your responses–systems–timing, for each.

The above list will not be comprehensive, it will miss out specific items associated with particular retail environments. It is the principle behind it which is important because:

(***1***) we are concerned here with using the trade-off evaluation to work out the specification itself;

(***2***) we must then describe the agreed process in detail, together with the ways in which we propose to measure its quality and effectiveness.

Clearly we cannot publish a specification in advance unless it is to start off the overall process as a discussion document, or in order to compare the service stores think they want (or think they are getting), with what you will jointly develop from the trade-off work at some later stage. Nevertheless there is some prior work you can do, which surprisingly is often ignored by otherwise quite perceptive companies.

You could take out your existing specification and employ some reasonably independent means of finding out two important things:

(**1**) Do your customers recognise it?

(**2**) Does your service match it?

By inference you will discover how appropriate your current services are and thus how much effort will need to go into the evaluation phase. Do not expect glowing testimonials, but comfort yourselves with the thought that at least you have had the courage to take the bull by the horns and ask the questions!

Cost

'In most retail distribution systems far too much effort is spent on controlling cost.' This foolish and irresponsible statement is obviously an attention-grabbing paradox, but worthy of some attention in spite of that. An alternative statement to this could be, 'An appropriate strategy is more beneficial than a cheap contract.'

Is that easier to accept? Yes, well, the idea behind both versions is to point out that if we have used a thorough examination of potential trade-offs to arrive at a robust and simple service specification we have achieved two very important steps:

(**1**) during the trade-off phase we have eliminated a great deal of waste and improved our joint cost-effectiveness;

(**2**) as part of the process of setting the service specification we have agreed, actually agreed, our working methods and quality objectives with our customers.

It follows that the costs will then be:

(***1***) already thoroughly understood and acceptable to both sides (if not, your trade-off phase was flawed);

(***2***) almost totally dependent on the specification already agreed and so not open to criticism by the customer.

Of course there will be opportunities to further reduce cost through refining methods, improving productivity, enhancing volumes but there should be no major surprises or missed opportunities for a while at least. The cost problem will largely disappear. Your rationale when challenged by other areas of the business with inter-firm comparisons will be:

(***1***) that your costs are as they are as a necessary function of producing a tailor-made service;

(***2***) this has been designed to save your stores more than it costs you;

(***3***) the process is well understood and has been audited by your finance colleagues to their entire satisfaction!

The most insidious influence on cost in retail distribution is often not operating efficiency, but organisational positioning or cultural problems. If the activity is perceived as adding cost rather than value then, curiously, that is exactly what it does. This is because the company culture tends to treat the added cost department as a dumping ground for its problems.

This means a variety of things from pushing underachieving managers into its ranks, or clogging up its resources with the accumulated buying errors of years or, more subtly, giving it the tasks that no direct supplier or contractor would dream of attempting, either at all, or at the revenue offered.

In contemplating an environment where trade-offs and service specifications can be openly discussed, we are assuming that the distribution function under consideration is not one of those downtrodden, underrepresented, budget-hugging organisations that have no clear role within the organisation other than to act as the butt of all its jokes. If this assumption is wrong then, in reading this far, you have been wasting your time. A retail distribution division which is simply trying to be a service to buyers and stores alike is bound to be a costly anachronism which will shortly fail, usually in a dramatic way which will seriously affect the health of the whole company. So, homily aside, what else can we usefully discuss about costs?

It might be worth starting by describing the scope of these costs. If we are going to use trade-off analysis as a regular feature of the way in which we manage the function, then it would be appropriate to use a definition of cost more akin to the logistics approach than that used in distribution. The reason for doing that would be because any small change that a buyer makes to the specification of an imported or locally sourced product, any change the merchandise or display department makes in the way the product is treated in the store, all impact on cost.

The logistics approach accepts this and has, as a result, an output identical to DPP which is simply the new name for an old technique. In practical terms this means that we need to be able to describe accurately all costs, from the moment the buyer and supplier have agreed the product specification (together with the consumer packaging if it exists – that which the final customer lifts off the shelf and which contains the product), to the point where that very consumer has paid for it, and is reaching out to carry the product out of the store. (Further still if there is returnable packaging or some form of warranty or maintenance required.)

The cost table, which can be much more detailed, is given in Figure 6.3. In order to calculate the DPP equation: take the full (bracketed) DPP cost; add the buying department cost (not on Figure 6.3) and a percentage for overhead (not on Figure 6.3.); take the sum away from selling price achieved for that product; and you have the DPP margin (if any!). This chart, by the way, is a useful trade-off checklist, since it contains all the main elements of the physical and administrative tasks involved. It should be used in conjunction with Figure 6.1.

Very early in this chapter it was agreed that you would need a proper costing database in order to begin the task of trade-off evaluation, perhaps now the importance of this task is more clearly established. To sum up:

- don't try to be *too* precise;
- try to make it product specific;
- try to make it usable practical data.

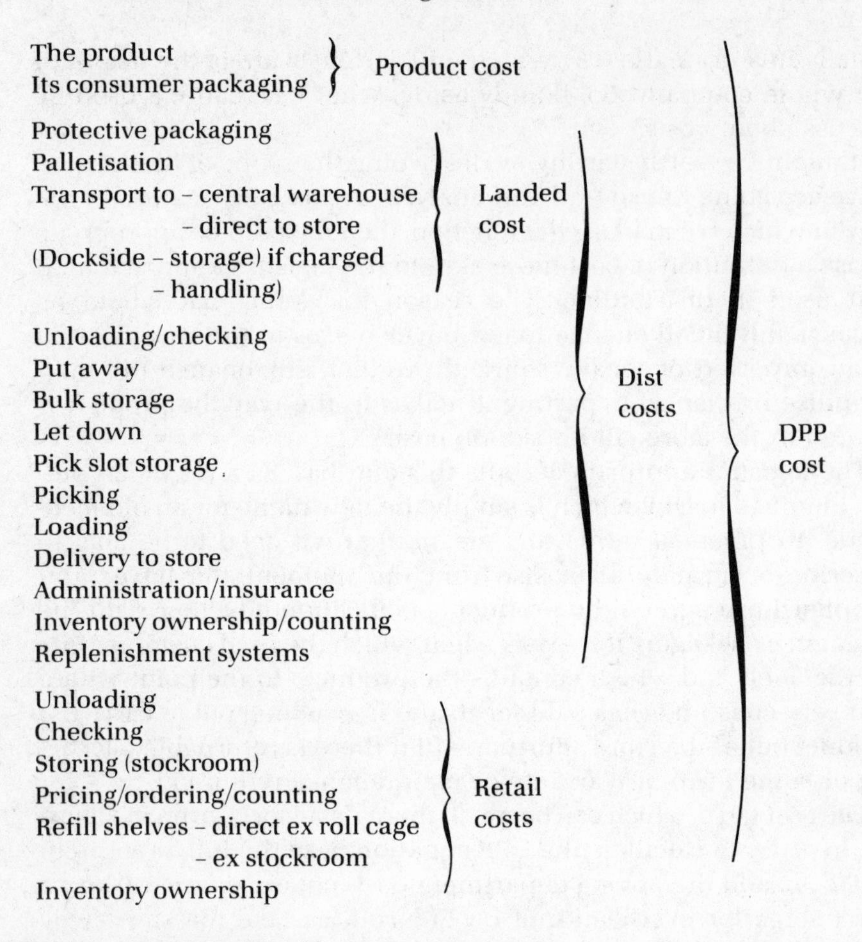

Figure 6.3: *DPP cost table*

The rest is applied common sense and a little lateral thought. Remember that there is, indeed can be, no ideal cost. The process of evaluating trade-offs will help you establish the potential for optimising your supply chain costs. Using old-fashioned productivity measurement will then help you ensure that you are applying the right methods as cheaply as you can. There is no short cut, no magic formula, no ready reckoner at the back of the book, only good solid supply chain management principles.

Summary

What I have tried to show in this chapter on trade-offs, service and cost are the relationships between these areas, the sequence in which they should be tackled and the valuable contributions these techniques can bring to your organisation.

It is important, if you truly want to achieve major improvements, that you break out of the narrow confines of a departmental approach, 'distribution' in 'retailing'. We have been trying here to see the biggest possible supply chain picture, to define, with others, our role in it, and to agree that role with the rest of the organisation. This agreement must include quality and cost criteria. Only once we have arrived at this point can we return to base, explain to our troops what the plan is, and set off to achieve it. It seems that trade-offs are the engine for change, improvement and the creation of methods and systems which will give you genuine and sustainable competitive advantage.

The service specification must represent a common understanding of what you are trying to achieve day to day. It must be achievable, it must be measurable and measured. Costs are what poorly managed or desperate companies worry about and try to cut. In our world optimum costs flow naturally from devising superior operating methods and managing them productively. They should not be capable of arbitrary or panic-induced reduction, because they should already be minimal. Further reduction should only be possible by volume increase or decrease, further method change or price reductions in fuel or packaging.

This whole area is one of great potential for rich cost saving and the creation of value added services. In many retail organisations it is still underexploited and undermanaged. It has become apparent in recent years that poor logistics have the potential to destroy or endanger a company and that the converse can transform a company into a successful organisation. Trade-offs, service and the consequent costs are at the heart of this logistical process. Ignore them at your peril!

7
Direct Product Profitability – A Supply Chain Philosophy

Alison K Pinnock

'DPP is one more piece of information, but it is not just any piece. The information generated in a DPP program can give retailers a quantitative way to be factual with information rather than depending on what you feel.'[1] David Diver, produce merchandiser, Hannaford Brothers, USA.

What is DPP?

There are many definitions of direct product profitability. Simply stated, it is a measure of the net profit an individual item of product contributes towards unallocated fixed costs and ultimately profit. To achieve this, the costs incurred by a distributor that may be directly associated with a particular product's handling and storage need to be identifed, and deducted from its profit generating capabilities, as shown in Figure 7.1.

The DPP methodologies identify the 'product causal' or 'direct product' costs in the supply chain, and allocate them to a single consumer unit of product.

An historical perspective

The DPP concept has been in existence for many years. In the early 1960s, in the USA, the consultants McKinsey and Co published a series of reports based on some initial work with General Foods. These set down a method of approach to cost allocation and profit measurement. Such studies, although not as detailed as current work, form the basis for today's approach to DPP.

In the late 1960s and early 1970s a major application was developed

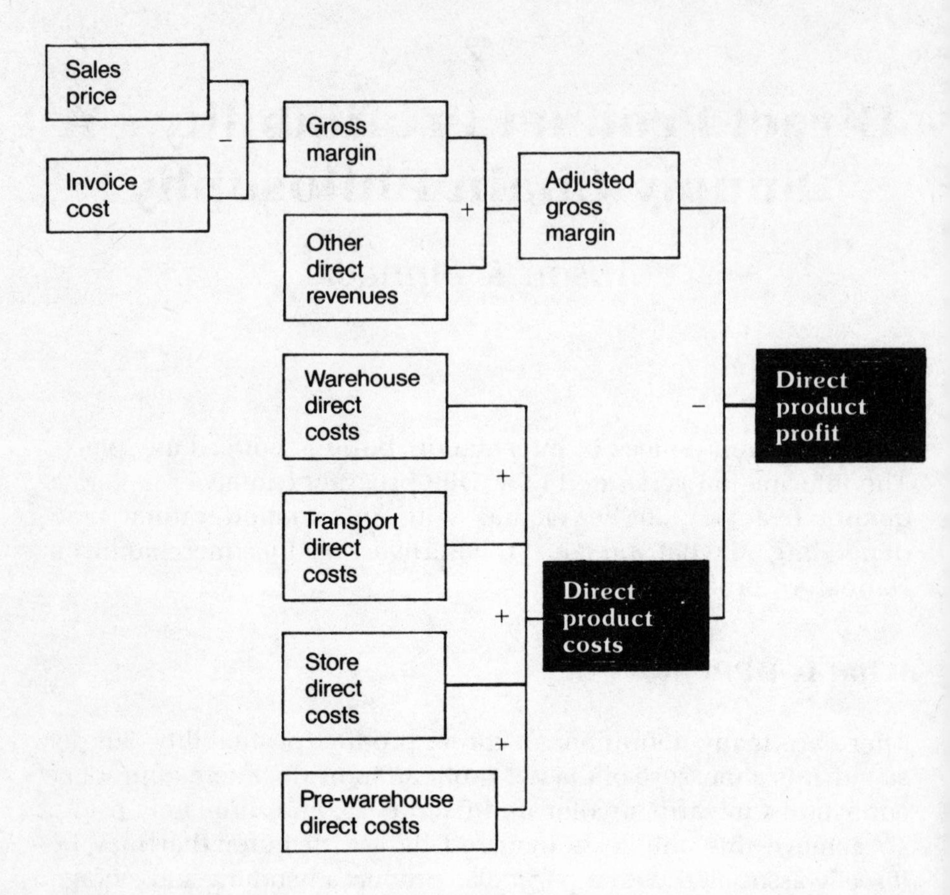

Figure 7.1: *Direct product profitability*

Source: Institute of Grocery Distribution

in a project called COSMOS (computer optimisation and simulation modelling for operating supermakets), co-ordinated by the National Association of Food Chains (a predecessor to the Food Marketing Institute, FMI).[2]

At about the same time, in the UK, similar studies were being carried out, most notably a study of the Health and Beauty Aids (H and BA) sector carried out by John Gordon and Associates in 1969, and updated in 1972. This was included in an Institute of Grocery Distribution (IGD) working party report in 1973 on space allocation and space management.[3] Further studies included the dairy cabinet and confectionery.

There was not much activity worldwide on DPP then until the early 1980s. With the advancement of data processing and in particular the widespread adoption of scanning by the retailers in the USA, DPP modelling had become operationally feasible, an opportunity taken up firmly by several companies. One of the most pro-active was the manufacturer Procter and Gamble, who advertised jointly with retailers to promote the use of DPP more widely.

August 1985 saw the release of the FMI's unified DPP method for dry grocery products in the USA, brought about by increasing calls for some form of standardisation of the technique. DPP could not become a 'common language' if a commonly understood model were not available. A combined effort of all facets of the food industry enabled a standard approach to obtaining DPP profitability information to be formed.[4]

In the UK, the American DPP model was not felt to be appropriate, so a steering group of manufacturers, retailers and wholesalers was established by the IGD to develop a model relevant to the UK grocery retailing sector. The UK unified DPP method for ambient temperature packaged products was launched in spring 1987. Subsequent studies have considered other product areas and their specific handling and storage peculiarities. These include frozen, chilled and health and beauty products.

There is one underlying philosophy to all DPP models, it is just the slightly different product handling practices and methods of approach that have caused or sometimes required alternative models to be developed. Only in one or two instances have there been fundamental differences in cost allocation. Under analysis, these have sometimes served to unnecessarily complicate the situation without having any significant impact on the results. When significant results are obtained, the differences have generally been useful for addressing a specific issue to which they relate.

Euro DPP method

Since 1985, manufacturers and retailers right across Europe have begun to study DPP methods. Some countries have translated existing models into their national languages, while others have developed their own methods of approach, as in the UK.

With the lowering of trade barriers across Europe getting ever closer, and with many companies now operating on a multinational basis, a need was established for a truly international approach to DPP. A European DPP method and model could support the cross-border transactions and international marketing programmes of the 1990s. For this, differences in national models needed to be understood or even eliminated. The starting point for this would be the harmonisation of the existing national models across Europe.

In response to the need for a common European approach, the CIES (the International Association of Chain Stores) co-ordinated an effort between the major European national trade institutes as a move towards the harmonisation of DPP, and the development of a joint European DPP methodology. The objectives to be achieved were:

- to establish a common methodology for Europe and to standardise DPC definitions;
- to produce a simple computer model incorporating the above standards;
- to share experiences and expertise across Europe.

The European DPP method was prepared through the joint technical co-operation of the national institutes of France (IFM), Germany (DHI) and the UK (IGD), with assistance from AECOC (Spain) and Touche Ross, international consultants.

This combined technical expertise on DPP facilitated a consistent methodology across the European partners. Where there were differences of approach for cost allocation, a 'party line' was determined and the differences therefore eliminated. For example, forklift costs have been included as part of the cost of movement activities, rather than with the more general occupancy costs.

The launch of the Euro model has also enabled a broader range of supply chain activities to be included in each of the national methodologies. For example, in the UK, the specific handling of display pallets through to the shop floor has been added, along with the handling of bottle returns – a significant cost element in the 'greener' countries of Sweden and Germany.

The European DPP method was launched towards the end of 1989, and has seen widespread uptake in the major project participant countries, but also across Scandinavia and in other EC countries such as Italy, and the Netherlands.

American enhancements

Over the same time period, work in the USA has extended their methodology to encompass a much broader range of categories and departments in the store, besides dry grocery. In particular, produce, fresh meat, bakery and delicatessen have been developed by the FMI in association with relevant trade organisations.

In these areas, the major problem encountered is with allocating costs to variable weight items, because a 'consumer unit' as such is difficult to define. The consideration of product shrinkage is also very important in these product areas, and can be a very significant element of cost.

Other FMI enhancements to the DPP methodology include:

- owner/operator and wholesaler;
- shrink/returns;
- coupon handling;
- display pallets;
- repackaging;
- cigarettes.

Similar extensions to the European DPP method will be considered in the early 1990s.

Improving profitability

Profit contribution has always been an important measure for product comparisons in the retail trade. Historically this has generally been taken as the difference between purchase price and selling price, namely gross margin. With the additional information given by direct product costing (DPC), a different perspective on products may be achieved, as is shown in Figure 7.2.

Different departments in the store achieve varying levels of gross margin profitability. Certain categories are known to generate low levels of gross profit, such as pet foods. Similarly, health and beauty products generally enjoy a relatively large difference between cost price and selling price. When, however, the direct product costs are taken into consideration, the levels of DPP may not correspond. A high gross margin product may also have high DPCs, such as

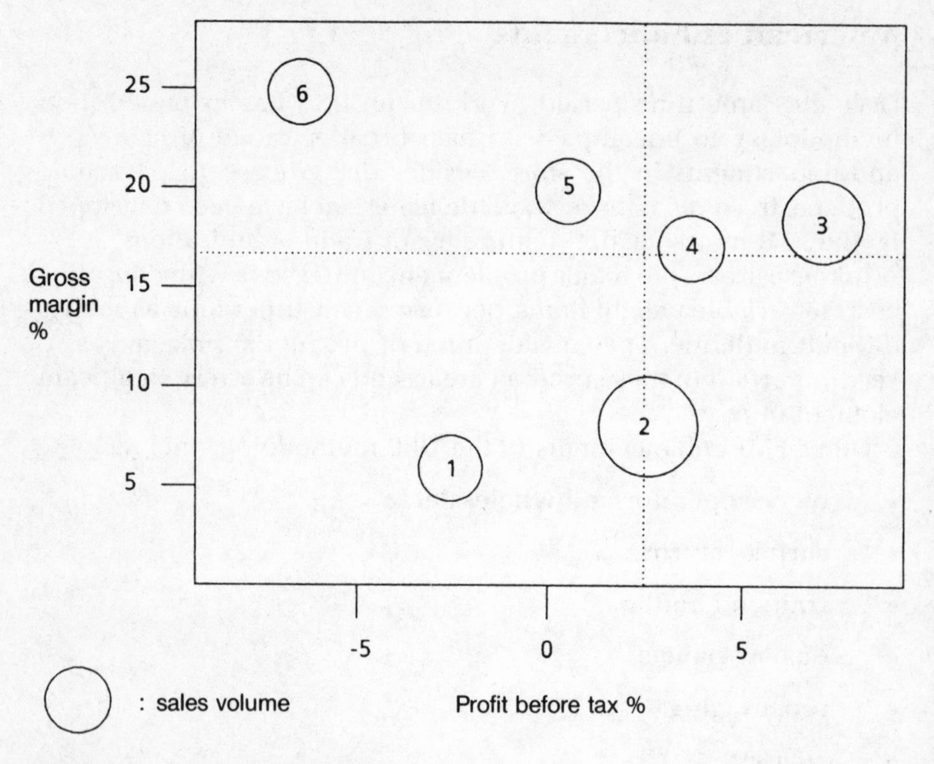

Figure 7.2: *Gross margin vs DPP*

product 6 in Figure 7.2. Alternatively, a low gross margin product may not have significant DPCs, such as product 2. The circle size in this diagram represents the sales volume of the product, giving a third dimension to the chart.

Direct product profit can be improved through either increasing the gross margin or reducing the direct product costs. For the former this can be achieved through increasing sales and therefore gaining from volume discounts, or by actually changing or negotiating new prices or costs.

The second approach naturally involves identifying the significant areas of costs and understanding each of their dynamics. For example, reducing distribution costs through more local buying; inventory and space costs can be optimised through computerised space management models; the consideration of delivery frequency, drop sizes and out-of-stocks can all lead to reducing costs.[5]

Fundamental to the interpretation of DPP results is the decision matrix. This relates the contribution of an item to its overall volume sales, as shown in Figure 7.3. The crossing point for the axes represents the average DPP per unit versus average weekly unit sales volume.

Various responses are available for a product falling into any one of these quadrants:

Winners

These products are performing well.

- Promote.
- Give prime display space.
- Reduce out-of-stocks.

Potentials

These products need sales stimulation.

- Promote.
- Give prime location on shelf.
- Reconsider price.

Traffic builders

Popular but costly to stock.

- Review handling.
- Reconsider price.
- Downgrade shelf location.
- Less promotion.

Losers

Are these items necessary?

- Reduce high areas of cost.
- Reduce shelf allocation.
- Reconsider price.
- Limit variety.
- Discontinue.

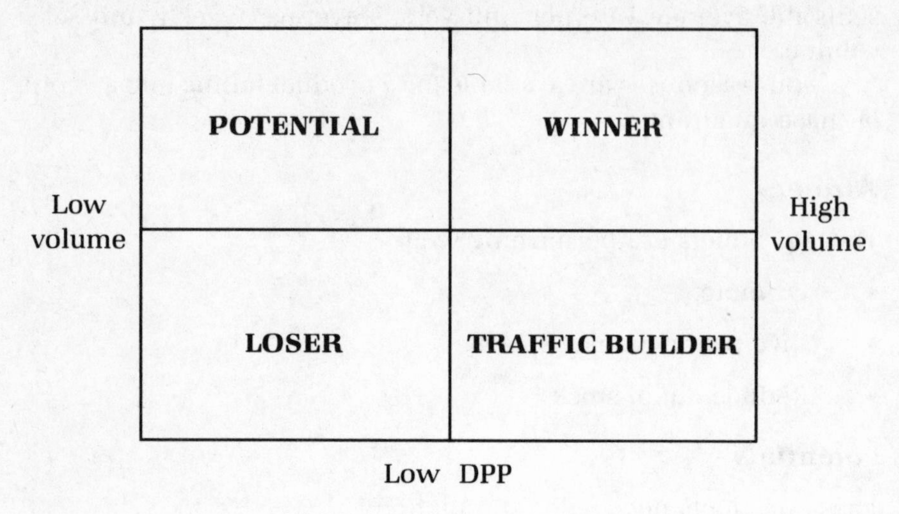

Figure 7.3: *DPP decision matrix*

These are just a few of the considerations one might consider in response to a product's position on the merchandising matrix.

Retail uses of DPP

The second industry survey on DPP in the UK,[6] a joint project between the IGD and Touche Ross management consultants, highlights the areas in which retailers and manufacturers are currently applying DPP techniques. The main use is in various aspects of merchandising – shelf space management, display and store layout – as shown in the rankings in Table 7.1. These results reflect the retailers' recognition that space is a scarce resource, and space profitability is a key strategic competitive factor.

Similar surveys have been carried out on an international basis by Touche Ross and this emphasis on space management is fairly common. The growth of space management software over recent years has certainly helped in promoting the use of DPP in merchandising.

A study was carried out in the USA in 1988 with Lucky Stores in northern California and Quaker Oats Ltd.[7] The aim of the project was to 'put new merchandising technology to the test', and publish the results through the FMI. The objective of the study was to determine the full practical value that can be realised from space management technologies and DPP. The study was designed to answer questions such as whether a category, or individual items therein, could be managed more profitably by using new space management technology.

Baseline DPP findings were used to identify general areas of opportunity for improved performance, through new category layouts. The following DPP performance measures were used:

- *DPP/unit* – measures the basic performance of an item or category in order to identify items that can most greatly improve profits from increased movement;
- *DPP/week* – measures the strength of profit contribution in order to help in shelf positioning decisions;
- *DPP/square foot* – measures the efficiency of shelf space utilisation in order to help in space allocation decisions.

The study resulted in increasing sales in the categories selected, in both value and volume terms, and more importantly DPP and gross profit were also improved. As a general rule, the quantity of space given to individual items and categories was primarily driven by unit sales. Space quality was assigned on DPP.

DPP developments in the UK have not just been restricted to the grocery sector. Boots The Chemist have spent several years develop-

Table 7.1. : *How is DPP being used by retailers?*

Uses	*Order of Priority*
Store layout	1
Display	1
Shelf space	1
Delivery methods	2
New product selection	2
Pricing	2
Promotion	2
Advertising	3

Source: IGD/Touche Ross Survey 1989

ing their in-house systems so that DPP information is available to their buying teams. In its early stages of development, DPP was used to consider total category contributions. This resulted in a change of strategy for stocking certain ranges, the most widely publicised of which involved the de-listing of petfoods, a category which was costing money to stock. Certain other factors needed to be considered before the decision was finally taken, such as the impact this would have on their petfood buying customers. This obviously cannot be measured using DPP.

Woolworths too have used DPP for range rationalisation. Identifying loss-making lines, and in particular the reasons why they do not contribute.[8] For example, grow-bags are no longer stocked since the stock-holding and space requirements far exceed any justification for carrying the line.

Both Boots and Woolworth have also used DPP for operational decision making – identifying how certain product ranges are best handled to satisfy high levels of service, but without holding excesses of stock. These manifest themselves in break-bulk operations and frequent deliveries to store in small quantities for certain product ranges.

Manufacturer uses of DPP

As DPP has been described so far, it appears predominantly to be a retail profitability measure for retailers. Many manufacturers in the UK appear to have this attitude – DPP is another weapon in the retailers' arsenal.

As with many of such decision support systems being used by the retail trade, it should be seen as an opportunity for manufacturers to better understand the way in which the retailers operate. In understanding their rationale, it is then possible to play the same game – anticipating the areas on which the retailers will focus, and using this as an opportunity rather than a threat.

Procter and Gamble recently commissioned Touche Ross to perform an independent study of the disposable nappy market.[9] The study helped in the relaunch of their market-leading Pampers nappies to the retail trade as distinct boy/girl ranges, a total of 14 products, instead of the previous 7, and occupying only 50 per cent more shelf space. Through the use of DPP they helped demonstrate to the retailers that the increased range more than justified the extra space and handling in terms of extra profit.

Still with Procter and Gamble, the launch of Ariel Ultra demonstrated the use of DPP as part of a 'total systems efficiency' philosophy. The new product uses 30 per cent less chemicals, 30 per cent less packaging and is also far more space efficient on shelf.[10] It thus gives better performance for the retailer as well as for the manufacturer. A more space efficient product gives better pallet and storage utilisation throughout the whole product supply chain.

Following a similar theme, Scott put an enormous effort into the design of a new outer case for Andrex toilet tissue with a view to reducing direct product costs.[11] The design changed from a 6 × 3 format to a 5 × 4 (giving 11 per cent more product per case). This resulted in the elimination of pallet overhang, which in turn gave better stability, less product damage and improved pallet utilisation – with 6 per cent more product per pallet.

Further ways of reducing costs for all products were identified in Scott's study. These included the more efficient utilisation of case cube, smaller case sizes for slower moving lines to reduce inventory holding, rationalisation of product ranges to eliminate 'losers', and a review of distribution channels – central warehouse versus direct to store. Costs throughout the supply chain were considered, inefficiencies were located and the source of the problem tackled.

Coca Cola and Schweppes Beverages took a more category-orientated approach to DPP when they suggested reducing the number of soft drinks lines from 41 to 18, and suppliers from 7 to 2.[11] Research from 1987 indicated that due to out-of-stocks, CCSB soft drinks lost sales for the retail trade were somewhere in the region of £10m. By comparison, some slower selling lines were heavily overstocked, and relatively expensive to administrate in such low quantities. A correctly balanced range was therefore paramount in rectifying this situation. In one particular retailer, changing the range as shown above improved volume sales, but more significantly, direct product profit was up 20 per cent.

Problems of implementation

The road of implementation for many has not been particularly smooth. One of the many criticisms from both manufacturers and retailers has been the availability of data and the difficulties concerned with their collection. Data take two forms, first the retailer cost and productivity information used to drive the DPCs, and secondly the product data used to allocate these costs on to the individual items of product.

Manufacturers argue that the former is a retailers' preserve, and therefore they are unlikely to be able to obtain it. Some retailers would also argue that it is difficult and too costly to gather in the early stages. For this reason a database of typical cost and productivity information has been developed by the IGD. This does not represent any one retailer, but gives figures which are representative of the industry as a whole, and may be used for comparative purposes.

Even given such a database, some cynics will dispute the value of non-specific retailer data. The value they refuse to see comes with a greater understanding of DPP and how it should be used. Using such data, it is essential to move away from talking in absolute values, and to consider the relative positioning of products against each other. Even inaccurate data, so long as they are reasonable, will treat all products in the same fashion, so rankings and relativities will not be invalid.

Product information in the main is more widely available. Much of the relevant information is gathered by space planning departments, when they exist. Detailed sales data is, however, again a retailer domain. This is used in the allocation of space occupancy costs, one of the more significant DPP costs for many products. There is a distinct move towards sharing more and more sales information as the use of scanning increases. As the retailers see the benefits of its use, this will undoubtedly open up further the dialogue on DPP-related topics. In the meantime, the market research organisations providing market shares and syndicated data will inevitably have an important role to play.

Retailer uptake of DPP has been relatively slow, due mainly to the enormous task of systems integration and the change in company culture which may ensue. As far as the systems are concerned, to perform such analyses on a regular basis for say 20,000 lines is a rather daunting task. It would obviously not be feasible to perform such analyses on a personal computer.

As DPP considers all aspects of the retail distribution system, it cannot be a stand-alone system, and needs to be integrated into all parts of the business that will use it. At a recent conference on DPP,[11] Asda said it was currently evaluating DPP and how best it could integrate it so as to harness as many benefits as possible. All the major retailers in the grocery sector are integrating a form of

DPP into their information systems; it is just a question of time before it becomes an everyday mode for business operation.

The future

Software obviously plays an important role in DPP analyses. As DPP becomes more widely used, software solutions are being developed for much broader applications. Linked directly into other decision-support tools, such as computerised space management and promotion planning models, enables a more technical, rather than seat-of-the-pants, approach to merchandise management to be taken. They cannot replace the role of the negotiator or marketeer; such developments just provide better information for making better decisions.

The FMI DPP model was programmed into space management software in the late 1980s. The 1990s should see the European DPP method integrated within the leading commercial packages, including both Spaceman and Apollo. Space management forms just a part of the overall decision-making processes that can be achieved through the use of DPP. Since DPP attempts to model the entire distribution channel, there are points throughout the chain where decisions can impact on the results achieved.

One enhancement that could be built into DPP modelling is that of space elasticities – the ratio of relative change in sales to relative change in shelf space.[12] Recent studies in the USA at a category level have identified those categories from which incremental sales can be achieved through increased shelf space. A model could be developed to optimise the DPP contributions per week through the better management of the space in store.[13]

Many of the retailers are looking to use DPP as a part of new product selection. Each buyer would therefore be able to access the programme and compare any new prospects with current competitive offerings. Where special deals are on offer, these can be evaluated to see if increased stock-holding costs are not greater than the discounts being offered.

Summary

Gross margin as a measure is very basic, but DPP allows for fine-tuning, through the examination of the whole supply chain, and understanding how a product incurs costs as it moves through the system.

DPP cannot be the retail panacea in terms of decision making, it is a usable tool to help make better decisions based on sound technical understanding of the supply chain. In many organisations there will be some items whose DPP numbers might otherwise warrant their removal, but because of intangibles they are vital to overall department or organisation success.

To quote Tim Hammonds of the FMI,[14] 'The single most important thing to learn about DPP is that it is an invaluable servant but an intolerable master.' It cannot make the decisions. It is a diagnostic tool with which one is pointed to areas of the product supply chain which may require attention. Action taken from such analyses should lead to an increase in profitability – to the benefit of the whole industry.

There is a danger that the ultimate consumer will be forgotten among all this technology. However, consumer and market research still remain important factors in a product's profile – with the final test being the consumer purchase. DPP should harness such information to help generate the best contributions for the retailer and the manufacturer, but not at the expense of the consumer.

'The secret of today's operation lies in information. The industry is now far more complex. It is carried out on a much larger scale. Under these circumstances management can only now effectively be done if there is adequate information and there is power in the system to use that information to good effect.'[15] Dr JA Beaumont, chief executive, Institute of Grocery Distribution.

Notes

(1) *Supermarket News* (1988) 'How DPP will apply to produce' 24 October, USA.

(2) Buzzell, RD, Salmon, WJ, Vancil, RF (1965) *Product Profitability Measurement and Merchandising Decisions* Harvard University, USA.

(3) IGD (1973) *Report of the Working Party on Space Allocation and Space Management*, May.

(4) Boyle, K (1987) *Direct Product Profit – A Primer*, FMI, USA.

(5) Aston, M (1989) 'Method trade-offs and DPP' *Focus on Physical Distribution and Logistics Management* 8(8), 24–28.

(6) Touche Ross/IGD (1989) *DPP: Results of the Second Industry Survey*, July.

(7) FMI (1988) *Space Management: Putting New Merchandising Technology to the Test* May, USA.

(8) IIR (1988) DPP Conference Papers, April.
(9) Touche Ross (1989) *Annual Review*.
(10) IGD (1989) 'Transcripts from convention '89 responsibility' October.
(11) IIR (1989) DPP Conference Papers, April.
(12) Competitive Edge (1990) *A Practical Application of Space Elasticity* January, Willard Bishop Consulting, USA.
(13) Phipps, JR (1988) 'Putting Profit in its Place' *Productivity*, October, USA.
(14) Hammonds, T (1986) *Unified DPP: A Model of Consistency* Progressive Grocer Executive Report, USA.
(15) IGD (1989) op cit, 17–25.

References

FMI, USA (1989) *DPP and Shelf Space Management: An Implementation Strategy*.
ISB, Germany *DPP – 1989 – An International Approach*.
Pinnock, AK (1986) *DPP – An Introduction for the Grocery Trade* IGD, February.
Progressive Grocer (USA) monthly.
Supermarket News (USA) weekly.

8
The Impact of Information Technology

Alan Slater

Applications of information technology within physical distribution activities are often limited to operational activities designed to maximise productivity rather than to address those issues of integrating the independent elements in the supply chain to maximise service levels and minimise costs in order to gain competitive advantage.

Introduction

Retail organisations may spend up to 20 per cent of their cost either directly or indirectly upon physical distribution activities, and all these costs are simply evaluated and easily controlled. Yet the distribution function is the least exploited area in which to gain real competitive advantage.

Such lack of awareness is difficult to explain, but may result from the fact that the distribution function is something which is out of mind because the majority of the activities happen away from head office or store locations and outside office and store working hours. A more likely reason, however, is that there is little or no tangible information about physical distribution costs and performance available within the organisation.

Most retailers evaluate sales and profitability information at store, departmental and product levels and allocate physical distribution costs as a percentage of sales value in a similar manner to other non directly controllable costs such as head office overheads. However, the introduction of 'direct product profitability' has led to the creation of data and the awareness that distribution costs differ between products in relation to differences in product source, rate of sale, weight, cube, temperature requirements, and length of the storage requirement before transfer to store. Data upon physical distribution costs per product have often been a major factor in direct product profitability exercises to determine that individual products incur substantial losses.

These basic costings are the tip of the iceberg of potential data available from within the physical distribution system to assist management to identify and achieve a competitive advantage.

Objectives

Applications for information technology within physical distribution operations may be targeted at a number of objectives including the following.

(***1***) *Accounting* for receipts, stock held, damages, obsolescence, despatches and returns. This information is mandatory and both the processes and data are checked annually by the auditors.

(***2***) *Operations requirements* such as order processing, order picking, and despatch. Traditionally order data are input manually (now being replaced by electronic data interchange in some product categories) and this order represents a trigger to provide instructions to undertake other tasks such as order picking. Further moves away from paper driven systems have been improved by the ability to communicate by various methods to operators of equipment such as forklift trucks, and this has led to the development and acceptance of internal 'paperless operating systems'.

(***3***) *Productivity* has been substantially improved both in the warehouse by the introduction of stock location systems and in transport operations by the introduction of systems for tachograph analysis and vehicle routeing and scheduling. In these instances productivity is achieved by replacing labour intensive manual systems with computer based systems, often obtaining data direct from other sources in order to avoid duplication of data input and the possibility of error.

(**4**) *Information* feedback upon supplier, operations or customer performance to management in exception report format. These monitoring systems rely upon the existence of a 'standard' and a programme which relates actual performance to standard in order to determine variations. For example, supplier orders may be checked upon receipt in accordance with such standards for: day/time requested; product ordered; quantity delivered in good condition; best before date; price per item; and condition of pallet transferred; and any variations on each order received, recorded and subsequently reported to the buyer as evidence for discussion with the supplier. Note that information collected in this instance is on an 'exception to standard' basis and is only of value if the buyer obtains, interprets and actions the data in discussion with the suppliers who have unacceptable levels of errors.

(**5**) *Integration* of the elements of the supply chain by sharing information from the stores to the warehouses and the suppliers, often transferred through electronic data interchange. Such information may be as simple as the retailer's warehouse informing a particular store of the product despatched and a forecast of expected time of delivery, to a retailer informing a supplier of daily sales of a particular product.

(**6**) *Automation* of particular machine routines in the system, particularly in the warehouse with the AGV (automatic guided vehicle) and the fully automatic crane, both of which are instructed to undertake particular tasks and monitored in the process of these tasks by computer programs with set rules and routines.

(**7**) *Planning* of retail activities, particularly optimum store sites from demographic data, may require detailed programs to cope with the complex algorithms and systems support in order to manipulate the vast volumes of input data.

These objectives are generally targeted at achieving competitive advantage by obtaining one or more of the following: lower costs; speed of data transfer; regularity of data transfer; and dependability of the information transferred.

Applications

Applications for information technology in the retail physical distribution environment are extensive, and cover all areas from the customer and 'front of store' throughout the supply chain to the 'suppliers' and often even further back to their raw material suppliers.

One significant fact is that most applications may either be designed to operate in a stand-alone mode to solve particular problems (for example, planograms to set shelf space allocations), or may be designed to link into other systems for data collection or information presentation (for example, a warehouse stock location system will extract orders from the order processing system and present the location of individual products on the order picking instructions).

However, maximum added value is gained where systems are interlinked, particularly in operational systems where the minimum volume of paper is generated and instructions are presented on a screen and confirmation of completed actions is given through a few simple keyboard strokes.

The catalogue of potential retail information systems is vast, and their suitability will depend upon such factors as: the product groupings and specialisation; the geographical locations; organisation size; and the competitive pressures. For large multi-product group retail operations the systems applications are complex and divide into a number of categories (defined in Figure 8.1) which may be described under a number of headings.

Store operations

Front of store

- The *customer database* is normally only successful in operations such as cash and carry where customers are restricted to members only, but has also been tried through preferential credit card systems, discount card systems and guarantee systems. The database helps define the profile of customers to assist with targeting future products and marketing.
- *EPOS* systems, which are based on line items data collection through bar codes, article numbers, magnetic number codes,

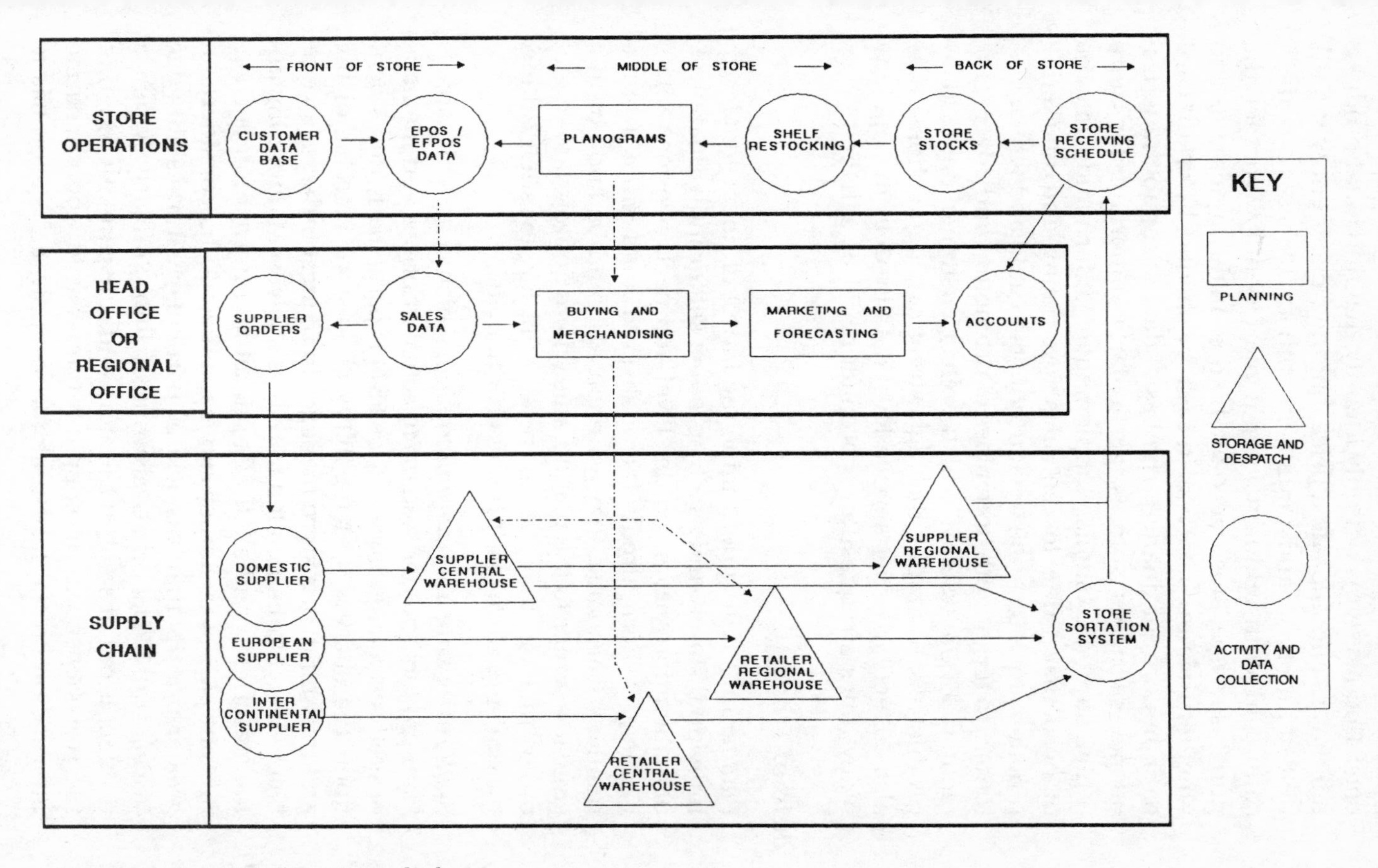

Figure 8.1: *Retail information links*

or alternative machine readable codes (for example, Kimble tags). Good systems not only identify the individual products purchased and allocate a price, but they also identify the till, time of purchase, and a number of other purchases automatically, and with additional input may identify whether the purchaser is a store account holder, male or female, and whether the purchase was in cash, by cheque, by credit card or some form of finance. The basic data of number and frequency of items sold is particularly important for store replenishment systems. Supplementary information may be of particular value to the sales forecasting and marketing functions to determine what products to hold and which customers to target with both types of promotion and advertising method. EPOS systems which collect customer demand by product (for example, the high street catalogue shops) may also collect customer service level data by determining how many times a request for a product could be satisfied.

Middle of store

- *Planograms*, which determine the layout of linear footage in individual stores, and as a by-product set for individual products the appropriate reorder level and pack size for replenishment. Where product is delivered to a store from a retailer's warehouse that warehouse should be laid out in a similar manner to the planograms where appropriate so that order picking may be in reverse order to shelf filling, maximising store shelf filling productivity.

- *Shelf restocking* and *merchandising*, which covers all aspects from product reorder systems to actual priorities and methods of shelf restocking. Store service level is particularly dependent upon the success and flexibility of in-store merchandising and the ability of a store manager to request orders above or below the volume needed to fill the shelves. Maintaining up-to-date pricing and shelf edge ticketing information is a significant part of customer service and could be considered a greater priority than restocking, particularly if the shelf edge prices and EPOS prices are out of line. Similarly, when a product is out of stock at the store and subsequently at either the warehouse or the supplier, then, based upon accurate information on the lead time for resupply, a decision has to be taken whether to leave the shelf empty or restock with the adjacent product.

Back of store

- *Store stocks* need to be checked regularly to detect such factors as pilferage, damage control, stock rotation, obsolescence (particularly where best before dates are marked) and pricing/ numbering if appropriate. Errors picked up in one store may indicate potential errors in others and should, therefore, be highlighted for specific attention. Particularly important is the analysis of customer, store and warehouse returns which, dependent upon source, could indicate a costly problem. New product lines deserve particular attention in order to detect problems early and in order to ensure satisfactory action is taken early.
- *Store receiving schedule*, which is a booking-in system to even out the receiving workload and ensure that not all the deliveries arrive in on the same morning of the week. This also allows the store management the opportunity of allocating priorities to receipts in accordance with store stock levels or restocking labour availability.

Head office or regional office

Buying and merchandising

- *Sales data* to provide pareto and seasonality figures by product line. This often shows a concentration on particular products and a narrow consumer's shopping basket, which implies the need for high service levels upon those items or product ranges, otherwise potential sales are lost. Analysis of sales data may also indicate to what degree service level may be maintained by the substitution of a similar product, or how price sensitive customers are with a particular product. Such data is particularly important to focus the attention of buyers, suppliers, distribution staff and store operations staff on those products which are both fast moving and provide a high contribution to the business. This implies that all staff throughout the supply chain are aware of the top selling products through the management communications process.

- *Marketing and forecasting* are particularly significant planning roles and analysis of historic trends will help ensure that correct quantities of product are purchased and delivered to store for the correct selling period. These forecasts may also assist distribution management to plan the use of warehousing and transport requirements, and store management to plan their layout changes and stock replenishment cycles. Far too often both distribution and store management are reactive to the current situation, when the opportunity existed to plan the required changes, if the salient information had been transferred from marketing or buying.
- *Supplier orders* and the control of the purchase ledger where the particularly important factors are: source of supply; location and date of first delivery; progressing method and communication of changes to the planned delivery schedules; method of delivery to warehouse and store; added value requirements in retailer's warehouse (for example, repacking or ticketing).

Supply chain

Warehousing and transport

- *Distribution operations* from supplier to store may involve an order processing through one or more of a number of types of warehouse including: the supplier's central warehouse; supplier's regional warehouse; retailer's central warehouse; and the retailer's regional warehouse. Distribution and store management may need to both know the exact supply route with the lead times involved, and the stock on hand plus stock in transit positions. There are a number of basic distribution functions which should be covered by each warehouse or transport operation. These may include the following.

Inventory management

- Receiving.
- Inventory control.
- Stock counting (including cycle counting).
- Stock transfers.
- Stock rotation.

Warehouse management

- Palletisation and pallet control.
- Storage and stock location.
- Labour scheduling and management.
- Material handling.
- Order picking (bulk and order levels).
- Order assembly and checking.
- Despatch system.
- Asset maintenance.
- Costing.
- Quality and performance monitoring.

Fleet management

- Vehicle routeing and scheduling.
- Tachograph analysis and driver records.
- Fleet administration.
- Workshop scheduling.
- Fleet maintenance and vehicle records.
- Fleet costing.
- Driver scheduling and management.
- Quality and performance monitoring.

In addition there is a requirement for each distribution function to inform their customer (either a store or another warehouse) that particular orders are being picked and the expected date and time of arrival.

The objectives of the systems support for each application area will differ in relation to the primary driving need for the system, but many individual applications seek to maximise a number of systems objectives – see Figure 8.2.

APPLICATION / OBJECTIVE	ACCOUNTING	OPERATIONAL REQUIREMENTS	PRODUCTIVITY	INFORMATION	INTEGRATION	AUTOMATION	PLANNING
FRONT OF STORE CUSTOMER DATABASE				■			■
EPOS / EFTPOS	■	■	■	■	■	■	■
MIDDLE OF STORE PLANOGRAMS		■					■
SHELF RESTOCKING ANDMERCHANDISING		■					
BACK OF STORE STORE STOCKS	■	■					
STORE RECEIVING SCHEDULE		■	■				
HEAD / REGIONAL OFFICE SALES DATA	■			■			
MARKETING AND FORECASTING				■	■		■
SUPPLIER ORDERS		■					
SUPPLY CHAIN DISTRIBUTION	■	■	■	■	■	■	■

Figure 8.2: Application and objectives of retail IT systems

Issues

There are extensive applications of information technology in the support of retail operations, but two significant factors stand out; first, the type of information needs differ between operational requirements and management requirements, and secondly, information technology crosses all organisational and functional boundaries. If the maximum competitive advantage is to be gained from the application of information technology then management must recognise and solve the differences between different types of information and the integrated information needs of each element of the supply chain.

Types of information

It is important to distinguish between those applications which support the day-to-day operations and those applications which support the decision-making process; since each type has different characteristics and demands.

Operational systems are primarily concerned with day-to-day activities and handle large volumes of data. The main requirements from the software and hardware are for availability, efficiency, accuracy and security. Software is often specially designed to meet the operational requirements and often lasts for many years because the rate of change in the requirement is slow.

Information to support the decision-making process, however, is different insofar as managers require different methods of presentation on a week-by-week basis, depending upon the emphasis they require. Decisions support systems are more successful when based upon a database, which extracts data from the operating system, and allows the management to manipulate it in the manner they wish in order to obtain whatever analysis they require.

Integration of the supply chain

The supply chain is essentially a number of independent activities (for example, storage is one activity and transport is another) connected together to transfer goods from their origin to the end user.

It is possible to optimise the costs and service level in one operation, and substantially adversely impact upon the costs and service level of another operation in the same supply chain. For example, if a warehouse could offer order picking one hour after receipt of order then costs may be minimised because orders could be picked and checked rapidly, but transport would be under pressure to despatch small loads on a regular basis, thus substantially increasing overall costs.

The key is to integrate all the elements of the supply chain to the single overall objective of minimum cost for a pre-defined service level. This implies that where appropriate an individual activity in the supply chain may be undertaken at below maximum efficiency in order that the whole supply chain be balanced.

There are many examples where the adoption of this principle would reduce overall costs and improve service level, but none is so significant as in stock management. The adoption of information technology in the form of 'distribution resource planning systems' (DRP) which address the question of balancing stock and physical distribution resources throughout the supply chain has proved to be of significant help in integrating the individual elements in the supply chain.

Integration throughout the supply chain is particularly simple for those retailers who are only dealing with 'own brand' goods, because they have the power to order goods when required, control stocks at all storage points from the manufacturer to the retail store, and control the times of transfer and transportation between individual elements within the supply chain.

In the case of branded goods, retailers are often at the mercy of the manufacturers, and vice versa, and each compensate for their lack of knowledge by increasing stock levels to secure sufficiently high service levels. However, if the retailers gave the manufacturers sales information by line item from EPOS by Electronic Data Interchange (EDI), and manufacturers gave retailers stock information in a similar manner, then both main parties would trust each other and overall stocks held throughout the supply chain could be reduced.

Thus, competitive advantage may be gained by the application of information technology to transfer stock data between the elements within the supply chain (EDI), and also to optimise the stock levels and resources employed throughout the supply chain (DRP).

Software selection

When selecting suitable software it is important to keep both the application and objectives in mind because this helps focus attention on the real needs of the organisation. Otherwise, there is a real trap in that after seeing one software solution with particular features which are memorable, rather than useful, the memorable features will cloud the mind from ensuring that all the basic requirements exist. This results in a difficult implementation programme and the credibility of the software house, or DP department, being questioned by operators who require specific functions which are not available.

The key to success is often at the supplier selection procedure which may contain a number of significant steps, from defining the requirement to review of the functionality, after six months or one year of implementation.

Definition of requirement

The first and most important element of software selection is to define the user requirement. This means listing in some organised way those functions each potential user of the system may require both now and in the immediate future.

The requirement should be defined in some detail, for example, when considering the storage element of a warehouse management system then a single requirement may be to provide user definable properties in order to allocate product to the most appropriate different physical storage types including:

- block stacking;
- pallet racking;
- drive in racking;
- mobile racking;
- live storage for pallets;
- carton live storage;
- shelving;
- carousels;
- multiple pallet storage;
- temperature controlled storage;
- end of aisle storage;
- ground floor storage.

These requirements may be defined and collected by a combination of interviews with potential users, visits to other appropriate sites, and discussions with potential software suppliers.

When a list of requirements is prepared the potential users of the system should be asked to identify whether each requirement is essential, desirable or useful. This information may form the foundation of a selection, scoring and ranking process insofar as the software selected must include all those requirements defined as essential.

The written definition of requirements represents a valuable reference point later in the selection and implementation process, because it provides the fixed goal posts and target to be achieved.

Supplier selection

The most difficult element of supplier selection is to decide whether to pursue a tailored system route or whether to opt for the adoption of an existing package.

The advantages of the package based solution may include:

- faster implementation;
- rapid integration of multiple locations;
- over specification in some functional areas;
- effective use of resources (particularly internal DP staff);
- specialisation of skills in the software house;
- cost-effective solution;
- secure implementation;
- low maintenance costs;
- low long-term risk of decline in support facilities;
- potentially greater hardware flexibility.

The basic disadvantage of the package based solution is that if the requirements are particularly specific then it will be difficult to find a package which meets more than 75 per cent of the essential requirements, and any subsequent conversion costs may be as expensive as developing a tailored system.

However, based upon the definition of requirements, it is a simple matter to produce a questionnaire for suppliers to identify whether their software would be suitable. The questionnaire lists the requirements and asks suppliers to identify whether their software offers the functionality required, whether it could be modified to offer the functionality required at low cost, or would not be able to offer the functionality required without signficant additional cost being incurred.

The answers from each software supplier could be analysed to rank the individual software packages by both functional fit (essential, desirable or useful) and availability fit (available now, minor modification or major modification). An overall software ranking could be obtained by the addition of rankings for price and support operations.

This procedure both defines whether the package based route is feasible and, if so, shortlists the suitable suppliers through the ranking process. In the event of needing to follow the tailored system solution a similar process will define the most suitable software houses to undertake the task.

The final selection must be at the detailed level from the shortlist provided and the factors included in the decision must include:

- functional fit (software and hardware);
- overall price (software, hardware and support);
- implementation time;
- suitability (cultural fit);
- business risk (size of organisation and financial standing);
- proof of ability (reference sites).

Implementation

Implementation of both a package based solution and a software house assisted tailored solution should be based upon a written contract with the supplier. Similarly, the in-house solution should be based upon a written plan.

The contract or plan should include:

- a written functional requirement defining at minimum that the essential and desirable functional requirements will be achieved;
- a timetable for implementation;

- a price or budget.

It should be possible to monitor progress against functional achievement, timetable and cost. The most significant factor to remember is that throughout the implementation the business must continue to operate efficiently; and this may imply parallel running of the existing and new system while all the software errors (bugs) are removed and while sufficient staff are trained upon the new system. It may also imply that while the new system is being prepared for implementation the old system will still require support, change and adaptation to the constantly changing business environment.

The implementation programme should also include such essential features as:

- user documentation;
- source code documentation;
- disaster recovery plans;
- supplier, in-house staff and customer information programme.

Post-implementation review

After six months or a year of full operation an operating system should be critically reviewed to determine whether the original essential requirements have been achieved, and whether there are any new requirements which should be added.

Normally, after some time of operation, the users will find alternative ways of achieving their requirements whatever data are presented to them, and it is essential that users are not incurring more expense because of system failures.

User requirements have a habit of changing, and software could easily become obsolete if valid new user requirements are not met. This may include evaluating the needs of suppliers or customers.

Conclusion

Competitive advantage may be obtained by those retailers who consider the significance of the objectives, the application and the selection of information systems. This competitive advantage will be obtained through better information flows throughout the supply chain and improved speed of decision making; all of which will reduce overall stock levels, reduce overall costs and improve overall service levels.

In the future one of the critical distinguishing features between retailers will be their ability to use information systems to support the physical distribution operation.

9

(a) The Changing Nature of Food Retailing

John Fernie

Introduction

In the last 10–15 years, the food retailing sector has experienced the most radical changes of all the sectors in UK retailing. In the 1960s and 1970s grocery retail outlets were small in size, located in traditional high streets and price wars were a predominant feature of companies' retail strategies. The 1980s have seen companies strive for a quality image. More product lines, many of which are own-label, have enabled grocery retailers to add value to generic products. This, coupled with efficient improvements in retail operations, has led to significant improvements in the profit margins of the major multiples in the last ten years. Further market opportunities are evolving as the public becomes increasingly aware of environmental issues. Indeed, if the 1970s was the decade of price wars and the 1980s the decade of quality initiatives, the 1990s could be the decade for the environmentally friendly product.

The total market for food expenditure continues to grow, but slowly. The success of many multiple chains during the 1980s can be largely attributed to new high quality square footage replacing lower quality square footage, therefore retail food sales increased by 68 per cent in value terms from 1980–7, but volume sales only increased by 19 per cent during the same period (Key Note, 1988). In addition to improving profitability of existing stores, the major grocery retailers have moved into new geographical markets either through organic growth or by acquisition. Consequently, the grocery market is highly concentrated in the UK with the top seven companies accounting for around two-thirds of sales. To experience continued growth, food retailers will either have to enter new overseas markets where concentration is less marked or move into new product areas. J Sainsbury has already taken such initiatives in the 1980s with the purchase of Shaws, a New England supermarket chain in the USA, the further development of Homebase, the DIY chain and the buy-out of Storehouse's share of Savacentre.

This chapter will discuss these changes in the food market prior to assessing the implications of such changes for the distribution of grocery products. The example of J Sainsbury will then be used in part (b) to illustrate the changes which have occurred to the company's distribution network in response to an evolving store expansion programme.

The power of the consumer

The changes which have occurred in food retailing have been largely in response to the changing needs of the UK consumer. With inflation running in the teens in the 1970s, price was an important consideration in consumer's choice of products and which stores to frequent. A decade later, the average consumer has enjoyed a 'real' growth in spending power of around 2 per cent per annum. Furthermore, the trends of more women working, increased car ownership and greater market penetration of freezers and microwaves in the kitchen have transformed our approach to food shopping. Not surprisingly, the frozen foods market and 'convenience' foods have exhibited much growth during this period. The consumer has also become more health and environmentally conscious, demanding better nutritional labelling and the stocking of organic biodegradable 'green' products.

The retailer response

In response to changing consumer demands, the food retailing sector has undergone considerable transformation during the 1970s and 1980s. Many high street names have disappeared, especially those taken over in the aggressive acquisition strategies of the Argyll Group and the Gateway Corporation, for example, Liptons, Hintons, Fine Fare and International Stores. (Now that Gateway has been taken over by Isosceles, most of the superstores have been sold to Asda.) These trends have resulted in greater concentration in the food retailing sector. The grocery trade is the largest within this sector and it has been growing at the expense of the food specialists, for example, in 1987 total grocery sales of £31 billion accounted for 81 per cent of total food sales, compared with 76 per cent of a £17 billion market in 1980 (Key Note, 1988).

Within the grocery sector, the multiples continued to increase their share (from 61 per cent in 1980 to 73 per cent in 1987) at the expense of the independents (25 per cent to 16 per cent) and the co-operatives (14 per cent to 11 per cent) (IGD, 1989). Table 9.1 shows how the grocery store network has been rationalised during this period. In 1987, 47,270 outlets were in operation, a 37 per cent decline in numbers in a decade. It should be noted, however, that in terms of percentage decline the multiple sector exhibits the highest rate – 39 per cent. Nevertheless, in all sectors the rate of decline has slowed down considerably in recent years with the multiple sector increasing its numbers in 1986–7.

Table 9.1: *Number of grocery retail outlets 1977–87*

Year	Multiples[1]	Co-operatives	Independents[2]	Total no of grocery outlets
1977	7,000	6,000	62,000	75,000
1978	6,440	5,760	59,000	71,200
1979	6,000	5,550	56,000	67,550
1980	5,700	5,250	53,000	63,950
1981	5,600	5,050	51,000	61,650
1982	5,430	4,630	48,000	58,060
1983	4,760	4,490	43,000	52,250
1984	4,380	4,230	40,850[3]	49,460
1985	4,290	4,120	40,100	48,510
1986	4,270	3,910	39,620	47,800
1987	4,280	3,820	39,170	47,270

[1] Multiples : 10 or more shops
[2] Independents : 1–9 shops
[3] Revised figure

Source: IGD, 1989

The rationalisation of outlets in the multiple sector and the apparent paradox of an increase in market share arises because of the development of larger stores, especially superstores. From 1977 to 1989 the number of superstores increased from 150 to 580 (Joseph, 1990) and these superstores currently account for around 25 per cent of a £42 billion food market (*The Grocer*, 19 August 1989). Experts disagree on the eventual saturation level and the time when this number will be reached. Key Note (1988) had estimated a figure of 650 by the end of the 1980s. Mintel claims that 710 will be in operation by 1991 on the basis of plans of the major operators (*The Grocer*, op cit). Mintel therefore does not expect saturation to be reached until the mid 1990s. Research undertaken by the Centre for Business Research at Manchester Business School involving panels of industry 'experts' produced equally inconclusive results (Killen, 1988). Around 50 per cent of the panel opted for a saturation figure of between 501 and 650 with 71 per cent choosing between 1991 and 1996 for the date of saturation.

The net effect of the move to larger grocery outlets has been the replacement of small stores by large supermarkets and superstores to give a major increase in overall selling space. For example, throughout the 1980s the average size of store opened by a grocery multiple was in the region of 20,000 square feet and the average size of store closed was around 4,000 square feet; the average sales area of a multiple has more than doubled between 1977 and 1987 from 5,248 square feet to 11,926 square feet (IGD, 1989).

With the advent of larger stores and the consumer's desire for less frequent but more 'bulk' shopping, product proliferation has occurred. NFC (1988) estimates that an average superstore of 30,000 square feet accommodates 10,000 lines compared with the 4,000 lines stocked by a 17,000 square foot store a decade earlier. Some operators, which have opened the largest superstores or hypermarkets, have devoted a greater percentage of sales area to non-foods (Asda, Tesco) whereas others (J Sainsbury, Safeway) have tended to venture into non-foods with products associated with the weekly shop. These stores come into the smaller size superstore category. This venture into new product areas is an attempt to improve profit margins. In food products, the high standards increasingly demanded by customers have been met with the development of fresh food service departments, in-store bakeries and delicatessens. In an effort to add value to traditional grocery lines, most of the major operators have followed the lead of J Sainsbury and Waitrose in pursuing own-label developments. Own-label share of current packaged grocery sales is around 33 per cent, but the optimal level of own-label to manufacturer's brands will soon be reached. Commensurate with these changes has been the trend to building up store loyalty rather than manufacturer's brand loyalty. Grocery retailers have been using their own quality brands plus other store attributes to differentiate their 'brand' from the competition. Image building and increased expenditure on corporate advertising have occurred to create individual trading identities. Retailers are now second only to the food manufacturing sector as the main advertising spenders in the UK. For example, J Sainsbury spent £5.7 million solely on own-label advertising in 1988 (IGD, 1989).

Success in grocery retailing would not have been achieved without the implementation of new technological developments, particularly in information technology. Effective supply chain management can now be achieved through innovations in information technology. Manufacturers and retailers can now respond much more quickly to market demand because of data capture through EPOS terminals (J Sainsbury is the leading scanning operator). Direct product profitability (DPP) models have been constructed to assess the profitability of products as they pass through the supply chain, that is, what are the costs associated with storing, transporting and holding products in-store, in addition to buying costs. Electronic data interchange has also facilitated links between suppliers and retailers, reducing costly paperwork. The market place is replete with software packages to improve existing retail operations from space management systems in stores and warehouses which optimise shelf and layout efficiency to vehicle routeing and scheduling packages which optimise delivery times from distribution centres to stores. Indeed, the changes which have occurred in distribution management in the last decade can largely be attributed to developments in information technology.

(b) Changes in the Physical Distribution of Food to Retail Outlets

David Quarmby

This part of the chapter is a revised version of a paper published in the Journal of Transport Economics and Policy, *January 1989.*

The competitiveness of the grocery industry has meant that companies are under pressure to contain costs while continuing to maintain or improve customer service levels. Although the grocery sector has improved net profit margins in the 1980s, good performers average around 6 per cent. Angus Clark, discussing J Sainsbury's operating performance, claims that 'efficient logistics and distribution contribute up to one per cent of this edge. Further improvements could increase this by another 0.5 per cent' (*The Director*, August 1989, 69).

The complexity of retail operations has posed challenges for distribution managers. The broad range of products offered in supermarkets, discussed above, has meant that products with different temperature regimes – ambient, produce, chilled provisions, fresh meat and frozen products and those requiring special security arrangements (beers, wines and spirits and some non-foods) have to be properly handled through the distribution chain. The constant evolution of the store network and of the ordering systems and delivery source, necessitates a continuous review of the distribution operation. The major strategic changes in grocery distribution, however, are related to the shift to own-label branding and the control which can now be maintained on the distribution operation through the power of information technology. These changes represent the following moves:

- away from supplier-controlled distribution networks towards retailer-controlled networks;
- away from own-account operations to contract distribution.

The move to retail control

The first trend can be illustrated as follows. A supplier-controlled network will typically involve trunk delivery from the supplier's manufacturing or processing factory to a large number of distribution centres, each serving a specific local area. From there, the supplier provides local delivery direct to the customer's retail premises. Sometimes there are two tiers of distribution centres or depots, but one tier will typically be only for transshipment of assembled orders.

By contrast, a retailer-controlled network is one in which the retailer controls the distribution centres – which will tend to be regional in scale, larger in capacity and fewer in number than in the supplier's network. Suppliers still deliver into the distribution centres; the retailer is then responsible for the goods and for their distribution to his own retail outlets.

Why is this trend towards retailer-control happening? The primary reason is that it is more cost efficient. At a retail-controlled depot, the economics of load consolidation, high vehicle fill and only one or two drops per vehicle must lead to lower resource costs than those incurred by the supplier in carrying out multi-drops of much smaller individual branch orders.

There are other reasons associated with the management of a professional retailing operation – quality of service, management control and flexibility. Quality of service embraces the total interface with the retail branch: puntuality of arrival of vehicles, conformity with handling systems, consistency of documentation, as well as the ability to meet standardised order/delivery cycles and the successful completion of orders within the agreed cycle. It has been difficult for many suppliers to match the disciplined requirements and quality of service offered by the retailer's established systems of delivery to depots. This has not been through any fault of the supplier, but often for reasons of sheer logistics and differing company policies.

Secondly, management control of inwards distribution to retail outlets is an essential feature of the management of shelf and branch warehouse stock levels, and of the matching of commodities to their appropriate order/delivery cycles and lead times. Management of supplier interfaces, both for physical replenishment and for documentary and financial controls, is easier when delivery is made into a small number of regional depots than into several hundred retail outlets. Management control of the supply chain is particularly important for perishable commodities, to maintain standards of quality and freshness.

Finally, flexibility is an absolute requirement for distribution in the highly competitive business of food retailing. The ability to respond quickly to changes in commodity distribution, to changes in commodity volume, to changes in order/delivery cycles, to seasonal variances, to supply problems, to transport and distribution problems, to changes in display methods – all this is required of a professional retailer-controlled network. Very few, if any, supplier-controlled networks have the capability to be as flexible. Yet it is this, together with the other two factors, which provides the basis for the high quality of food and of service to the customer at low cost; thus it makes a large contribution to sound profitability.

In 1982, the volume of distribution into all types of retail outlets was almost equally divided between the three main participants (National Economic Development Office (NEDO), 1985).

	per cent
Retail-controlled distribution	35
Delivered wholesale	33
Cash and carry	3
Supplier-controlled distribution	30

Proportions are expected to move further in favour of retail-controlled distribution, with 44 per cent forecast for 1990, at the expense of supplier-controlled; at the same time, the delivered wholesaler, meeting the needs of small and medium-sized outlets, is likely to decline in favour of direct deliveries to such outlets by suppliers. Recent developments by Tesco and Asda to bring most goods into depot distribution mean that all the main UK food distributors now control their own distribution. Sainsbury's has depended for decades on a high level of depot distribution which now runs at nearly 90 per cent of volume sales.

An indication of the relative efficiency of retail-controlled systems is given by the following indices of unit costs of transport, stockholding and warehousing (NEDO, 1985):

Retail-controlled distribution	100
Supplier-controlled distribution	190
Delivered wholesaler	250

Control by retailer and supplier compared

The significance of the move towards retail-controlled distribution is that it uses transport in a different way. As explained above, the economic advantage arises because of the consolidation that takes place at the retail-controlled distribution centre. In food, for example, goods from a very wide range of suppliers are received and stored; then orders for individual branches are picked (retrieved), assembled and delivered, to meet standardised order cycles and delivery schedules.

Commodities held at different temperatures – chilled, frozen, ambient and produce – are assembled and delivered in mixed loads, according to rules, during the course of a trading day. The objectives are to meet the branch requirements for perishable goods early in the day, and to achieve optimum use of transport.

Delivery to branches is mostly a trunking operation – single load, single drop. The contrast with the typical supplier-controlled operation, basically multi-drop, is striking. The principal impact is on the amount of time available for driving from the depot to the point or area of delivery. In trunking, the time spent in unloading can be as little as 10 per cent of the driver's day, so the driving time between depot and branch can be up to 45 per cent of his day in each direction.

By contrast, a typical multi-drop could take up as much as 30 per cent of the driver's day in driving between drop locations, 40 per cent of his time in waiting to deliver and unloading, and only 30 per cent in 'stem' driving – 15 per cent in each direction – between depot and delivery area. The range reachable from one depot by trunking could be up to three times as much as by the multi-drop system.

The difference between supplier-controlled and retail-controlled distribution can be illustrated dramatically with an illustrative 'model'. Suppose there is a region consisting of five retailers, each retailer having 50 supermarkets which could be served from one depot. Each supermarket sells 1,000 cases/day in a five-day week; goods come from 25 suppliers in equal quantities; one roll cage holds 20 cases; a large vehicle holds 50 roll cages.

Model A: supplier-controlled distribution

The demand from each of the 250 supermarkets on each of the 25 suppliers is 40 cases/day, which is 2 roll cages/day. This involves 25 drops/day from one large vehicle, which for geographical reasons is unlikely to be practical. If all the goods are short-life perishables, the daily delivery requirements can only be met by a larger number of smaller delivery vehicles such as, for instance, a 20-roll cage capacity vehicle working 10 drops.

Non-perishable commodities would be on a less frequent cycle, say twice a week, so each large vehicle would make ten drops of five roll cages each; the retailer would have to hold more stock.

If half the suppliers send perishables and half non-perishables, the transport requirement for each supplier, and in total, is

	Each supplier	Total
12.5 suppliers: perishables	25 small vehicles	313 small vehicles
12.5 suppliers: non-perishables	10 large vehicles	125 large vehicles

The 'stem' time available for a ten-drop journey is at best one-third of that available to the retailers' own single-drop transport, as explained above, so the territory that each supplier's depot can cover is at best one-third in radius. If the region is such that each retailer can service its own branches from one depot, then in model A each supplier needs three depots. The average depot size for each supplier of perishables will be 8.33 vehicles, and for each supplier of non-perishables 3.33 vehicles. In practice, some trade-off would be made between the number of drops/the 'stem' time/the number of depots/the number of vehicles. For instance, the supplier of non-perishables might manage with two depots if the number of drops were reduced to five and twice the number of 25-roll cage vehicles were used. The average number of vehicles per depot would then be ten.

Model B: retail-controlled distribution

For each of five retailers, one depot serves 50 branches. All suppliers deliver into each of the five depots (instead of into two or three of their own depots under model A). Each branch receives 1,000 cases/day, in 50 roll cages, equal to one vehicle load. The furthest branches in the region take a whole driver's shift to complete the return journey; for nearer branches two or in some cases three return journeys can be completed within a shift.

If the average number of return journeys per shift achievable is, say, 1.67, then the transport requirement is:

Each retailer depot	Total
30 large vehicles	150 large vehicles

This requirement is met from a total of five depots, with 30 vehicles per depot. Both models assume one driver's shift per vehicle. If delivery windows allow, this can be assumed to increase; there is more scope for this under model B, because the 'stem' time out on the first journey and back on the last can be outside branch receiving hours. The two models are compared in Table 9.2.

Table 9.2: *Comparison of models A and B*

	No of vehicles	No of depots	Average depot throughput
Model A			
Perishable	313 small	37.5	3,300 cases/day
Non-perishable	125 large	37.5	3,300 cases/day
		or 25	5,000 cases/day
Model B			
Total	150 large	5	50,000 cases/day

The characteristics of the retail-controlled operation are:

- small number of large depots;
- use of large vehicles;
- single drop, trunking;
- large geographic region covered from each depot.

In this illustration, one distribution centre with 30 vehicles is required for each of the five retailers. This type of operation is typically planned around, and heavily dependent on, the motorway and primary route network.

The characteristics of the supplier-controlled operation are:

- large number of small depots;
- use of smaller vehicles;
- multi-drop, local delivery;
- small area covered from each depot.

In this case, the 25 suppliers need 60–70 depots, and a mix of large and small vehicles totalling nearly 440. The key point is that the transport and warehousing efficiency of the retail-controlled network is much higher than that of the supplier-controlled network.

The move to contract distribution and the power of information technology

The other main trend is the move from own-account operation to contract distribution. In one respect, it is a natural response to the decline of suppliers' own distribution activities and the consequent move into 'third party' distribution by what were the distribution divisions of suppliers. It also reflects, however, the retailers' policy of choosing to concentrate investment in their mainstream business of retailing, and to contract out distribution, rather than investing in own account warehousing and transport infrastructure. It also gives more flexibility to the retailer to adapt this network to changing business needs.

Perhaps most fundamentally, the decline of own account operation and the growth of contract distribution reflects the power of information technology to substitute 'control by information' for 'control by doing it yourself'. For example, systems used by Sainsbury's for branch ordering, depot replenishment, stock control and the picking (retrieval) and assembly of individual branch orders, mean that the effective control of activity in one of their contract depots is exactly the same as that in a Sainsbury-owned depot. The on-line computer systems which control all this enable head office management to monitor, through their screens, the progress of the day's work, as well as stock status, suppliers' deliveries and despatches to branches, in real time in any depot, however physically remote. The performance of the distribution network is therefore transparent to the ownership of the distribution resource.

The significance of this is that it creates a 'market' for fully-integrated and professionalised distribution. There has been a free market for road transport since the deregulation – the abolition of quantity licensing – in the 1968 Transport Act, but a market for the total distribution service has been more recent. The significance of the existence of a market is that it makes reaction and adjustment to change of both the client and the provider that much easier and quicker. In particular, it means that a particular retailer's depots can more readily be relocated and/or expanded as a result of growth and development in the business, or indeed of major changes in the road network.

Relationship with the road network

The previous section has described how the shift from supplier-controlled distribution to retailer-controlled has changed the nature of the transport and warehouse operation – to larger vehicles, from multi-drop local delivery to single-drop trunking, and from a large number of small depots each covering a small area to a small number of large depots each covering a large region. It also described how the shift from own account to contract distribution has enabled distribution networks to respond flexibly to significant changes in the road network.

Locations too are different. Supplier-controlled or wholesale distribution into retail outlets tends to have more depots in or near towns, so that the number of drops can be maximised with relatively small 'stem' driving time. Retailer-controlled distribution, based on single-drop trunking (or full trunkers) delivering to a more limited number of branches, will tend to have fewer depots; these will be located on or near the primary road network, and probably away from large towns, to take maximum advantage of the much longer driving time available in the shift.

An example: the Sainsbury network

Location of principal Sainsbury depots, for example in relation to the supermarkets, illustrates the dependence on the motorway and primary road network. The most dense location of branches is in Greater London and the home counties, including the south coast and East Anglia. The next most dense area is in the Midlands; then come the region to the north, as far as York and Lancaster, and south Wales and the south-west. (*See* Figure 9.1.)

Three principal depots – at Buntingford (on A10), Basingstoke (on M3) and Charlton in inner south-east London – serve the first area; Droitwich (M5/M42), Middleton on the north side of Manchester (for M62), Yate to the north-east of Bristol (for M4/M5) and Corby (between M1 and A1) serve the others. These mostly carry a full range of chilled goods, produce, frozen and ambient grocery and non-foods, and each has a 'patch' where transport geography

Figure 9.1: *Location of Sainsbury disbribution centres (contract and own account)*

reflects the delivery disciplines of 'overnight' perishables and produce.

Fifteen other depots carry a generally complementary range of goods, on similar and different order cycles and lead times; it is significant that seven of these are very near the M25 (the London orbital), and a further three are within easy striking distance of it. Slow-moving ambient foods are nationally distributed by two depots, and slow-moving frozen foods by another two.

It is fascinating to trace the historical growth of Sainsbury branches from the early days, in the late nineteenth century and the first quarter of this. Before the turn of the century the company moved its depot to the Blackfriars site, just over the river from the City of London, where the head office still is today. At that time branches were being established along the main radial routes out of London, within the catchment of horse-drawn transport, and subsequently of motor lorries. The original concentration of branches on, for instance, the main Brighton Road out of London can still be detected in the present locations of supermarkets.

For a while, branches in the home counties and on the south coast were served by the pre-eminent primary network of the nineteenth and early twentieth century, the railways. The logistics of handling bulk perishable foods, assembled for specific branches, on and off the railway was challenging, to say the least.

Today the road network allows branches at Plymouth, Exeter, Swansea and Bournemouth all to be served from a principal depot near Bristol. Lincoln, Lancaster, Chester and Whitley Bay are served from Middleton, near Manchester; Dover, Eastbourne and central London from Charlton in inner south-east London, and so on.

The operational requirement is to receive into depot produce and perishable goods up to 2000 hours, to receive in mid-evening the branch orders placed earlier in the day, and to commence assembly after 2200 hours, with first vehicles generally away after 0100 hours. Most branches receive first vehicles between 0400 and 0700.

Conclusion

This brief overview of the evolution of Sainsbury's distribution operation illustrates how the logistics of supplying the branch network have evolved over time in response to changes in the UK socio-economic and spatial environment. Sainsbury's has been consistently at the forefront of UK food retailing with a consistent record of 20 per cent annual profit growth. Distribution has played an important role in this success. The network of distribution centres shown in Figure 9.1 has evolved as the company expanded north and west away from its south-east base. The initial depots were own account but the majority of Sainsbury's depots are now provided by contractors. The power of information technology allows the company to control a contract depot such as Middleton in the same way as the largest own account depot, Basingstoke.

The move by the food and, more recently, electrical and other retail sectors to contract distribution has created a market for distribution services among other things; enabling distribution networks to react and adjust more readily to changes in the road network. It was shown that contracting out and the move to retail-controlled networks are together bringing about major changes in the use of freight transport, most importantly by increasing the size of vehicles and making the operation more dependent upon the motorway and primary route network. Improvements in the road network allow for better scheduling with more predictable journey times, a deterioration of the network, for example through congestion, leads to unpredictability and greater cost.

References

IGD (1989) 'Food retailing' *Distribution and Technology* June, 1–8.

Joseph, M (1990) 'Superstores trading profile' *Grocery Market Bulletin* July, 1–7.

Key Note (1988) *Supermarkets and Superstores: an industry sector overview*, Key Note.

Killin, V (1988) *UK Grocery Retailing in the 1990s – Consensus on Consolidation* Centre for Business Research, Manchester Business School.

National Economic Development Office (NEDO) (1985) 'Factors affecting the cost of physical distribution to the retail trade' unpublished report prepared for NEDO by Kearney Management Consultants.

NFC (1988) *Looking at Dedicated Distribution* NFC Contract Distribution Report.

Quarmby, DA (1989) 'Developments in the retail market and their effect on freight distribution' *Journal of Transport Economics and Policy* January 75–87.

10
Supply Chain Management in Footwear Retailing

Philip T Hammersley

This chapter is a revision of an earlier paper given at the sixth annual IT Conference at Leicester Polytechnic on 26 April 1990. The author would like to acknowledge the help of Steve Beattie of Coopers & Lybrand, Deloitte.

Introduction

The reader will be well aware of some of the problems which face retailers today – low or negative growth in consumer spending and rising labour and occupation costs. Footwear retailing is no exception to the general situation, but additionally some other pressures and trends have to be addressed.

The sector is substantially overshopped and as each of the multiples either by choice or *force majeure* does what it can to correct this, we find that our efforts are negated by the increasing availability of shoes in non-specialist outlets – chain stores, clothes shops and fashion boutiques.

Since 1980 the footwear share of total consumer spending has fallen – substantially so in the last three years – and the average price of shoes in real terms has risen by less than 10 per cent. The reason for this is the growth in imports which have increased by 80 per cent in ten years and which now account for two-thirds by volume of the UK market.

This has led to the development of a complicated international network of sources – my own company, for example, trades with several hundred suppliers in over 40 countries in all of the continents of the world with the exception of Australasia. If we add to this the consumers' demand for increased choice and frequent change it is clear that footwear retailers face the 1990s with a set of conflicting requirements:

- a flat market and escalating retailing costs through the combination of the various factors of the demographic time bomb, uniform business rate and high street rents;
- the drive to increase gross margins to compensate for this and because of the fear of becoming uncompetitive by raising prices, achieving this by buying cheaply from distant overseas sources;
- the high cost of stocks both directly and through the space they occupy because the consumer wants choice and variety and hence a wide selection of product.

In the past when similar circumstances have arisen, the traditional action has been to cut overheads, run half-price sales and hope that the competition collapses before you do. No doubt such actions will be taken in the future, but it is becoming obvious that the chain of supply of goods to our shops – something which many of us have taken for granted – demands our attention, as a source of cost reduction and improved service.

The objective for this chapter is to outline the supply chain management opportunities that exist for retailers into the 1990s. An overview of the evolution of the supply chain is necessary in order to identify the major opportunities that exist for shortening or simplifying the supply chain by assessing the value of lead time. Then, consideration of some of the key issues involved will be reviewed, including the importance of costs, both within and outside the business, and identification of those costs which are vital to the success of the business will be made. Finally, the implementation of a supply chain philosophy will be discussed, in particular the need for supplier partnerships and manufacturing agreements in addition to the development of an appropriate corporate culture to take advantage of the opportunities offered by the supply chain concept.

Supply chain perspective

The concept of the supply chain is not a new one. As a chain of companies trade with each other they move goods from the original supplier to the shop and there is both a movement and a storage of information as well as materials. However, historically, either whole businesses have only been engaged in part of the supply chain, or those that have spanned a number of parts of the chain have not fully integrated the activities along it. For example, in the UK prior to major retailers setting up their own central distribution networks, suppliers were often responsible for direct distribution to shops and in some cases they still are. Those suppliers, however, had two separate functions within their businesses looking after different parts of their supply chain – a materials management function to source raw materials, plan production and control work in progress and a distinct and separate finished goods distribution network which delivered to the high street (*see* Figure 10.1).

More recently, some retailers have moved into central distribution through two or three stages. Retailers who received direct deliveries from suppliers into their retail stores ran out of space and started to develop a network of larger stock rooms on-site and then later off-site in edge of town locations where space costs were considerably cheaper. These operations were often run by store managers and their staff who lacked the depth of distribution-related skills to control these units effectively.

The increase in costs that resulted from the mushrooming of stockholding, and the poor service levels that were inherent in these arrangements, forced retailers to reconsider their distribution strategies and this led to a major shift towards central distribution. Central distribution for retailers by the 1980s had developed as a corporate support function in its own right, operating as a cost centre. The distribution management focused on the task of managing efficiently the physical resources represented by a warehouse and transport fleet, the responsibility for resourcing and stock holding remained firmly in the hands of the buyers and merchandisers, and the distribution-related activities in retail outlets remained under the control of retail operations management. This approach, because it is not co-ordinated through the chain, has the disadvantage that while each part may be working to its maximum efficiency in operational terms, the supply chain as a whole almost certainly will not be operating as effectively as it could in ensuring that goods arrive at the shop at minimum cost and in minimum time.

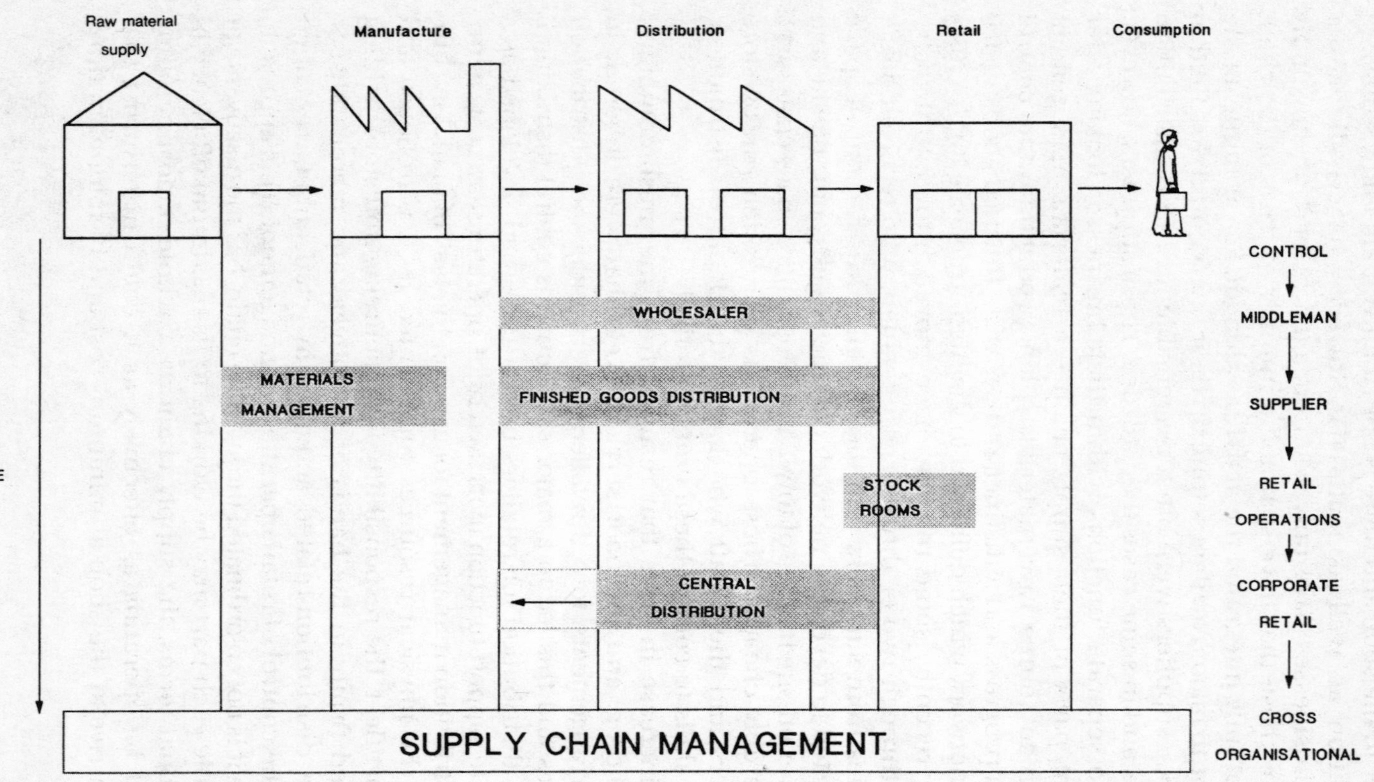

Figure 10.1: *Evolution of supply chain*

The traditional view of the supply chain

So what are the characteristics of the traditional supply chain? It is essentially a number of traders or businesses operating more or less independently. For instance, in this simplified example, an original supplier of components or raw materials sells on to a manufacturer who in turn then sells to a distributor or perhaps another intermediary, and so on to the final consumer. Each business unit is unrelated to the supply chain as a whole and merely trades with its supplier and its customer and attempts to negotiate the most favourable terms with both of them. Inevitably, this means an accumulation of stock at each stage in the chain as a means of ensuring the service to the downstream customer and there is also a broken flow of information (*see* Figure 10.2).

The results speak for themselves (*see* Figure 10.3). Each company in the chain seeks cost reduction within its own business, largely in isolation from both its suppliers and customers, and this inevitably leads to companies which, although trading with each other, are nevertheless working to different objectives. This naturally results in conflict and an example of this is often seen in the relationship between the buyer and his supplier, which can become adversarial when based solely on the how much/too much principle of negotiation, and the power of the retailer over the manufacturer which has built up through the 1980s has encouraged this kind of relationship. The result of these independent operations is poor service and an unnecessarily high level of costs – the inevitable consequence of a disjointed supply chain.

It is worthwhile to examine the lowest price mentality in more detail because this has been fundamental to the way in which retail business has been run, and has affected, detrimentally, its supply chain performance.

Importance of cost visibility

It is fair to say that for most retailers one of the main objectives for the buying function is to maximise gross margin by negotiating the lowest price available from suppliers for a particular product (*see* Figure 10.4). It is assumed that maximum gross profit leads unfailingly to maximum net profit because the lack of sophisticated systems within the business means that the variety of costs which are incurred in wholesaling and retailing cannot be allocated on a true

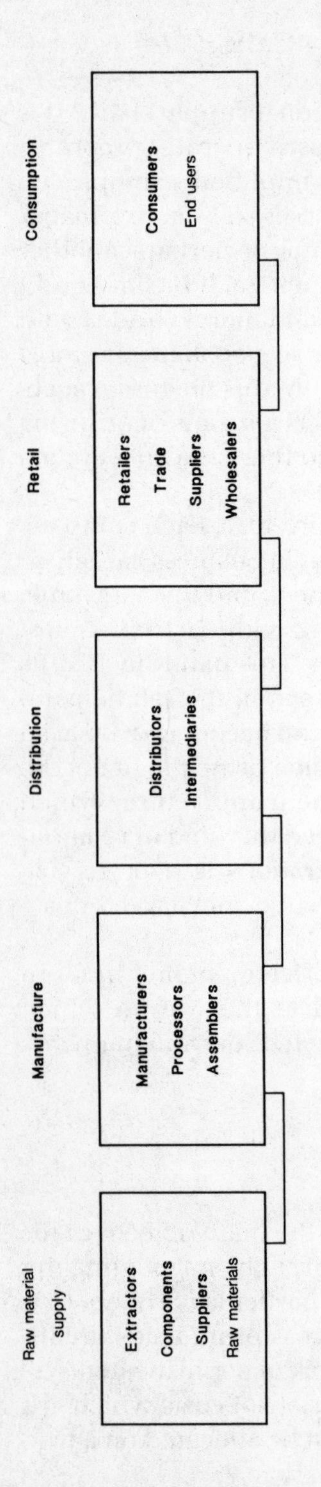

Key characteristics:

- A number of traders in the chain
- Each is an unrelated business unit
- Stock buffering at each stage
- Broken information flow

Figure 10.2: *Traditional view of the supply chain*

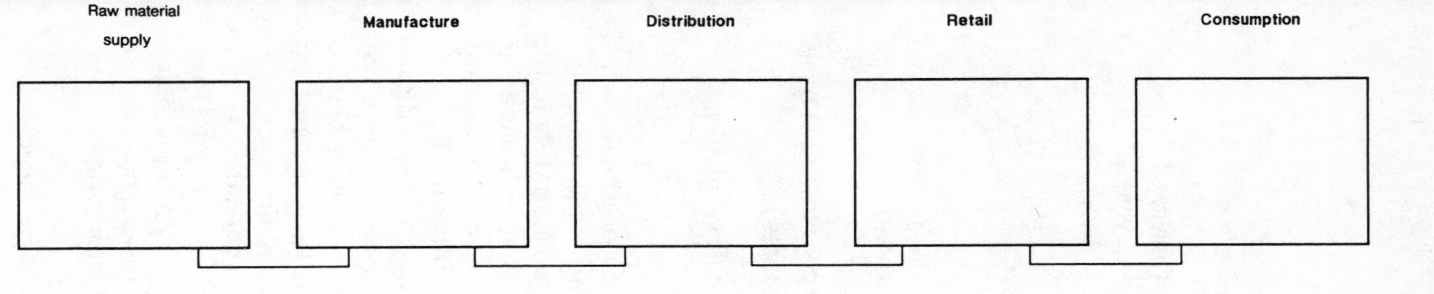

Result:

- Cost reduction sought by each company in isolation
- Conflict between companies
- Poor service and high cost a natural consequence

Figure 10.3: *Traditional view of the supply chain*

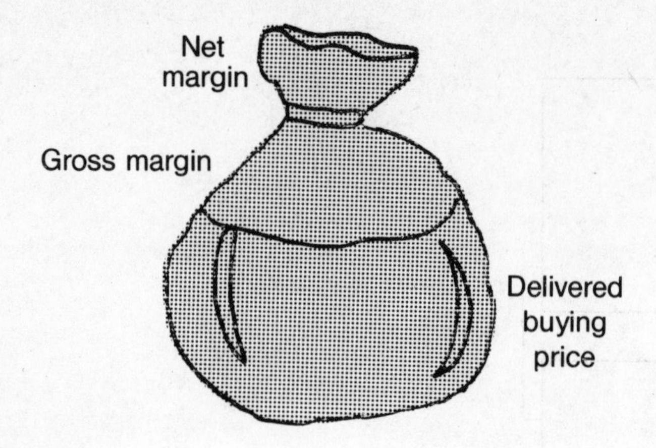

This was because:

- Make-up of delivered buying price not known
- His operating costs lumped together as an overhead
  - fixed in the short run
  - systems not sophisticated enough to allocate on a true cost basis
- Crude sales and stock information from retail stores

Figure 10.4: *For the retailer the traditional measure of profit was gross margin*

basis either to individual products or indeed to product groups. This results in many of the operating costs being lumped together into an overall overhead which is treated as fixed, certainly in the short term. In addition, the lack of good information relating to sales and stock from the retail shops makes the task of measuring the profit performance of products even more difficult.

In many cases, retailers survive on open-to-buy systems driven by sketchy and inaccurate stock and sales information often collected by value at product group level. Mark-downs, clearly detracting from profit, are given budgets along with the sales and the stock. If the budget permits, mark-downs are taken either to create additional open-to-buy or to reduce the value of the stock so that the stock budget can be met.

The emphasis on gross margin gives buyers very simple objectives to which they can work and the justified importance of good product selection gives the buying function a strong power base within the business. Buyers clearly see their prime objective as being to get the best deal from their suppliers but the needs of the customer, and hence the requirements of the retail outlets, in terms of service and stock allocation, are viewed as second order issues for which other parts of the business are responsible. In addition, within the business, we have a variety of discrete functions intent on cost reduction. Overhead reduction programmes are planned in central administration, distribution and in retail outlets, but the actions of buyers driven by their gross margin performance targets, can create extra costs down stream within the business. For example, the desire for lowest prices may lead to single large buys, creating demand for space throughout the business both in the shops and in the warehouses. It also is the case that some of these overhead reductions, while justified in terms of operational efficiency within the department concerned, may act against the most effective operation of the supply chain and cause an increased cost elsewhere, either directly or through a build-up of stock.

Looking ahead into the 1990s, what will change? There appear to be three significant issues. Most important of these is that retailers now have available, for the first time, accurate and timely item level sales data flowing back from stores. The introduction of EPOS systems is the major innovation which has allowed a genuine step change to take place. It is expensive and there are implementation problems, although fewer than might be expected, but it is now for many retailers the means by which we can get item level sales and stock data which is more accurate, more quickly available and more easily used.

The main benefit of EPOS to British Shoe is that of stock control. Replenishment is much more accurate and timely and as a result the stock on our shelves is more likely to match the demands of our customers. It is also possible to introduce flexible pricing, both by time and geographical region, so that sales opportunities can be rapidly tested and evaluated. And of course there is a saving of head office costs because the information on operations within the branch is transmitted as part of an integrated data processing system. The branch is able to provide an improved service to the customer for stock enquiries and the manager has to hand a very effective means of managing both his staff and his stock within the branch.

The second major change is that suppliers are having to improve their performance. They understand that, to remain competitive, they must be much more highly responsive to retailers' demands, and they must therefore work both to reduce new product lead times, and also the time it takes to make repeat orders.

The third change has arisen out of retailers' need to drive cost out of the supply chain. We have to understand better the cost build-up within our business and also, and perhaps more importantly, externally back through the supply chain.

These issues are important ones that clearly form part of a wider set relating to how managers run their business and try to exert influence over their suppliers and customers. But they have been highlighted for two reasons. First, because IT is the technology which enables these changes to be made and second because they are good examples of how the review of the supply chain provides a framework of thinking for profit improvement.

Identifying the key costs

There is a very real need to create a cross-functional environment which gets people at all levels of business looking not just at the job they are doing, but much further afield. It is this inquisitiveness about how their actions can affect the costs in other parts of their business, and also those of their suppliers and customers; that causes managers to rethink how they should service their customers. What are the key costs within the business?

Our gross margin is calculated by deducting the cost of goods delivered from the retail selling value. The important discipline is for managers to understand what costs eat into that gross margin, how large they are, how accurately they are measured and which of them can be controlled. A number of the costs are controllable and of those which can be influenced by buying, range planning and sourcing decisions, those relating to mark-downs, returns for poor quality, warehousing and distribution, and stock in the warehouse and the shop can be identified (*see* Figure 10.5).

In addition, if the right shoes are not in the right place at the right time, sales will be lost and because of the high level of costs which in the short term are fixed, the effect of this on the bottom line can be serious. Last year we carried out a survey in a number of our shops to determine the degree to which we were able to meet the needs of people coming into the shops. On average 50 per cent of those coming in were clearly browsers who wandered through the shops without even picking up a shoe; of the remaining 50 per cent, two-thirds obtained shoes and one-third received some

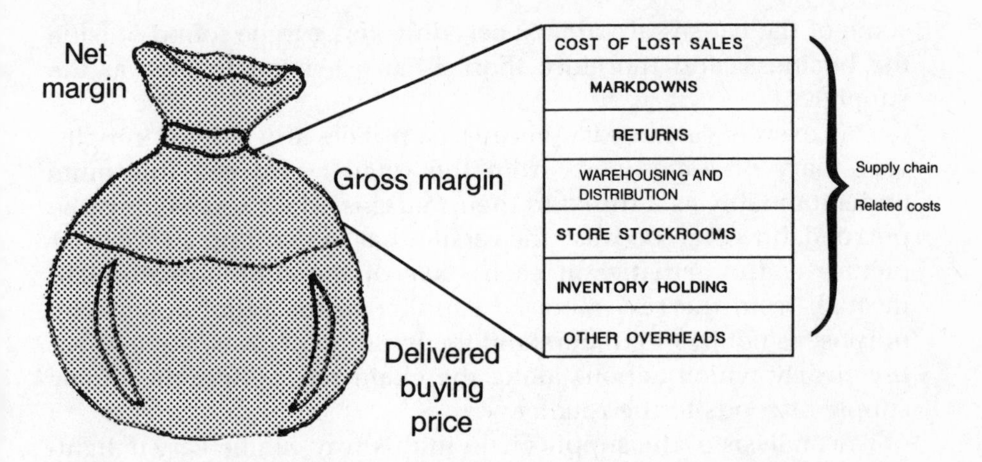

- Many of the costs that erode gross margin can be influenced
- Understanding and measuring the costs is a key step
- What most influences them?
- Probably a need to look externally to resolve these questions

Figure 10.5: *Costs internal to the business*

form of service but rejected what was offered principally because the style they wanted was not available in their size.Thus, of those customers who intended to buy, one-third left the shop empty-handed. These results are very close to those achieved by a major retail chain in France where a similar survey was carried out. This is a factor which is difficult to quantify accurately because a customer may buy from another shop in the town belonging to the same company but nevertheless stock-outs must represent a loss of profit to any business.

It is possible to increase our stocks to avoid these lost sales. But end of season mark-downs are already high and represent a loss of gross margin of over 20 per cent. So we have the unfortunate – and unprofitable – combination of a large percentage of lost sales and a significant amount of stock which cannot be sold at full gross margin.

The understanding and measurement of these costs is a key step to assessing their relative importance and it is vital to determine what influences them most. Is it buying practices, or supplier failure to deliver, or ineffective management of operations within the business, or one of a number of other possibilities? The fact is that some of the causes are almost certainly going to be found outside the business, and therefore there is also a need to look at the suppliers.

This exercise is not easy, because suppliers are, at least initially, very wary of approaches from the retailer and see this quite understandably as a threat to their margins. The exercise must be pursued, however, because the retailer has to build up a very clear picture of the activities at each stage of the supply chain right through from the raw material supplier to the retail outlet. The purpose is not just to understand the build-up of costs, but to identify clearly which actions along the chain most effect the timely supply of goods to the retailer.

The analysis of the supply chain in this way can be very enlightening because it exposes costs that can be controlled but which are normally hidden in the purchase price paid to suppliers. For example, with a complex supply chain, each time stock changes ownership, the build-up of costs is absorbed into the buyer's business as a total purchase cost and is treated in the accounts as the cost of goods sold. This process continues at each transaction along the supply chain, and as a result the retailer has no picture at all of proportion of the total cost incurred along the chain by each component (*see* Figure 10.6). For example, it is interesting to note that in this example the total logistics-related costs of each stage in the supply chain exceeds the retailers' own costs of that function. This information in detail is vital to the retailer for strategic decision-making, because once he has the right information to hand, he is able to deal with the cost benefit trade-offs that exist in any supply chain. For example, there will be clear trade-offs between service and inventory, or between speed of response and logistics costs, or between more regular replenishments in smaller quantities, versus the manufacturer's cost of changeover.

But alongside all of these supply chain trade-offs there is probably one consideration which, more than any other, is vital for success.

The value of time

In a traditional supply chain, where orders are placed up the chain through a number of intermediaries, and deliveries come back down through a similar route, the elapsed times between the placing of the initial order by the buyer and the delivery of the product can be very lengthy. This is particularly true of certain industries

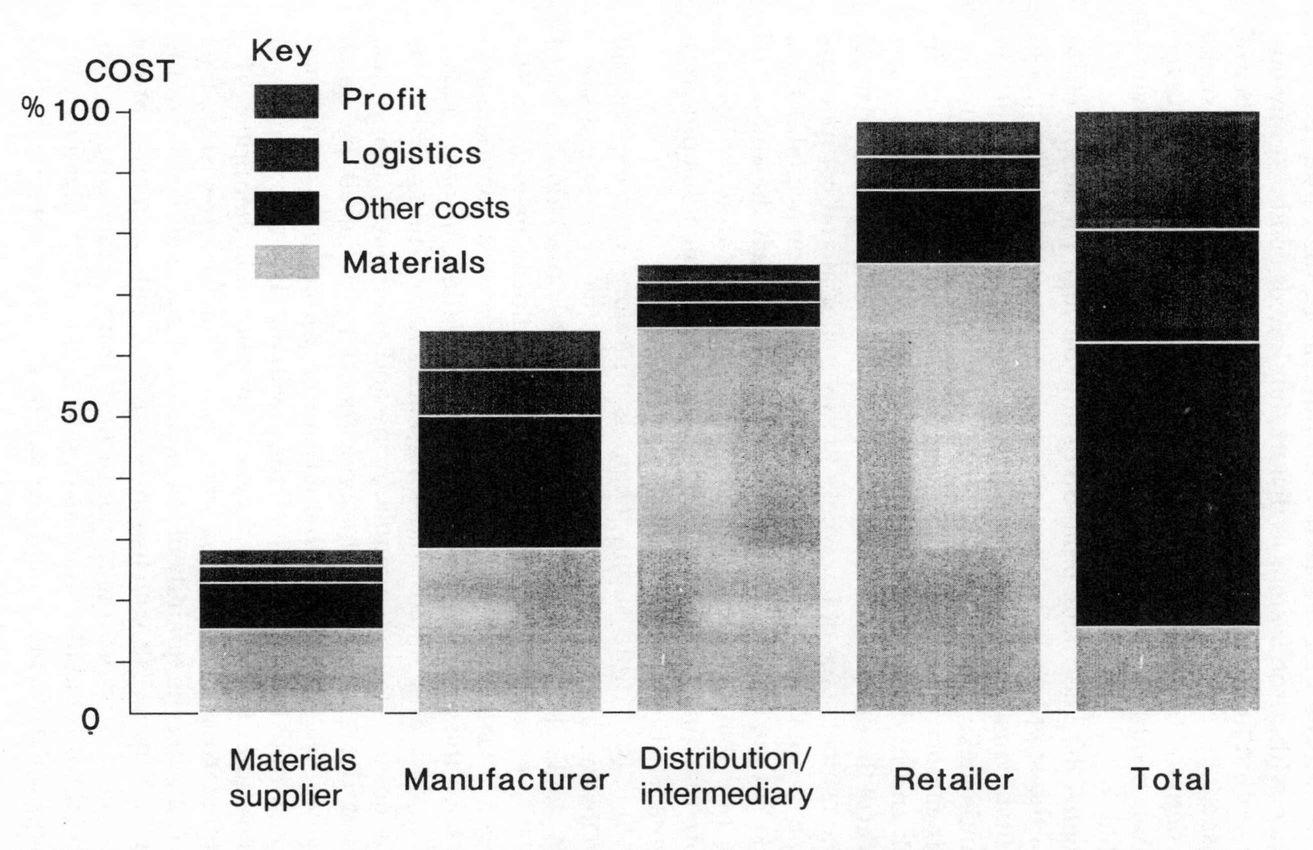

Figure 10.6: *The external costs which normally conceal a series of trading transactions*

where, because of changing fashions and market conditions, an in-stock system is inappropriate and make-to-order conditions apply. Not only is this in essence a contradition in satisfying the market but the longer that the lead time interval is, the more that can change within the system to distort the flow of goods. At any one time within the pipeline of supply there will be a large number of transactions, resulting in high variability of demand at each stage. The demand for more frequent change from the consumer, and the shorter product lifecycles which result, exacerbates the whole problem.

Figure 10.7 shows the build-up of time through the supply chain from the supplier of components and raw materials – through to the final consumer. In each operation the numbers represent – in an anti-clockwise direction, the time taken by or in order planning, the in-factory process time and the time the finished goods are in stock and in delivery. The overall elapsed time of 21 weeks is not typical of the delay between a retailer ordering a shoe and receiving it as the critical stage of ten weeks in raw material and components supply is not visible to him, as these items are often available from stock. But the overall 21 weeks does represent fairly the amount of time raw materials and finished product are within the system before reaching the shop and the cost of stock which this time represents is, of course, carried by the product.

A long lead time supply chain is therefore very exposed to changes in customer needs. As a result this can create lost sales, large stocks through the chain and also heavy mark-downs, all of which have a direct impact on the profitability of the retailer. The answer is clearly to work towards systems and supply networks that have the primary objective of reducing the time of response.

The Shoe and Allied Trades Research Association, which has members in retailing, manufacturing and component supply, has carried out analyses of the benefits to be achieved by quick response. They concluded that if restocking time could be reduced there would be a substantial improvement in gross margin of which some at least could pass to the supplier in higher prices. The benefits arose by improving sales as a result of fewer stock-outs and reducing the quantity of shoes marked down at the end of the season. The overall conclusion was that if only a quarter of the stock had an improved response time from nine weeks to four weeks the profitability, as measured by gross margin divided by the average value of stock, would increase by 27 per cent and naturally if

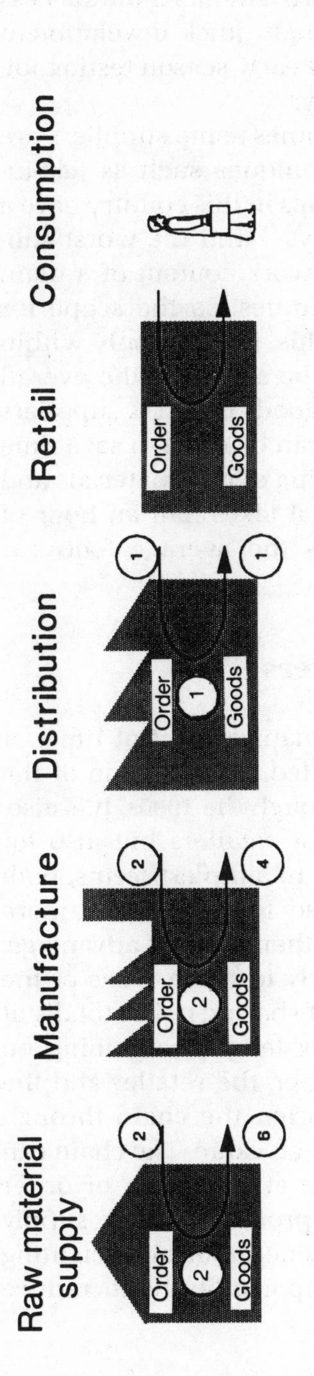

Figure 10.7: *What should we try to influence along the supply chain?*

half the stock were on a four-week response time the improvement would be over 50 per cent.

In addition there are further margin improvements if the success rate of new styles can be improved through quick development using CAD systems as well as some form of early season testing followed by bulk ordering and rapid delivery.

As part of the drive to reduce response times some suppliers are beginning to employ quick response techniques such as just-in-time. At present, the best of the shoe factories in this country have a throughput time of about ten working days – and the worst substantially longer – and yet the measured work content of a plain ladies court shoe amounts to only 32 minutes, so the scope for improvement is substantial. Having said this, it is not only within the manufacturing cycle where time can be saved, as the overall time between date of order and receipt of goods from UK suppliers can be as much as nine weeks – so much can be done to save time in the planning process and in the resourcing of raw materials and components. It must be noted that while it takes half an hour of direct labour to make the shoe, it takes the average footwear retailer about 22 weeks to sell it.

Building partnerships with suppliers

Retailers can expect to see the effective management of time, or 'time-based competition' as it is often called, become one of the major differentiators for their business through the 1990s. It is also, however, a major opportunity not only for retailers but also for their suppliers. But much has to be done. In simplest terms, both the retailers and their suppliers will need to work much more closely together and accept that this is to their mutual advantage. This in itself is a major hurdle, particularly in those areas of the business, such as buying, where the idea of sharing risk is totally at odds with the traditional stance of arm's length bargaining on price and delivery date. By working together, the retailer and the supplier will be able to simplify and shorten the chain through bypassing intermediaries who add cost but no value. The chain can also be shortened by taking a fresh look at the areas of order administration, planning, the production process and the supply routes to the retailer. For example, the benefits of air freighting high value products to meet a selling opportunity or to reduce stock holding can be substantial.

The retailer and supplier must share the risks and costs, as well as the benefits, of working together to their mutual advantage. The risks may include some joint commitment between supplier and retailer to raw materials or components which allow the manufacturer to reduce dramatically his response time without his carrying the total costs of redundant stock. The costs of this exercise to a retailer, if the sales of the product are well below his forecast, are far less if the raw material has to be sold at a discounted price than if the finished product has to be sold at half-price – or a gross profit of zero.

Finally the new partners will need to use IT as the enabling technology, both in terms of gathering information from within the retail business from systems such as EPOS, and transmitting this, after appropriate adjustment, to suppliers by using EDI. The latter can be used for sending forecast sales demand and buying orders up stream, delivery information down stream, and for transacting invoices and payment (*see* Figure 10.8).

The objective is to use these technology breakthroughs to enable the whole supply chain to be driven from the most recent sales data at item level. Besides the technology issues, there can be fears on both sides concerning the passing of confidential data, and, as with the sharing of risk, success will only be achieved through a new relationship, which is based on trust and the expectation of mutual benefit.

Developing a flexible organisation

In addition to finding the most profitable solutions and the technically correct ones, we also have to manage change within the business to make sure things happen. This is fundamental to success and the key areas of management structure, the training of existing staff, the recruitment of new specialists and an open and flexible management style are as important as the selection of the best computer systems. If attention is not given to the human resource issues then beneficial change will not be achieved.

The management structure of the business must reflect and permit the change in management priorities which a more responsive business demands. There are those who would respond to this by the appointment of a logistics director whose task it would be to manage the flow of goods from supplier through to shop. The author does not believe this to be practicable as it would interfere

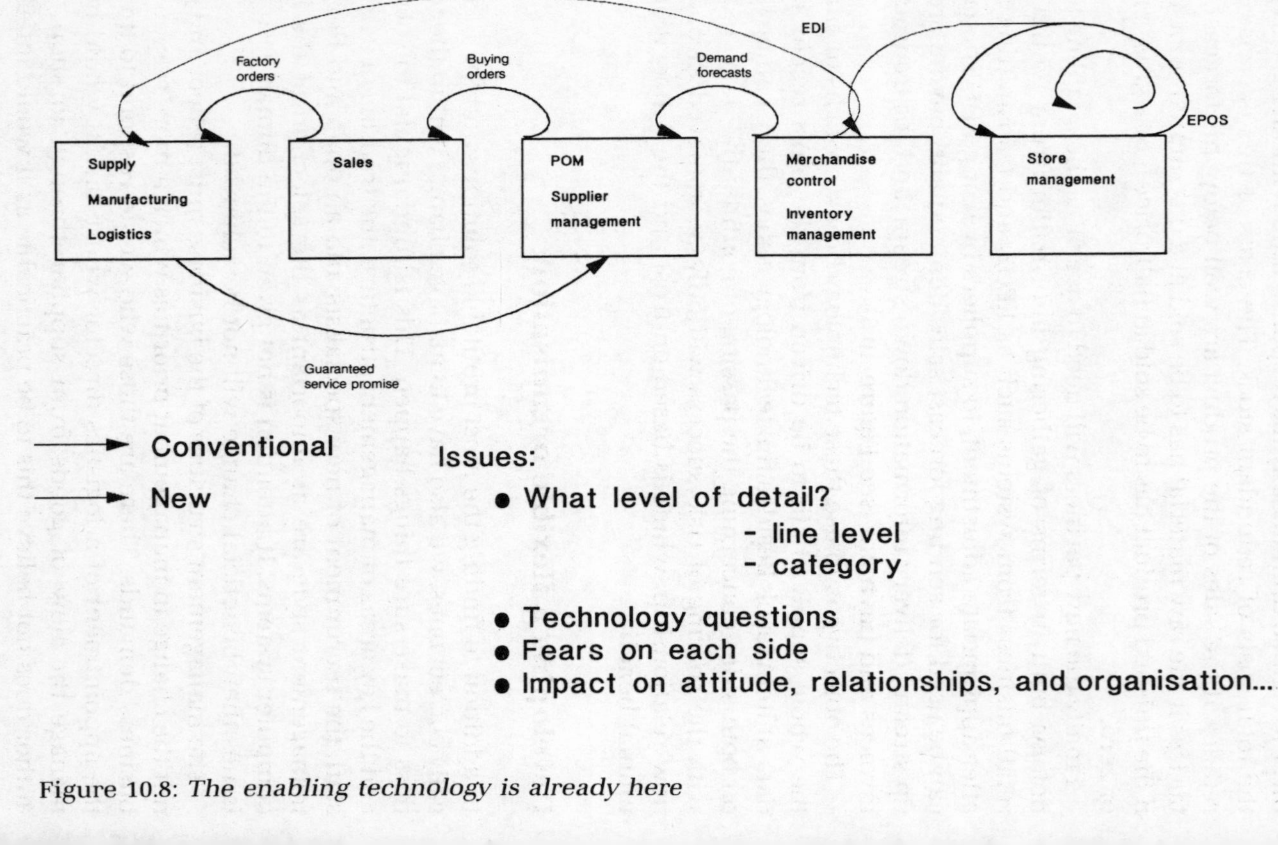

Figure 10.8: *The enabling technology is already here*

with the functional responsibilities of buyers, merchandisers, distribution management and retailers – and lead to a form of matrix management about which, for good reasons, we hear very little these days.

The supply chain issue should be part of every business plan and each functional manager should have clear objectives to ensure quick response. It is, however, necessary to have a function with a clearly defined responsibility for providing logistics services such as freight forwarding and shipping and this can be extended to the co-ordination of the chain across the business unit to ensure that new practices are tested, evaluated and introduced.

Top management – the chief executive and his team – must be committed to the objective of managing the supply chain, as they already manage every other activity. The marketing strategy of a business is understood by all functions within it and this forms the basis of the objectives of each functional department. So it must be with the supply chain – each part of the business must work to the common aim of reducing time – and to do this effectively each must understand the operation of its neighbours in the supply chain.

It is now the time to discuss the question of management style. Because the supply chain crosses so many functions and because there should be no such role as a logistics-supremo, it is essential that openness exists between the functions. The operation of each part of the business is the concern of all of the business, as the strength of the supply chain is also that of its weakest link. The merchandisers and buyers must work closely in planning the ranges and ordering the goods, the merchandisers must understand the needs and opportunities of the retailers, the distribution team must take part in the planning of intake and know which products have priority and why – and so on. The supply chain is in fact a loop and each part of it is dependent on the others.

There are many ways in which the necessary changes can be made. The key message is that, after the critical stage of analysis to identify where the best returns can be achieved, it is important to set up a series of trials, each with an operating manager as its leader and with clear objectives and tight timing. Some ideas will not work – and these must not be seen as failures but rather as part of the process of finding out and moving forward.

In this discussion an outline has been presented of the requirements for each of the building blocks which an organisation needs

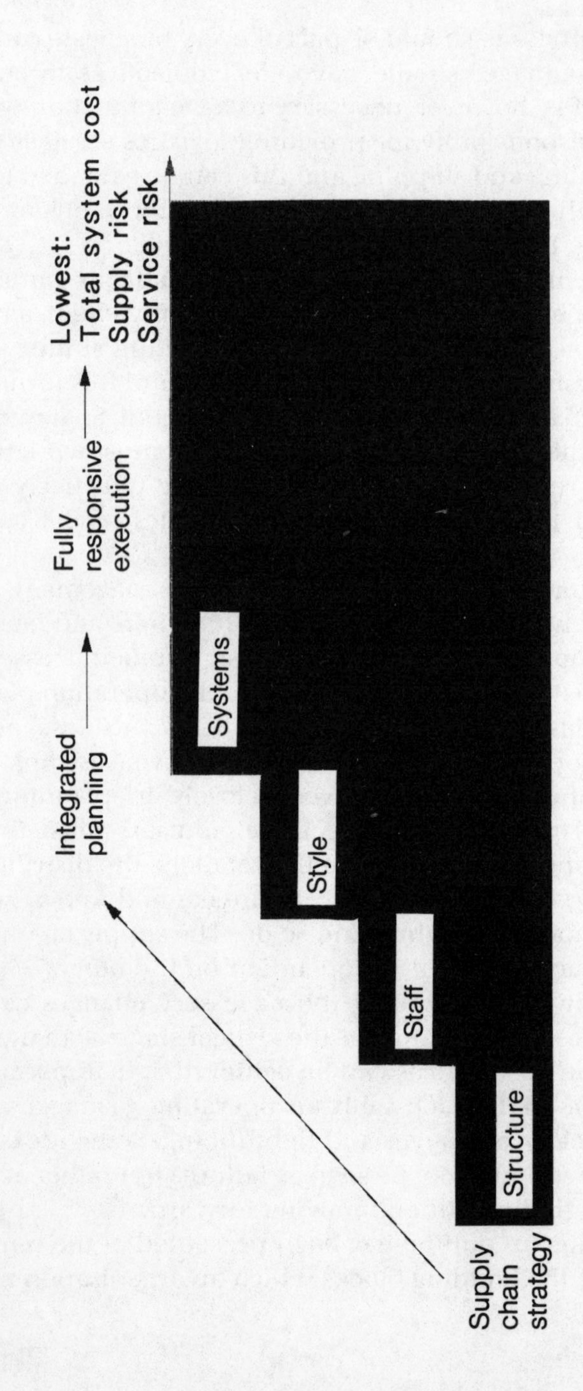

Figure 10.9: *The building blocks for a flexible organisation able to respond to the supply chain challenges*

if it is to develop an effective response to the supply chain opportunities – the structure of the business, the quality and attitude of the staff, the management style set from the top and the computer based systems which facilitate the change (*see* Figure 10.9).

All these requirements contribute to the shortening of the chain of supply and all have to be considered by retailers if they are to achieve a satisfactory profit from the buying and selling of goods – and not just from the fortunate inheritance of freeholds and long leaseholds. In conclusion, another opportunity exists which is not only to the benefit of those directly concerned but will also reduce our balance of payments deficit and strengthen the economy. The UK manufacturing industry is, by virtue of its proximity to our markets, particularly well placed to meet our needs for quick response. In labour intensive industries, such as knitwear, textiles and footwear, low labour cost countries have an obvious advantage. But it takes us at least 13 weeks to obtain shoes from Taiwan or Indonesia and at best only three or four weeks from a factory in Leicester. The opportunity is obvious, the resources are available – we only need the will and application to make it happen – and the benefits will not only be to our customers, our staff and our shareholders but also to the economy of the UK as a whole.

11
Retail Warehouse Operators – The Comet Case

Trevor Thomas and John Fernie

Introduction

Of the major changes which have occurred in UK retailing during the 1970s and 1980s, the rise of the retail warehouse operator has had the most notable physical impact upon the retail environment. It is difficult to accurately assess the true scale of this phenomenon because of definitional changes over time, from the term discount retail warehouses in the early years, to retail warehouse parks and, more recently, retail parks. This chapter will briefly chart the development of the retail warehouse concept, the changing nature of logistics management within this sector, concluding with a case study of one of the pioneers of this form of trading – Comet, part of Kingfisher plc.

Retail warehousing

As the suburbanisation of retailing activity gathers pace in the UK, retail warehousing has become a major element of the out of town exodus, accounting for 50 million square feet of gross floorspace in 1989 from 2,026 warehouses (Clive Lewis, 1989). Deemed to be the second wave of decentralisation by Schiller in 1986, the retail warehouse has gone from strength to strength, while superstore developments (the first wave) and regional shopping centres (the third wave) have met with greater hostility from downtown traders, consumer groups and planning authorities. Indeed, much attention has been focused upon the physical and economic impacts of superstore proposals whilst the less than aesthetic 'sheds' of the early warehouse operators received planning approval (see Brown,

1989; URPI, 1988). Yet, Dawson and Broadbridge (1988) claim that food superstores will account for only 600 out of 3,195 superstores and retail warehouses in operation by 1990/1.

The reasons for this relative immunity from planning objection can be traced to the early years of the concept. The earliest schemes were termed 'retail discount warehouses' and URPI (1978) produced definitions for the three main types of discount operator – electrical goods, DIY and carpets/furniture. In planning terms confusion arose regarding whether such operations should be classed as retail or warehouse in the use classes order (de Main, 1978). As the pioneers of retail warehousing began to look for purpose-built premises instead of converted premises in the early 1980s, they quickly found local authorities to be fairly supportive of their proposals. Why? In the first instance, the UK was in the throes of recession in the early 1980s and the local authorities were more receptive to any new investment. Indeed, many schemes at this time were proposed in industrial estates and enterprise zones, which had good road access. Second, the types of goods sold in these warehouses were bulky and often of low value, requiring storage space and large amounts of ground-level car parking for customers, many of whom would take home goods in their cars or rented vans. Third, retail warehouses were 'in town' developments. Although they were not town centre schemes, they were on edge of centre or on the periphery of towns, usually accessible from a ring road. This encouraged more positive planning than was the case with superstore proposals and later regional centre schemes, which occasionally conflicted with green belt policies of local authorities.

In his excellent review of retail warehouse parks, Brown (1989) argues that the third phase, post 1985, has been one of trading up, eradicating the architectural 'shed' image and integrating stores in a well-planned, landscaped retail park. Note the abandonment of the downmarket term 'warehouse'. A retail park as defined by Hillier Parker (1990) is 'at least 50,000 sq ft gross lettable retail area, and built and let as a retail entity. It should be sited outside the town centre and contain at least three retail warehouses, defined as single storey retail units of at least 10,000 sq ft. The centre should also include some purpose-built pedestrian area or joint car parking facilities'. By the end of 1989, 174 retail park developments had opened, representing over 20 million square feet of retail space. (Table 11.1). Hillier Parker estimate that another 80 schemes will open in 1990. The impact of retail parks on overall shopping provision can be gauged from figures from 1989. The 71 schemes, representing over eight million square feet, accounted for 57 per cent of all shopping centre floorspace opened in that year.

Table 11.1: *Retail parks – 1982–9*

Year	Number of schemes	Annual floorspace opened (sq ft)	Average size (sq ft)
1982	1	93,000	93,000
1983	3	306,000	102,000
1984	–	–	–
1985	5	554,000	110,800
1986	10	1,357,000	135,700
1987	30	3,784,000	126,133
1988	54	6,399,000	118,500
1989	71	8,110,000	114,225

Source: Hillier Parker, Retail Parks, 1990

There is no reason to doubt that growth of retail park developments will continue, albeit at a slower rate than in the late 1980s. The bouyancy of this market can be attributed to the appeal of retail parks to a widening range of retailers. Retail parks are no longer the domain of DIY and furniture retailers. By the mid 1980s the concept was being embraced by toy, leisure, motor accessories and shoe retailers. More recently, traditional high street retailers have been locating in retail parks (Marks and Spencer, John Lewis, Next, Burton) and other complementary services have followed (cinemas, fast food restaurants, showrooms and financial services). Schiller (1990) illustrates the pace of change in this sector by comparing tenants of the newly opened Fosse Park near Leicester with those of the Retail World retail park in Team Valley, Gateshead in 1987. In this park, 11 out of the 16 units are occupied by furniture or carpet retailers; at Fosse Park only 3 out of the 14 traders are in furniture or DIY with eight selling comparison goods normally found in the high street.

Changing patterns of distribution

Commensurate with the changing profile of tenants who occupy retail parks, retail distribution by the operators is moving to embrace supply chain management philosophies. The traditional retail discounters traded on price, more than the quality of shopfitting or the ambience of being in a shopping centre. Many of these companies, especially Comet which provides our case study, advertised their offerings in the local press to entice customers to their rather unattractive surroundings. As retail warehouses, stock-piling was encouraged with volume purchases being delivered direct from manufacturers.

By the early 1980s, when retail warehouses had become more upmarket, the move to centralisation of distribution gathered pace; with greater control of stock through the supply chain more space could be given over to showrooms. Some of these operators, B&Q, Comet, Homebase and Payless, became part of larger multiple retail groups which had well established distribution networks with appropriate management expertise. Not surprisingly, Homebase, part of J Sainsbury plc, was the first DIY retailer to centralise part of its distribution operation. Sainsbury has always been at the fore-front of grocery distribution in the UK.

Now that the term 'retail warehouse operator' embraces much of UK retailing, most of the companies which belatedly moved out of town, for example Marks and Spencer, Burton, John Lewis, with established distribution operations, will ultimately benefit from reduced costs in delivering to more accessible sites than to sites in congested town centres. The remainder of this chapter charts the distribution strategy of a 'traditional' retail warehouse operator, Comet, as it moved to a centralised distribution policy in the late 1980s.

The Comet strategy

In February 1988 the chief executive of Kingfisher stated in his report 'The Group's Future Direction', that at Comet, '. . . this year we are creating a central distribution system which will enable us to reduce stock-outs, improve buying margins and release stock-room space – enabling us to create a new generation of electrical superstores.'

During the period of implementation of the strategy from March 1987 to completion in March 1989 Comet's operating profits grew from £17 million for the year ended January 1987 to £26 million for the year ended January 1989; and for 1988/9 the profit growth of 26 per cent in the tough trading climate was recognised as being partly attributable to the first full year of successful control of its own distribution and supply chain.

At the present time in the UK the effects of high interest rates on retail spending are causing slackening sales demand, which in turn have resulted in a big build-up of excess stocks. With gloomy forecasts for the UK retail sector, the need for a greater emphasis on a clear corporate strategy to manage the assets and people more productively, and to an even higher level of efficiency, has never been greater. Also customers are becoming increasingly insistent on value for money, both in quality of goods and in higher levels of service – they are less attracted by promotion-driven offers.

Any corporate strategy, in order to be successful, must be clearly understood and have full commitment from all levels of management throughout an organisation, but most particularly from the main board of directors and principal policy or decision-makers.

Where were we and where did we want to be?

In 1985 Comet had a turnover of £350 million from 200 stores – 150 of which had direct delivery of the total product range comprising both white goods (jargon for washing machines, dishwashers, etc) and brown goods (meaning videos, TVs, etc.) while the remaining 50 stores had at least some direct delivery of smaller cube products. There was no distribution or inventory control function in the organisation and just one stock controller at the head office.

The formation of orders and stock within stores was buyer-driven and much of the management data available was from manufacturers, who had their own interests at heart. Comet stores were visited by a large number of suppliers, their carriers, sub-carriers and transport intermediaries of one sort or another, which made inventory management virtually impossible, plus diverting the attention of store managers and their staff away from their job of selling.

During this time the company continued to expand and, with the system of direct deliveries, stock imbalances in the stores were exaggerated and stock availability was falling. Many of the 200 stores simply could not cope with the increased range and spiralling inventory levels, and the company suffered from the practice known as 'squirreling' – or managers hoarding stock, which prevented any sub-distribution or allocation between parent stores and their satellites. Many stores ended up with insufficient fast-selling lines and too many slow-selling ones.

The situation was not helped by the Comet policy of having retail units out of town, where stock-piling was commonplace and accepted, due to large back room areas.

To sum up, the lack of control of the supply chain, both internally and externally, was causing severe overstocking and stock imbalances and, most importantly, lost sales opportunities.

The decision to consider a project for improved stock control and distribution came in late 1985, and when one of the authors joined Comet, in 1986, as distribution controller with the task of devising a new strategy, the greatest ally in assessing and proposing it was the significant attitudinal change that had taken place at board level. The recognition that there were better ways of organising Comet's business was vital to the success of the strategy, particularly as the business was planned to expand to 300 stores and £500 million sales.

The first decision was to test the assumptions and viability of a central composite distribution strategy, which would result in major systems development and redesigns, together with the setting up of three distribution centres – in Scotland, the south-east and the north-west; followed by the planning of the team that would be required to implement the strategy. The right people had to be in place first before the implementation of Phase I of the strategy.

Initially lobbied by internal personnel to join the distribution group, it was vital not to end up with 'square pegs in round holes' as the appointment of high quality graduate-calibre people was essential in the formation of a small but highly skilled team.

Finally, an assessment of existing resources was necessary, plan the strategy, and present the case to the board: why Comet needed a new distribution and supply chain strategy, which would be based on the principles of third party contract distribution, automatic branch stock replenishment and purchase order management systems.

The need for a clear strategy

The need for the strategy was dictated by three main problems within the business:

- poor stock availability across the product range and between the retail outlets, which resulted in lost sales opportunities;
- increasing stock levels, leading to unnecessarily high working capital investment; and
- the need to maximise the sales and profits per square foot of Comet's retail outlets.

The success or failure of the strategy, therefore, would be judged by its impact on mitigating and resolving these three critical business problems.

A strategy based on three regional composite distribution centres (RDCs) would enable Comet to manage its stock more effectively in the future, resulting in increased service and sales to customers and reduced stock levels. The objectives therefore, were to:

- define a 'service mission' in terms of stock availability at the retail branches;
- to determine the best stock management practices to meet that service mission, at least total cost; and
- to ensure the benefit of the investment in the RDCs would be fully realised.

The objective that was to prove the most difficult to achieve and the most contentious with buying, marketing and retail operations colleagues was the first. The debate on what is the optimum correlation of stock investment to stock availability still rages on – but some reasoned assumptions had to be made in order to plan warehouse capacities, vehicle and staff resource levels, total stock within the supply chain, lead times, frequency of order call-off from suppliers, etc. In particular the combination of reduced supplier lead times with increased delivery frequencies would allow us to react more rapidly to unexpected changes in demand. This in turn would result in improved stock availability at the retail branches.

Moreover, it is good practice to keep reviewing the service mission, refining it to seek higher sales penetration through a higher service mission, or to differentiate the service mission targets to reflect the relative priorities of different products within a business marketing mix – eg alpha products, 95 per cent (core range of autowashers, freezers, TVs, videos, those products in those price bands that must never be out of stock), beta products 85 per cent and gamma products 25 per cent – or some other similar matrix.

The strategic logistics options should be driven by this service mission, which should be agreed at board level, and documented before any attempt is made to design supply chain mechanisms. Indeed the supply chain design should target lead time reduction, while at the same time improving the service mission, and inventory reductions will follow as a natural consequence. Bland or arbitrary stock reduction targets, such as 'reduce forward weeks' stock by two weeks' can cause severe problems if the full logistics mission is not fully understood in conjunction with the retail service mission you are trying to achieve.

The service mission concept in retail distribution is all-important to a successful implementation and performance measurement of any new distribution strategy. It is also one of the hardest on which to secure cohesive top level agreement, as it raises questions of accountability, personal management interest, ownership of stock and such other issues which cut across the full spectrum of the retailing key functions – buying, marketing, sales, operations, finance and distribution.

From the service mission you can then calculate the level of company stock required to achieve it – for instance at a service mission of 90 per cent – total stock of eight weeks is required, and at 95 per cent the stock required would rise to ten weeks. This disciplined approach can often result in a company operating at significantly reduced stock levels allowing it to either:

(a) operate from a smaller working capital base with direct benefits on the profit and loss account; or
(b) improve the service mission even further and thus hopefully improve sales; or
(c) invest in a wider range of products within slow turnover stores with slow stock turn characteristics.

But to achieve all this the company must realise the enormous cultural change impact in two areas; first within the business, which can take up to three years to fulfil and second outside the business by managing your suppliers and convincing them of the improvements to their business that will result with the introduction of better supply chain disciplines: for example, allowing visibility of forward forecasts enabling better production planning; co-operation on load planning for RDC intake and stock presentation and configurations to suit the receiving RDC.

Managing change effectively

Any change of distribution strategy within a retail environment demands single-minded commitment to implementation, not only by the key personnel, but also by the board. The cultural shock and fear of loss of control as a result of change can cause a perfectly well-reasoned, logical strategy to be blown off course for the wrong reasons. Thus, one had to be prepared to overcome the natural resistance to change and stand alone – while persuading colleagues that a professionally run distribution and logistics function within the company could solve some existing problems and produce accurate information on which to base better business decisions.

The critical path, action plans and contingency plans for managing a change of strategy have to stand up to severe scrutiny from external consultants, as a necessary check and balance to give comfort to any subsidiary or holding company board of directors. The investment in any retail distribution strategy is immense, but equally the pay back can be high, given clear objectives and top level understanding with commitment.

The pilot scheme was the RDC in Scotland opened in May 1987 to feed 35 stores, achieve stock availability on key lines to over 92 per cent; increase sales in our base stores by more than 3 per cent per annum, all within agreed cost budgets. Fortunately, all these objectives were achieved, which resulted in the approval to implement the balance of the strategy. Thus, the south-east depot, serving 110 stores, was opened on time, in May 1988, having only been given a 12-week timetable; and finally, the third and last RDC in the north-west, serving 150 stores, opened in September 1988, again on a 12-week timetable. In isolation, the start-up operations above would have been a big task but, in between these start-up operations, Kingfisher made two acquisitions; – one of 100 additional stores adding 25 per cent more volume and, six months later, a second acquisition adding 15 stores in Northern Ireland – which created its own particular brand of logistical problems.

These acquisitions required us to reappraise all our assumptions of capacity, store configurations, routeing, etc, within our original strategy and at the same time incorporate the closure of two RDCs acquired in the acquisition which did not fit with our strategy.

Systems, database and IT

Increasing demands for higher and more specific or targeted service levels, by product group and by classification of branch, have led to the need for sophisticated systems providing operational data from an accurate, timely and secure database within any retail distribution network. The power of information systems – to collect, transmit, collate, analyse and report is absolutely critical to a clear and meaningful use of operational data and performance indicators.

At Comet the strategic change to central distribution allowed the use of existing EPOS based systems to greater effect and to introduce new systems; we innovated first by basing our strategy on a unique automatic branch stock replenishment system at line item level, designed in-house between the distribution group and MIS department; the algorithm operates to agreed optima based on branch profiles and rates of sale for each line item in each store, so that the variability of demand for any product can be catered for, within the safety stock levels required to meet a given service level; and secondly we have designed and implemented a purchase order management system (POMS) which will enable Comet to manage its stocks more effectively. POMS allows the distribution group to:

- forecast monthly requirements by product, by supplier;
- suggest monthly national orders, allowing buyers to confirm previous 'order indications'; and
- suggest weekly order call-off quantities, allowing the intake to the RDCs to reflect the latest demand forecasts.

Thus the systems driving distribution are all 'forecast driven'. Moreover, considerable detailed analysis was done to determine lead times from the source of supply of the product, as this would be a key determinant of the amount of safety stock needed. At Comet sources are from the UK mainland (79 per cent), Europe (8 per cent) and the Far East (13 per cent) and typically the lead times were between two and six weeks for UK suppliers, two to three months for European and six months for the Far East. Our targets were to reduce these excessive lead times to one week for UK, three weeks for Europe and three months for the Far East. With central scheduling being introduced, together with the operation of purchase order management system on the opening of the third and final RDC, these targets were met for the principal suppliers in the UK and we negotiated ex-works scheduling and call-off from our principal European white goods manufacturers – the Far East remains to be completed. The savings in stock investment plus the increased stock availability in the warehouses was considerable, availability moved from 45 per cent pre weekly call-offs and central scheduling, to over 72 per cent post these changes. Similarly, branch availability improved from mid 70 per cent range to mid 80 per cent range for the company's total range of products – key lines remained over 92 per cent.

In an operationally complex and inter-dependent organisation it is easy to get hung up on internal politics such as perceived loss of control, power, etc and, more significantly, who can really be held accountable for what? Interestingly, during the implementation of the strategy, several heated debates and discussions occurred with buying and marketing colleagues on such issues as who is responsible for stock, etc – and once it was pointed out that the whole system was driven on forecasts, which were the sole responsibility of marketing colleagues, and that distribution operated the whole supply chain based on these forecasts, the perceived power and control rested with marketing – but the real power and control was behind that particular throne!

Why third party?

One of the key parts of the central distribution strategy for Comet was to operate the distribution network through third party contractors – the principal reason was the opportunity cost of capital; we earn higher returns on capital invested in our stores and stock than on capital invested in warehouses and vehicles; furthermore, our overall return on investment (ROI) is higher than our contractors', thus giving us an opportunity cost of capital benefit.

Other benefits include the ability to use specialists, familiar and experienced in responding to rapidly changing volume throughputs, and demanding store service levels. This resulted in the appointment of Exel Logistics (part of the worldwide National Freight Consortium plc) to operate the largest depot and another large contractor to run the two smaller depots. We were also able to distance ourselves from the day-to-day management and industrial relations aspects of the warehousing and transport operations, preferring instead to control the operations and the contractors with a few highly skilled individuals from the centre, relying on accurate and timely management information by exception from the RDC.

Furthermore, by sharing out total throughput between two of the major operators in the industry Comet has helped to create a market place for distribution services – with all the gains of market forces and constructive competitors, creativity, innovation and flexibility. There is a mutuality of interest in improving the productivity standards within warehouse and the utilisation levels of the transport resources.

Management structure and skills

The importance of defining the job descriptions and objectives that are required within a retail distribution network – particularly where you are changing strategies and cultures as radically as did Comet – cannot be overemphasised. Recruitment of the right people is always a key quality of any company, but it is particularly so in logistics, where the 'chemistry' within the department and within the other key functions is so important, as good communication should be a byword of any logistics department wanting to be effective.

Comet did not have the right skills at head office and decided to recruit; we were thus looking for first-class, highly-skilled people. First, two graduate inventory managers were appointed, one from an automotive parts company, and another from a major food/hardware retailer. Both members of the team had systems, inventory control and some warehousing experience and were of the calibre now necessary in the distribution industry.

A senior operations manager, a vital part of the strategy was also needed, because he would provide the link and control between Comet and the third party contractors. He was appointed ten months after the beginning of the strategy period. He came from the contracting industry and, as such, was a poacher turned gamekeeper!

The final appointment was a shipping manager to look after direct European and Far East imports, and once again the quality of selection was vital. Each member of the senior logistics team had to earn his own respect. Most of the team were brought in from outside, incorporating specialist management skills not available to the company before.

The extent of the changes in functional responsibility, education and understanding that had to occur cannot be underestimated. Managing the strategy successfully demanded high levels of operational skills, particularly on designing, implementing and controlling the systems required to:

(a) calculate amounts of safety and working stock needed at the warehouses and in the branches;
(b) forecast future product demands; and
(c) replenish product stocks at RDCs and in branches, including such requirements as designing and operating the methodology for scarce stock allocations – to ensure the supply of such product was maintained to those branches where the product sells fastest and avoid replenishing slow turnover branches – or in fashionable jargon 'the right product, at the right place, at the right time'!

Finally, in managing this change it was necessary to build computer based models to help question and adjust stock depths, stock ranges, demand variability, store grading, store profiling, space planning, etc – none of these concepts or techniques had been used or were understood by the management prior to the introduction of the strategy. Within the logistics group a galaxy of models was developed to enable us to use 'what if' techniques – models such as:

- a model for automatic replenishment system, or MARS;
- profiling levels up to optimum, or PLUTO.

Again these are key parts of managing the strategy successfully.

Future maximisation of the strategy

Central distribution and disciplined supply chain management techniques are now a way of life at Comet; the cultural change and developmental costs incurred during the implementation stages are being eliminated as the distribution and logistics function matures company-wide. The whole strategy was designed to be implemented as minimal risk (no capital invested/third party contractor solution), self-financing – by obtaining significant staff, vehicle and property savings, plus supplier discounts from forcing improved in-bound logistics costs on them, and above all to give a competitive edge in the electrical retailing industry by obtaining higher stock availability (90 per cent +) on a lower stock base (> ten weeks forward sales) and company distribution costs lower than competitors. On all accounts these objectives were met, with the exception that the lower stock objective was taking longer to achieve, particularly on the consumer electronics or brown goods side of the business.

As to the future, fine-tuning of the strategy will be an ongoing feature and a number of areas were identified:

(a) 'Opportunity agreements' with the third party contractors to obtain the best productivity and utilisation efficiencies for the benefit of both parties.

(b) Extend the ex-works strategy for direct imports from mainland Europe, shortening lead times and eliminating break bulk and consolidation operations; and utilise vehicle routing techniques to operate UK supplier collections ex-works, both of which will give further gross profit margin opportunities.

(c) Network opportunities with the after-sales service division utilising the newly established integrated distribution function to rationalise and centralise the service centres for stock refurbishment, repairs, damages and spares.

(d) Further refinements of the warehouse replenishments, stock profiling and stock service mission – all of which impact on the control, sourcing and efficiency of the total distribution and logistics operation, thus driving productivities and utilisations *up* and cost *down*.

The change in strategy has benefited all players in the supply chain – the suppliers, because the supply chain is simpler, better planned and enables them to manage their own stocks and material flows more effectively; the branch managers, through better availability and higher sales; and the customers, from having a wider range in stock in the stores at the time he or she wishes to purchase – and at the right price! All of this is geared to the retailer's overall aim of 'total customer satisfaction'.

References

Brown, S (1989) *Retail Warehouse Parks* Longman/Oxford Institute of Retail Management.

Clive Lewis and Partners (1989) *Midsummer Retail Report* Clive Lewis.

de Main, JD (1978) in URPI *Discount Retail Warehouses* U6, URPI, 21–30.

Dawson, JA and Broadbridge, AM (1988) *Retailing in Scotland, 2005* Institute of Retail Studies, University of Stirling.

Hillier Parker (1990) *Retail Parks* May, Hillier Parker Research.

Schiller, R (1986) 'Retail decentralisation – the coming of the third wave' *The Planner 72* (7) : 13–15.

—(1990) 'Recovery in site' *Shop Property* July, 22–3.

URPI (1978) *Discount Retail Warehouses* U6, URPI.

—(1988) 'Retail planning inquiry decisions: recent trends' *URPI Information Brief* 88/7.

12
Physical Distribution Management in Mail Order – The Grattan Case

David Brady and Julie Harrison

Introduction

Mail order is ubiquitous in today's society – leaflets fall from colour supplements and through our letterboxes. Yet it is not the traditional mail order that our grandmothers knew, with agents, brown paper packaging and two-week order cycles – it is a vibrant and exciting home shopping market with glossy targeted catalogues and; ultimately, the upmarket *Next Directory*.

The purpose of this chapter is to examine the role of physical distribution management (PDM) systems within mail order, specifically examining those within Grattan – the home shopping division of Next plc – and to ask whether these are the key to our success. This examination is particularly apt for two reasons. First, home shopping has no product as such; it produces the catalogues to sell goods that have been bought from other suppliers and, therefore, the essence of its being is to distribute goods. Second, Grattan is radically converting its old warehousing systems into a brand new £55 million complex, thereby encouraging greater investigation of distribution systems.

This analysis will centre around three areas:

- home shopping: the market and its changing nature;
- physical distribution management and competitive advantage;
- a case study of the role of distribution management within Grattan/Next.

Home shopping: the market and its changing nature

Home shopping has benefited from vast changes over the 1980s, and in order to fully understand these, it is necessary to discuss the sector by looking at the following; what it is, how it developed, its changing face and the market place.

What is home shopping?

Home shopping is 'the provision of goods directly by a company to a customer in response to an order', (Jordans, 1983: 4). The order could have been generated in a number of ways: general catalogues, direct catalogues or personal shopping, supplement one-page offers or specialist magazines, but the essence of mail order is provision – the final point of the distribution system being the customer's home.

This definition can be enhanced by tracing the development of mail order, for this dictates its characteristics.

The development of home shopping

All businesses or companies are the product of their development, and to this rule home shopping proves no exception – how then has home shopping developed?

The development of home shopping within Britain can be traced back to the early nineteenth century. American mail order was born out of necessity; the necessity to supply a widely spread population with vital goods – the reduction of distance. UK mail order, however, emerged from another necessity, that of poverty – the reduction of payments. Forerunners to the catalogue system were the 'Watch Clubs' of Yorkshire. These were established by Fattorinis of Leeds as a method by which a group of men would club together each week to buy a watch and allocate this through the drawing of lots until each member possessed one. By the time sufficient watches had been bought the clubs had become social institutions and Fattorini began to produce a catalogue selling a range of goods, but still permitting payment by weekly instalment (Kay, 1987: 143).

With the offer of household goods, these catalogues became the accepted method of purchase. The system involved a fixed period for payments, products were simply packaged and the catalogue owner – the agent – earned a commission for administering and delivering orders to a circle of customers. Thus, the traditional face of mail order came into existence. In 1910 Fattorini formed Empire Stores and, after a family split in 1912, Grattan was established – both of these mail order houses are still in existence.

What then were the characteristics of this traditional mail order and how have these changed with the advent of modern home shopping?

The changing nature of mail order

The characteristics of mail order pre 1980s were the following:

Agent
Seller to a large circle of customers (on average 12) who distributed all pre-packed parcels, collected returns and payments and received a commission for doing so; mainly female from C2DE socio-economic group.

Customer base
Mainly female from C2DE socio-economic group and northern based.

Credit
Given to all customers, a main selling point.

Catalogue
A large 1,000 page 'shop window' simply presented, selling department store products with a heavy bias towards practical goods.

The main competitive advantages of this mail order system were threefold; the three 'Cs of convenience, credit and commission' (Retail 1986). How then have these characteristics changed?

Agent
Seller to an average of three customers (immediate family circle), still acting as an agent to these, selling through the main catalogues. Many buy on a personal shopping basis – direct to a customer.

Customer base
More widely spread throughout the socio-economic groupings, but still mainly female. Customer base increased in the south-east, eg through *Next Directory*.

Credit
Still offered in general catalogue and personal shopping, but not in

the growing numbers of direct catalogues, ie Grattan, Direct, Kaleidoscope.

Catalogues

A greatly enhanced variety of goods available through:

- the main catalogue under a new title and cover (*Grattan Direct, Personal Shopping* – Littlewoods);
- selected parts of the main catalogue under specialist headings (*Streets of London* – Grattan, *You & Yours* – Grattan);
- catalogues with a selection of goods not available in main catalogue (*Bymail* – Jeff Banks and Freemans);
- direct response – one-off offers;
- direct mail targeted at a specific selection of customers through its merchandise (*Kaleidoscope* – Grattan);
- an upmarket version of the catalogue aimed at AB socio-economic groups (*Next Directory* – Grattan/Next).

(Empire Stores company information – 1987).

These changes in mail order came largely as a result of the recession in the late 1970s, which caused one of the general mail order companies to register a loss, and were made possible through the application of computerisation and technology to all aspects of home shopping. It is best assessed by the comparison of a northern housewife in the 1950s distributing goods purchased from a 1,000 page general catalogue to a large circle of friends, to the young professional female who bought her working clothes from the glossy and upmarket *Next Directory* in the 1980s.

Any analysis of home shopping could not be complete without looking at the sector itself – its size and its structure.

The market

Home shopping is a sector of retailing which in 1989 had an estimated turnover of £3.8 billion, which represents 3.3 per cent of all retail sales. Despite this size the market is dominated by only six companies: Great Universal Stores (GUS), the largest with approximately 40 per cent of the market, followed by Littlewoods with 25 per cent, Freemans and Next/Grattan each have 12–14 per cent with the remaining 10 per cent shared between Empire Stores and N Brown. The catalogues are as shown in Table 12.1.

Home shopping is a wealthy sector of retailing dominated by few companies, and it is also a sector which offers a variety of 'products' in the form of specifically targeted catalogues which ensure maximum marketing advantages. *Next Directory* was a watershed in home shopping, representing the tightening relationship between the high street and mail order.

Before using a case study to examine the role of PDM within Grattan/Next, it is first necessary to briefly define PDM and how it can influence a company's success.

Physical distribution management and competitive advantage

Writings on the theories of physical distribution management could, and often have, filled books, let alone chapters of their own. For the purposes of this analysis, it is necessary only to outline theories appropriate to competitive advantage, with further clarification through a case study on Grattan's own distribution management.

Table 12.1: *Leading mail order houses*

Company/Parent	Catalogues
Grattan/Next	Grattan, You & Yours, Look Again, Kaleidoscope, Streets of London, Next Directory
GUS	John England, Great Universal, John Noble, Trafford Myers, Marshall Ward, Kays, Selection, Kit
Littlewoods	Brian Mills, Janet Frazer, John Moores, Burlington, Peter Craig, Littlewoods
Freemans	Freemans, Together, iSiT, SW5
Empire Stores	Empire, Just 4 You
N Brown Investments	JD Williams, Shopping Sense, Angela King, Showcase, Heather Valley, Ambrose Wilson, Oxendale, Dale House, Country Garden/ Kitchen

Source: RTR (1989: 32)

To 'distribute' is to 'dispose in various directions' (*Oxford English Dictionary*, 1969: 43). It is the aim of any system of distribution to allow physical possession of a product through product availability by delivering the right product in the right place at the right time. What is important is that this possession, place, product or time are as the customer has perceived them, for it is in the fulfilment of those perceptions that a distribution system earns its keep.

Physical distribution systems exist as a member of a business system made up of many parts, whether they be marketing, finance, or production, and as such serve as a sub-system to the whole. The ultimate aim of all business systems is profit through sales, by achieving the competitive advantage of a perceived differentiation from their competitors.

'The nature of the competitive advantage should be based upon those elements which maximise differentiation from competitors and those are usually based upon customer perception of added value aspects of retail's overall offering' (Walters and White, 1987: 30). This concept of 'added value' is further pursued in the case study and is the crux of any analysis on a company's success. Added value can be achieved through a number of variables: customer service, product, speed of delivery and quality, all of which can be influenced by each part of the business system. 'Systems thinking' is as equally applied to a business system as any: changes in a sub-system will impact on the system itself, and thus it is for distribution.

Distribution systems within Grattan/Next – a case study

Many case studies suffer from a dearth of information and the wish to emphasise the study by restating facts. Therefore, we must state a clear aim. Having accepted the concept of added value and the achievement of this through competitive advantage, the aim of this case study is to ask how distribution systems of Grattan operate to achieve this. The study will centre around three sections: the group structure, and distribution within this, the distribution system itself and an analysis of the resulting added value.

The group structure

Next Retail and Grattan merged in June 1986 to pool their areas of expertise – for Next these were merchandising and marketing, for

Grattan it was the computerisation and distribution systems. The structure which has currently emerged is shown in Figure 12.1, with distribution and computing operating as services to the whole group.

Distribution systems

Distribution within home shopping comprises two elements, warehousing and transportation, which operate to:

- receive deliveries from suppliers and store until items are needed to fulfil orders;
- receive returned items from customers and make them fit for stock – if this is not possible out-sort for disposal as soon as possible;
- 'pick' items to fulfil customer orders;
- pack and despatch orders to customers;
- deliver orders to customers' homes;
- offer maximum service to the customer at the minimum cost.

NEXT RETAIL	NEXT DIRECTORY	GRATTAN CATALOGUES	KALEIDOSCOPE	SCOTCADE	SPECIAL OFFERS	'YOU' MAGAZINE	ETC
DISTRIBUTION							
COMPUTING SERVICES							

Figure 12.1: *The group structure of Next plc*

This case study will centre around Listerhills, the £55 million warehousing complex which will serve the home shopping division – Gratton, Kaleidoscope, Scotcade, leaflets, special offers, and boxed goods for *Next Directory*. Hanging garments will be handled at a separate site, as will Next Retail distribution. This analysis centres around the new complex because of the opportunity it provides for studying the relationship between distribution and competitive advantage.

Before assessing this impact we have to look at the systems themselves – past, present and future. In this instance the past systems are pre-Listerhills, the present are those employed in Listerhills and the future any enhancements to these.

Past systems (pre-Listerhills)

Traditionally, distribution within mail order has been labour-intensive with low levels of rationalisation and application of technology to methods of work. The predominant reason for this was their location in northern industrial towns which had high unemployment and a surfeit of disused textile mills. In addition, Grattan emerged as a very successful company after the Second World War, and the temptation was to buy a number of sites to house the growing warehousing operations. The transportation of goods was by delivery of the pre-packed parcel to agents, via the post office.

Therefore, the warehousing systems of Grattan in the late 1970s/early 1980s were spread over a number of sites with transportation occurring from each. In the early 1980s these systems were computerised to allow batch picking and packing from random locations and a carousel tilt-tray was introduced as a sorting device within packing, supported by a conveyor system.

The physical limitations of this system (Figure 12.2) meant that the functions of bulk receiving and store, returns and picking/packing occurred at three different locations, with additional warehousing for Kaleidoscope/Scotcade and palletised merchandise. There were a number of disadvantages from this system including:

- high costs of transportation between sites;
- high labour costs with multi-handling of stock;
- time delay between errors and effect;
- minimum of three days from receipt of goods to packing of items to fill an order;

- assumptions that led to 'out of stock' situations, of primary annoyance to all customers.

As well as the application of computerisation to these systems, enhancements were also made to the transportation system through:

- the use of super agents who receive single items and packing materials to their home, and are paid for each parcel that they pack and deliver;
- the increase of Grattan's own deliveries rather than the use of the post office.

However, despite these improvements, the distribution system within Grattan had severe limitations and these impacted on customer service, bringing about the decision to build Listerhills, and transfer operations.

Present – current Listerhills operations

The implementation of Listerhills is currently being completed – the returns centre operates fully from site, and for the spring/summer 1990 catalogue all goods are being received and all orders despatched from the complex. A period of dual operations followed by a running down of the old sites is currently taking place at the main distribution centre and the pallet store. Figure 12.3 shows the work-flow which will occur within Listerhills. A brief description of these systems is as follows:

Appointments

Goods and delivery times are booked on to computer and validated against contract details. After validation bay-time is allocated for unloading – no unappointed vehicles will be accepted unless previously agreed with the stock controllers – approximately 30 per cent of deliveries were inaccurate with the old system, with a high toll in costs of storage and handling.

Receiving

Goods are unloaded in two forms: cartons and pallets, there is a separate receiving and storage system for each.

Cartons

Barcoded on arrival and fed by conveyor on to man-rider cranes within the carton store. The cranes are then directed by computer

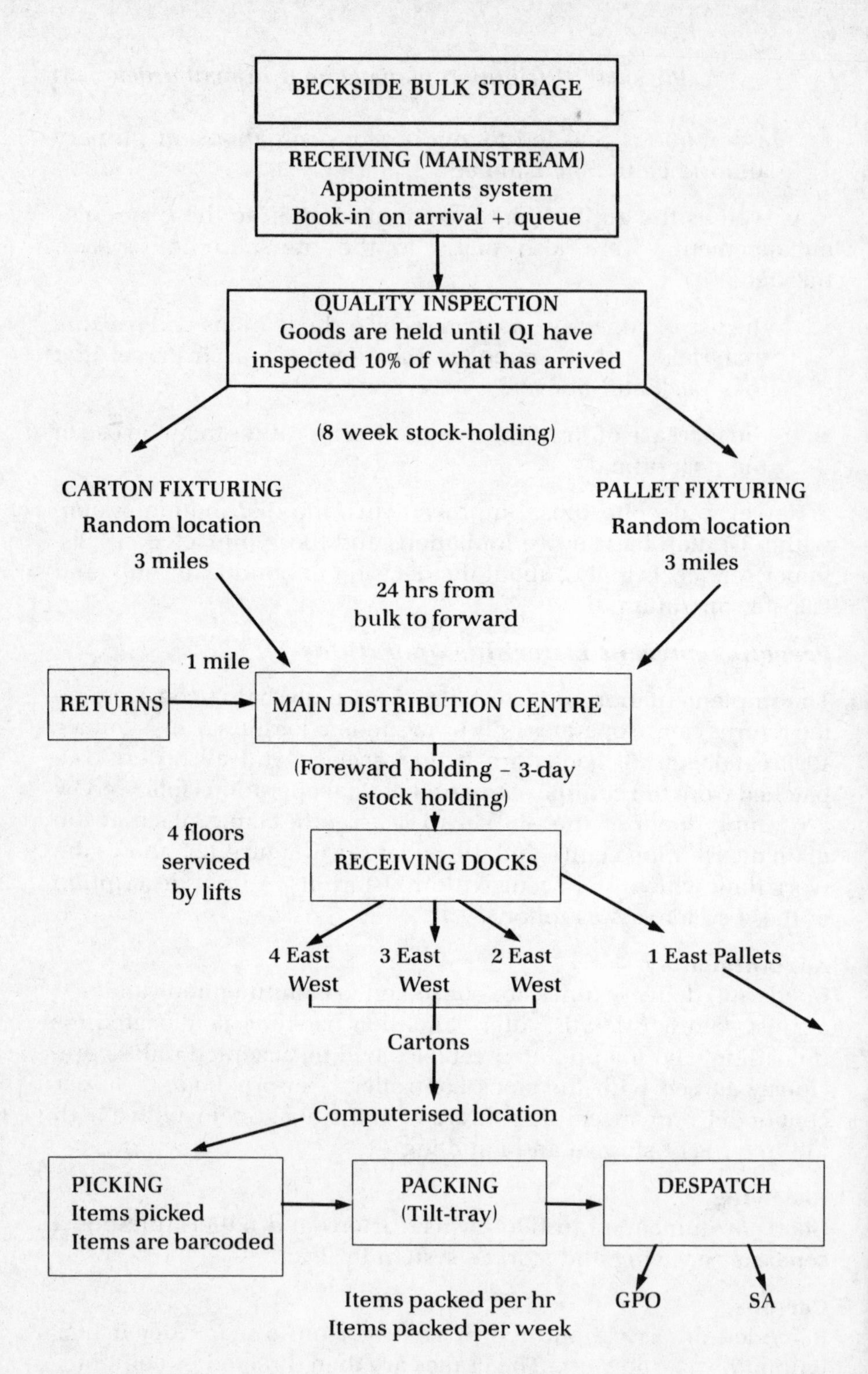

Figure 12.2: *Distribution system pre-Listerhills*

to spare locations where the driver confirms 'put-away' using a light pen. Time and date stamping through the barcode allows rotation of stock within the location management file.

Pallets

Pallets are removed from lorries and checked for dimension – to prevent stock being damaged these are shrink-wrapped if necessary. All pallets are barcoded with a time and date stamp, and are then taken by automated guided vehicles (AGVs) to automated cranes and are placed in an available location identified by computer within the pallet store high bay.

Bulk storage to forward (replenishment)

Forward is where items are picked to match orders and goods are called to forward when stock levels fall below a pre-set standard. Pallets are transferred by the cranes on to AGVs and into pallet picking.

Quality inspection

To avoid bottlenecks, goods are placed straight away into bulk storage in 'quarantine', and when required in forward are inspected, in the case of cartons this inspection rate averages out at one in ten. Some suppliers are identified as 'good' and are allowed past without inspection, ie 'monopoly' who have very stringent quality control checks themselves.

Forward picking

Cartons are removed from chutes and put into appropriate locations, with confirmation of put-away achieved by the reading of the two-carton barcodes and location label. These are opened for items to be picked from.

Pallets are placed by man-rider trucks whose display screens show the next available location, and put-away is confirmed by laser gun reading the pallet and location barcode. Information available through this confirmed put-away allows perpetual inventory of stock.

Orders are picked according to a 'walk' of barcoded labels – the picker picks an item and places a barcoded label on it and places it on a conveyor for packing. Within pallet picking, items are picked to 'fly' sheets if they are going straight to despatch and 'walks' if they need packing with other items.

Packing

Packing receives goods in chutes via the tilt-tray in batches. Separate orders are identified and packed as such, and these are placed on a conveyor to despatch.

Despatch

Parcels are placed on a tilt-tray which drops parcels into appropriate super agent or GPO sacks, which are loaded on to trucks from chutes. The sacks are dropped into the correct chute through the use of a laser barcode reader and a tilt-slat conveyor.

Transportation

Remains a mixture of Grattan own deliveries to super agents with subsequent house delivery, and the use of the post office, with all packing being done in-house. The super agent network operates through a series of 12 depots within the UK, with the initial sort being geographical for depot and then a subsequent sort for super agents.

Future

The future of distribution management within Grattan is two-fold. In the short term it is the completion of the implementation of the five warehouses into the Listerhills complex, and in the long term the enhancement of these systems in terms of utilisation of space and productivity.

Having identified the distribution management systems employed within Grattan, and remembering that the ultimate aim of distribution is to act as a sub-system of Grattan's business system to increase our competitive advantage, what value do these systems add?

An added value result?

What added value to the customer do these distribution systems achieve or how do they enable differentiation of the product by competitors? Porter's 'value chain' is a useful tool in identifying areas where productivity is essential in achieving margins, and how improvements in the former can enhance the latter. By using Porter's value chain we can display Grattan's business system in Figure 12.4.

Thus distribution has a key role in the achievement of profitable productivity, but is this so in the adding of value to achieve differentiation? To assess this, Figure 12.5 shows a model of the value chain adapted from Walters and White (1987).

The chain shows that added value is perceived by customers but these perceptions are enhanced by product based decisions, trad-

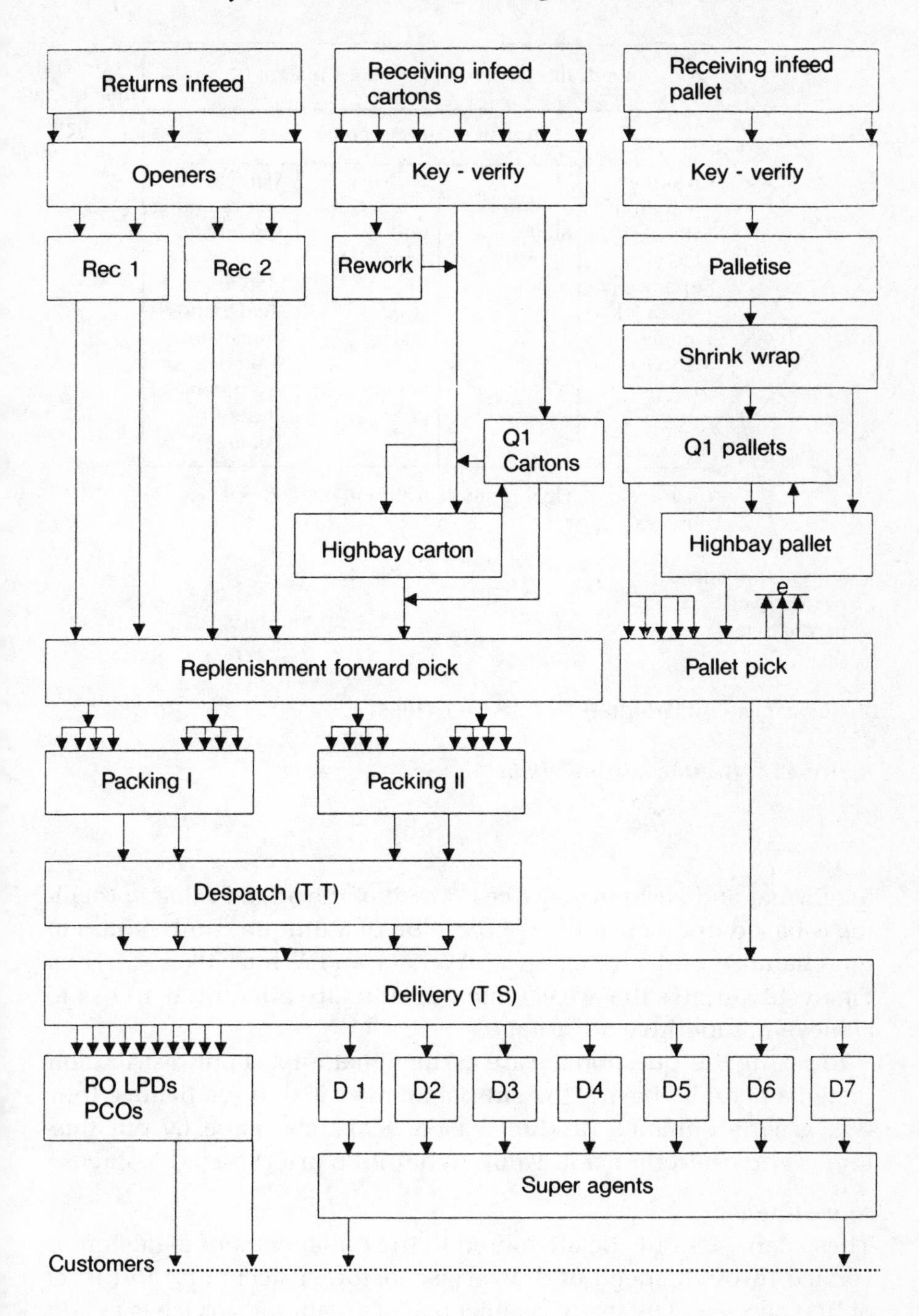

Figure 12.3: *Flow diagram – Listerhills*

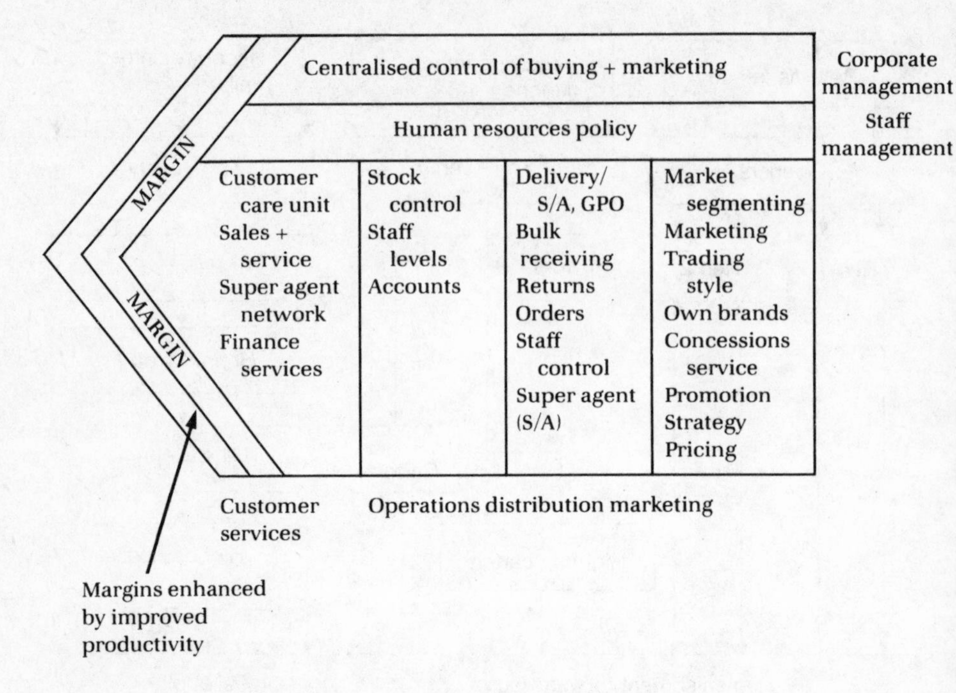

Business system: Adapted from Porter (1985)

Figure 12.4: *Grattan's value chain*

ing format and customer services: 'Much of the added value in retailing is based upon customer perception of a unique combination of merchandise and trading style' (Walters and White, 1987:32). Thus Figure 12.5 shows the areas which Grattan are attempting to use to achieve competitive advantage.

In asking this question we are asking what impact our distribution systems actually have – the simple answer is that we believe they will greatly enhance product based decisions made by our customer and, therefore, add value. What then are these advantages?

Advantages

These can generally be attributed to the enhancement of customer service through speed of deliveries, customer accounts, and level of first service. 'The primary objective of customer service is to add value to the existing retail offer and increase the relative differentiation between the company and its competitors' (Walters and

White 1987: 246). This is achieved by Grattan's distribution system by:

- increasing the speed of delivery: it is the intention to implement live processing of orders, rather than overnight, so that the order cycle is greatly reduced. Before live processing of orders the system will increase this speed by reducing the movement of stock between sites. Once live processing is in place, Listerhills will be able to achieve 48-hour delivery, a long way from the 'allow 28 days for delivery' of traditional mail order;
- enhancing customer accounts: the input of returns details at source allow the speedy and accurate updating of customer accounts with queries out-sorted at that point;
- increasing level of first service: this is done in two ways, the traceability of stock through barcoding will remove the acceptance of orders against inaccurate stock levels, and the distribution system allows the immediate processing of stock through receiving and quality inspection if any orders are held;
- reducing the order cycle time, through live processing;
- increasing the standard of the product itself, achieved by in-

INCREASED ADDED VALUE

CUSTOMER PERCEIVED ADDED VALUE

Assortment:	Ambiance:	Support:
coherence + co-ordination availability, continuity, quality, style, service, products, packaging	convenience excitement effectiveness	credit services parts replacement service staff: – number – ability
Product based decisions	Trading format	Customer services

Source: Adapted from Walters and White (1987)

Figure 12.5: *Adapted model of value chain*

house packaging for all parcels and the control over suppliers achieved by unitisation;

- increasing availability of stock, and thereby preventing the 'no-stock' situation where customers' orders are released against items in the warehouse which are not in location, resulting in a 'to follow' notice being issued to customers. These are prevented because: accurate traceability of stock prevents orders being accepted against 'assumed' stock levels and the use of barcoding for confirmed put-away will prevent the release of orders until stock is in place;
- improved communications with customers through the speedier release of information by the computer systems.

All of these result from the distribution management system employed by Grattan and the changes within it. By referring to Figure 12.5, we can prove the added value perceived by the customer.

Conclusion

In conclusion, as a company, Grattan exists to achieve profit through the selling to customers of required products – the intention is to maximise profit by minimising costs and maximising competitive advantage.

The Listerhills warehouse complex will increase this advantage through increasing the speed of delivery, the level of first service, the standard of the product and enhancing customer information. As such, the distribution systems are operating as an essential part of the business system in achieving added value and thus competitive advantage.

Grattan produce no product – the company is a distribution network receiving goods and orders and packaging the former to satisfy the latter. While distribution systems are not the sole key to Grattan's success, they provide an approach to undoing the first latch.

References

Empire Stores (1987) 'Empire Stores and mail order', Company Information January.

Harrison, J (1988) 'Mail order: market restructure and technological change' Final Year Project School of Industrial Technology, Bradford University.

Jordans Survey (1983) *The British Mail Order Industry* Jordan & Sons Ltd.

Kay, W (1987) *Battle for the High Street* Piatkus Books Ltd, London.

Oxford English Dictionary (1969) Clarendon Press.

Porter ME (1985) *Competitive Advantage* Free Press.

—— (1980) *Competitive Strategy* Free Press.

Retail (1986) *Retail* Spring.

Retail Trade Review (1989) 'Mail order' in *Retail Business* September.

Walters, D and White, D (1989) *Retail Marketing Management* Macmillan Press Ltd.

Index